STAR-SPANGLED HOCKEY

CELEBRATING 75 YEARS OF **USA HOCKEY**

D1441705

KEVIN ALLEN | FOREWORD BY **JEREMY ROENICK**

Copyright © 2011 by USA Hockey

No part of this publication may be reproduced, stored in a retrieval system, or transmitted in any form by any means, electronic, mechanical, photocopying, or otherwise, without the prior written permission of the publisher, Triumph Books, 542 South Dearborn Street, Suite 750, Chicago, Illinois 60605.

Triumph Books and colophon are registered trademarks of Random House, Inc.

Library of Congress Cataloging-in-Publication Data

Allen, Kevin, 1956–
  Star-spangled hockey : celebrating 75 years of USA hockey / Kevin Allen.
    p. cm.
  ISBN 978-1-60078-613-6
  1. Hockey—United States—History. I. Title.
  GV848.4.U6A55 2011
  796.962—dc22

                            2011015077

This book is available in quantity at special discounts for your group or organization. For further information, contact:

Triumph Books
542 South Dearborn Street
Suite 750
Chicago, Illinois 60605
(312) 939-3330
Fax (312) 663-3557
www.triumphbooks.com

Printed in China
ISBN: 978-1-60078-613-6–Paperback
ISBN: 978-1-60078-687-7–Hardcover
Design by Patricia Frey

Contents

FOREWORD

When I was 10, I wanted to be Mike Eruzione. When I watched him score the winning goal against the Soviets at the 1980 Olympics in Lake Placid, I was inspired to be a hockey player.

The on-ice celebration of USA's greatest hockey triumph—with Jim Craig wrapped in Old Glory—may have had even more impact than Eruzione's wrist shot. Certainly I wanted to score like Eruzione did, but what intrigued me was the idea that someday I might be able to know the exhilaration that the American players shared as they reveled in the upset.

Frankly, my fascination with players raising the Stanley Cup came about because of the emotional Lake Placid scene I witnessed on my television screen. I loved watching the chaotic scene on the ice, and the euphoria that was etched in the faces of players as they tossed their sticks and gloves high into the air. I loved seeing the big pile of players that resulted from their attempts to hug each other. It is a very visual memory. I wanted to know that feeling. I wanted to know what it was like to win a championship. I wanted to know what it was like to represent my country on the biggest stage. I wanted to know what it was like to celebrate with teammates who had become like a band of brothers.

The 1980 team's success changed our lives in so many ways. It was a symbol of American pride and perseverance. Almost every American player in my generation has said that he was inspired by watching the Americans win in Lake Placid.

We can all remember where we were when Eruzione launched the shot that changed his life and our country. I was at a friend's house because my Richfield (Connecticut) Bruins team had a game scheduled that night. Not wanting to miss a second of action, we put on our equipment in the living room, in front of the television.

There was no way we were leaving the U.S.–Soviet Union game until it was over. I even had my skates on in the living room. After Al Michaels made his famous "Do you believe in miracles" call, we stayed to watch the celebration and then ran to the car in our skates.

The funny aspect of the story was that when we arrived at the arena there wasn't a soul around even though it was game time. Everyone had stayed home to watch the game. But right after we squealed into the parking lot, a line of cars followed us. The game was delayed, but there was a buzz in that arena about what the Americans had accomplished at Lake Placid.

From that day forward, I wanted to play for my country. Today, I am proud that I was a member of the generation that helped transform the American program into a world power. When I started playing for USA Hockey national teams, we were always a fifth-, sixth-, or seventh-place team. It was considered an upset if we finished higher than that. We changed the American hockey mentality from hoping to win to expecting to win.

Clearly my generation's drive was born from the fact that the most important win in American hockey history happened when we were at an impressionable age. Interest in hockey grew in America after Eruzione found the net. Because we had more teams registered to play, we had better competition. Better competition created better players.

Plus, my generation had the love of the game. We wanted to be great players, and we wanted to be on great teams. With players like Mike Modano, Keith Tkachuk, Doug Weight, Chris Chelios, and Brian Leetch—among others—the American program developed its own swagger. We adopted a Canadian mentality about playing. When we showed up at tournaments, we feared no one. We expected to be tougher, faster, and more skilled than the other teams, even the Canadians. We respected the Canadians and hated them at the same time. Every time we faced the Canadians in those years we improved. That's how we helped change the American program.

When I was playing for the U.S. Olympic team in 2002 and we lost to Canada in the gold-medal game, I was devastated. But today I say that Olympic experience was one of my career highlights. Now that the sting of losing has worn off, I can see that winning a silver medal at the Olympics is a monumental accomplishment. The best athletes in the world go to the Olympics, and I was there.

I thank USA Hockey for that opportunity. I thought it was appropriate that when I entered the U.S. Hockey Hall of Fame in 2010, former USA Hockey executive Art Berglund entered the Hall with me. He was the first person from USA Hockey to call me and give me a chance to play at the national level. He believed in me, and we both believed that American hockey was going to thrive under our watch.

Today, I think there are many of us that are very proud of how far the American program has come from the days when we needed a miracle to be successful. Today, when an American team, young or old, walks into an arena it expects to be the best team in the arena. ∎

Jeremy Roenick
May 2011

USA HOCKEY
INTRODUCTION

When it comes to spreading the gospel about American hockey, Lou Vairo is an evangelist. After becoming coaching director for the Amateur Hockey Association of the United States (AHAUS) in 1978, Vairo often preached about the sinfulness of not inviting players from nontraditional hockey states to national development camps.

He insisted players from the Sun Belt region needed be invited, even though administrators from Northern programs thought his idea was preposterous.

"One of the most important aspects of national development is giving kids the chance," Vairo would say. "The kid from Dallas may talk funny to you and wear spurs, but he needs to get on the ice with a kid from Virginia, Minnesota, and beat his ass so he can know that he can play too."

Thirty-three years later, on February 26, 2011, Blake Geoffrion played for the Nashville Predators against the Dallas Stars to become the first Tennessean to play in the NHL. Geoffrion's Nashville teammates included Jonathan Blum, who was the first Californian to be drafted in the first round of the NHL draft. Geoffrion's debut came about a month after Carolina

Hurricanes owner Peter Karmanos predicted that the youth program in Raleigh, North Carolina, was close to producing NHL draft picks.

Just seven weeks before Geoffrion took the ice for the first time in the NHL, the U.S. National Junior Team won a bronze medal at the World Junior Championship using players from 12 different states, including California, Pennsylvania, Maine, and Nevada. Jason Zucker, who was on that U.S. squad, grew up playing hockey in Las Vegas, starting out on inline skates. He was selected in the second round of the 2010 draft, making him the first Nevada player to be drafted in the NHL. Two rounds later, Florida native Andrew Yogan was drafted by the New York Rangers.

This all came during the 2010–11 season when Americans claimed 20 percent of NHL opening-day roster spots for the first time in league history. That number should be on the rise, given that 26 percent of all players drafted from 2007 to 2010 have been American. In 2011 a record 11 Americans were drafted in the first round.

The 2010–11 season also marked the first time that USA Hockey had reached 100,000 registered players in the 8-and-Under age category.

On December 9, 2010, a college outdoor game featuring Michigan State at Michigan, in Ann Arbor, Michigan, drew a world-record crowd of 104,073. In that game, Michigan had a line that consisted of players from Texas (Chris Brown), Arizona (Luke Moffat), and California (Scooter Vaughan). On January 1, 2011, the outdoor Winter Classic game featuring the Washington Capitals vs. the Pittsburgh Penguins, in Pittsburgh's NFL stadium, became the highest-rated televised NHL game since 1975.

American junior hockey has advanced to the point that, in 2010–11, the United States Hockey League drew more than 1 million fans for the 11th consecutive season. The Lincoln, Nebraska, franchise in the USHL averaged more than 4,200 fans per game. In 2009–10, 248 USHL players had Division I commitments to play college hockey. The North American Hockey League drew almost 600,000 fans and also had a significant number of future college players.

American hockey has come a long way since 1969 when the United States sent more men to the moon than to the National Hockey League. In 1969 there were two Apollo missions with six astronauts making lunar orbits. In 1969 Tommy Williams and Doug Roberts were the only American players with regular NHL jobs, although Larry Pleau and Bobby Sheehan would come to the NHL later in the 1969–70 season.

For a long time, the growth of American hockey moved glacially, mostly because there were not enough rinks or qualified coaches. Gary Fay, the first AHAUS coaching director, conducted a study in the 1970s that showed that 85 percent of America's youth hockey coaches were fathers who never played the game. "Today, teams are still coached by fathers, but a lot more have played the game at a fairly high level," Vairo said. "That has changed our hockey."

Today, some of the top young Americans, such as New Jersey's Zach Parise and Nashville's Colin Wilson, are sons of former Canadians who settled in the United States. Paul Stastny, the No. 1 center on the 2010 U.S. Olympic Team, is the son of Slovak legend Peter Stastny. John Ramage, captain of the 2011 U.S. National Junior Team, is the son of former NHL player Rob Ramage, another Canadian who settled in the United States.

"One important aspect of American development is that Canadian players have liked American women," USA Hockey's Art Berglund once joked.

When Vairo holds coaching clinics, he always sincerely thanks all the Canadians and Europeans in attendance for their countries' contributions to America's hockey melting pot. "The hockey volunteers in this country are the real heroes of U.S. hockey development," Vairo has said. "We have good employees and good leadership. But if we didn't have parents hauling kids and buying equipment, we wouldn't be where we are."

Today, former NHL superstar Mario Lemieux coaches a youth team in Pittsburgh. Former New York Rangers Mark Messier, Brian Leetch, and Mike Richter are registered USA Hockey coaches.

Volunteerism goes beyond coaching. Four-time U.S. Olympian Angela Ruggiero was only introduced to the sport because of an ambitious registrar in Pasadena, California. Ruggiero's father, Bill, was only planning to register his son for youth hockey, but the registrar, needing to fill rosters, convinced him that he would get a good financial deal if he registered the entire family.

The 2010 Thayer Tutt Award, one of USA Hockey's highest honors, was given to Wally Kormylo for his work as a skating coach. It is

Star-Spangled Hockey

estimated that Kormylo taught skating to more than 50,000 kids during 60 years of hockey service. In 1953 Kormylo was the first hockey coach at the U.S. Air Force Academy. Neal Henderson also won the Tutt Award for serving as head coach of the Fort Dupont Ice Hockey Club, a minority program in the Washington, D.C., area.

The symbol of Canadian hockey might be a child skating on a frozen pond. The symbol of American hockey might be a high-mileage automobile with low resale value. There are plenty of tales about parents driving their kids two hours one way to practice. That's what some U.S. hockey parents endure to find a high level of competition for their children. Former NHL player Jeremy Roenick entered the U.S. Hockey Hall of Fame in 2010 and recalled that his father, Wally, gave up a career advancement and took a pay cut to move his family from Virginia to Massachusetts because he knew his son needed better competition. Before the move, Jeremy had to commute from Virginia to New Jersey each weekend to play for a junior team.

"We would put him on People's Express airline every Friday for about $59 one way to New Jersey," Wally Roenick said. "But sometimes we had to send him to Boston or Detroit. We probably spent $25,000 that season."

Even today, in some parts of the country, it's still not easy or inexpensive to find quality competition. To better prepare himself to make the NHL, Californian Emerson Etem worked out in the summer with famed trainer T.R. Goodman, who has a stable of NHL players. To get into Goodman's program, he had to travel from Long Beach to Venice Beach. He started with 6:00 AM roller-skating, followed by two train rides and a bus ride to get to the training site. It was two-and-one-half hours one way, and he did it six days a week for three consecutive summers. It paid off, because the Anaheim Ducks drafted him 29th overall in 2010.

"The sport has come a long way," said USA 1980 Olympic hero Mike Eruzione. "The sport used to be just about kids from Massachusetts or Michigan and Minnesota. But we have players coming from everywhere. We just haven't had a Wayne Gretzky yet."

America might have already had a Gretzky. His name was Hobey Baker, and he played at Princeton almost 100 years ago. He may have been the most talented American to ever play the game, and this is where we will begin the story of American hockey history. ∎

In 1981, the Decathlon Club of
Minnesota began presenting the
Hobey Baker Memorial Award to the
outstanding collegiate hockey player
in the United States. (Getty Images)

HOBEY BAKER MEMORIAL AWARD
PRESENTED ANNUALLY TO THE OUTSTANDING COLLEGIATE HOCKEY PLAYER
IN THE UNITED STATES BY THE
DECATHLON ATHLETIC CLUB OF BLOOMINGTON, MINNESOTA

HOBEY BAKER
Hockey's First American Knight

In the idyllic days before the Great War, journalists viewed Hobey Baker as the embodiment of America—or at least of what they thought America should be. The golden-haired Princeton star athlete was as handsome as he was talented, as noble as he was fearless, as daring as he was cunning. With his lion's heart and poet's soul, he was bursting with confidence, yet stardom humbled him in a way that no one quite understood. Hobart Amory Hare Baker was the favorite son for whom all Americans longed. Whether returning a punt or flying up the ice with the puck on his stick, Baker persevered with a passion and courage that hadn't been seen on college campuses before he arrived at Princeton in 1910.

Newspapers weren't content to merely report Baker's hockey and football exploits; they glorified them through headlines and prose that brought romance and idealism to all that he accomplished. To the media, Baker was an artist whose runs with the football or dashes with the puck were like lines of poetry to be savored and enjoyed. They were smitten with Hobey Baker like amorous teenagers doting upon first loves.

"If it is possible to say of any man that he was beautiful, it may be said of Hobey Baker because he was beautiful of body, soul, and spirit," *New York Herald Tribune* writer Al Laney wrote more than 40 years after Baker had graced Princeton's ice.

During football season, sportswriters referred to Baker as the "blond Adonis of the gridiron."

Baker may have been the model for the All-American boy. He was F. Scott Fitzgerald on skates, minus the highbrow cynicism. Novelist Fitzgerald was actually Baker's contemporary at Princeton. It is believed that the Allenby character in Fitzgerald's first novel, *This Side of Paradise*, is modeled after Hobey Baker. Fitzgerald presumably dressed down Baker slightly for his work of fiction, because Baker was almost too flawless for a good fictional tale. Baker dominated college hockey from 1910 to 1914 the way Wayne Gretzky dominated the NHL in the early 1980s.

At a time when America had finally grown accustomed to flying machines roaring overhead, Baker's skates must have seemed as if they were powered by warp drive. He was a dazzling skater with speed that amazed those who witnessed it for the first time. When the puck found the blade of his stick and he began his trek up the ice, a buzz would move through the crowd, as if they were about to witness magnificence born before their eyes.

The rules of seven-man hockey were perfect for Baker's talents. With no forward passing allowed, Baker, playing rover, had license to carry the puck coast-to-coast many times during the game. As a youngster, he had perfected his stick handling by practicing on darkened rinks. The puck clung to his stick as if attached by a magnet.

The *Boston Herald* couldn't have imagined the level of talent that players such as Gordie Howe, Rocket Richard, Wayne Gretzky, and Mario Lemieux would bring to hockey in coming years. But at the time, the newspaper unabashedly called Hobey Baker "the greatest hockey player who ever lived."

Baker played hockey and football in much the same way—with an open throttle and a refusal to recognize that his playing style might be dangerous. In 1912 he was named an All-American halfback, putting him on the same team with the legendary Jim Thorpe. Like Thorpe, Baker was also an accomplished drop-kicker whose skill was invaluable in an era where the forward pass was just becoming a part of football strategy. His kicking skill resolved several gridiron stalemates in Princeton's favor.

Baker's daring style was most apparent as a punt returner. Sure-handed and unafraid, he would stand well beyond where the punt would come down to assure he could be in full gallop when he cradled the ball in his arms. Fans would gasp as the ball, Baker, and the defensive ends would all arrive virtually at the same time. More often than not, Baker would elude his would-be tacklers and dart to the outside for a touchdown romp or long gainer. Sluggish offenses were the norm in that era; hence, Baker had plenty of opportunities to dazzle crowds with his unique and exhilarating punt-return style.

That bravado also showed on the ice when he attempted to stick-handle through defenders, most of whom would resort to physical attacks to slow him down. The news accounts from that era make frequent references to Baker jumping over sticks and legs to fill the opposing net. One report claimed Baker had 30 of Princeton's 42 shots on goal in a game against Yale. Even the elitist *New York Times* often waxed poetic about Baker. Describing his performance as a rover in a 7–5 win against Yale on January 17, 1913, an unnamed correspondent for the *Times* said that Baker "was all over the rink skimming up and down the ice like a shadow."

That game had been tied 5–5 at the end of two regulation 20-minute halves. In the extra period, Baker scored a goal with a spectacular end-to-end dash, during which "he carried the puck to every part of the ice surface without being stopped."

"Baker had regained his second wind and he started as dazzling an exhibition of skating as had ever been seen on the rink," the unnamed correspondent wrote. "He started a series of zigzag dashes across the rink.... He was going so fast that the Yale players went down before him." He was clearly like no athlete reporters had ever seen, yet their fascination seemed to transcend his skill. They were disarmed by Baker, intrigued by him.

Baker was a well-spoken lad when he arrived at Princeton in 1910 after establishing himself as a schoolboy legend at St. Paul's School in Concord,

New Hampshire. He was well trained at St. Paul's because the school's coach was Malcolm Gordon, now a member of the U.S. Hockey Hall of Fame. Gordon is viewed as an American hockey pioneer who helped formalize the game in the U.S., because he wrote out the first set of rules in 1885. Early accounts of Baker's athletic successes at Princeton speak of a "twinkle in his eye" and an impish grin that no doubt served him well whether he was wooing the ladies or charming professors, who probably were as fascinated with him as the rest of the Princeton campus.

Born into Philadelphia high society, Baker arrived at Princeton with a well-defined set of values and ideals for his athletic involvement. During four years of hockey at Princeton, he had only two minor penalties, despite the fact that he was manhandled, roughed, and whacked with sticks in almost every game. Most opposing teams correctly figured that the way to stop Princeton was to stop Baker, and some teams resorted to tactics that were on the outside edge of the rule book. But to the astonishment of his teammates, Baker never retaliated. No matter how rough the contest, he shook opponents' hands after games.

In one football game, Dartmouth All-American Red Louden was rendered unconscious in a failed attempt to stop Baker. Not only did Baker carry Louden off the field himself, but he was almost too upset to return to the game. Only the thought of letting down his teammates convinced Baker to return to the contest. To Baker, there was no value in winning unless an athlete played honorably. He so loved the team concept that it bothered him when journalists would refer to Princeton as a one-man team, and he detested when friends or teammates exaggerated his accomplishments.

Strikingly handsome and always nattily attired—usually in a Norfolk jacket—Baker was a dashing figure on campus. One can imagine that he looked the way a younger Robert Redford did in the movie *The Great Gatsby.* Baker was a person most people wanted in their circle of friends. No one knew exactly what Baker was going to do with his life, but they were relatively sure he was going to be a success.

Standing 5'9" and weighing about 160 pounds, Baker wasn't physically imposing. But he was a superbly honed athlete who was said to be as proficient at golf, track, and swimming as he was at football and hockey.

The only other American hockey player drawing a high degree of attention in that era was Francis "Moose" Goheen of White Bear Lake, Minnesota, who created his own hockey legend in the Midwest. He was two years younger than Baker and began making his mark as a rover and defenseman with the St. Paul Athletic Club just as Baker was finishing up at Princeton.

But the fact that Baker's games were usually covered by the *New York Times* gave him a much broader reputation as America's best hockey player. He was, at the very least, on the same athletic level as the great players of Canada, such as Cyclone Taylor, who was known to Americans because he had made tour stops in New York and Boston.

Baker dominated a sport that was relatively new to the American public. Unlike in Canada, where seven-man hockey had known some level of notoriety since the 1860s, U.S. hockey was really still in its infancy when Baker began drawing attention as an extraordinary player at Princeton in 1910.

In the early 1890s, college athletes were playing what they called "ice polo." The idea was the same, except each team used only five players, and the object of their attention was a ball, not a puck.

Some American college tennis standouts brought back hockey after a challenge match between Canada and the U.S. in 1895. The earliest documented college game was between Yale and Johns Hopkins in 1896.

Hockey had also taken hold in Pittsburgh before the turn of the century with the introduction of the Western Pennsylvania League and the Interscholastic League (though a fire that destroyed the Schenley Park Casino rink temporarily stalled the game's growth). The sport was also gaining popularity in Michigan's Upper Peninsula. In 1904 a dentist named J.L. Gibson began America's first pro league. Called the International Hockey League, it included the Calumet-Larium Miners, the American Soo Indians, Pittsburgh (Pennsylvania), the Canadian Soo, and Houghton.

By the time Baker arrived at Princeton, ice hockey had a strong foothold, especially on the East Coast, where Baker's name gained considerable prominence. American "amateur" hockey had been thriving, although the rosters of those teams often included many Canadians who had come south for the promise of under-the-table payments.

According to the *New York Times*, Baker had several offers to turn pro after he left Princeton. Later reports suggested he turned down $3,500 from the NHL's Montreal Wanderers. That would have put him in the salary neighborhood of Taylor, who the *New York Times* had called "the Ty Cobb of pro hockey." Taylor made more than $5,000 when the Renfrew Millionaires lured him to play for that club team.

Baker's decision not to become a professional player following his career at Princeton isn't surprising, given his circumstances. First, professional hockey wasn't viewed as being quite the honorable vocation that it is today. Second, Baker's upper-crust background and Princeton degree suggest that the money offered in those days wouldn't overwhelm him. Third, a professional career would probably have forced him to play in Canada. The Pacific Coast Hockey Association's first American team had arrived that year in Portland, but somehow it just doesn't seem likely that America's greatest player would abandon his East Coast lifestyle to play professionally for a team called the Rosebuds. As much as Baker talked of hockey being a team game, he certainly must have appreciated that his greatest fame was with those who watched him play for four years at Princeton.

The logical choice to further his career was the St. Nick's amateur team out of New York, which he joined after his graduation in 1914. The St. Nicholas team was a major hockey attraction before his arrival, but with Baker on the squad, it drew even more attention. Newspapers made reference to limousines lined up outside St. Nick's arena on the nights Baker would play. With an Ivy League college connection, hockey had become a high-society sport. When St. Nick's won a game against the Montreal Stars in the 1915 Ross Cup series, the *Montreal Press* wrote, "Baker cooked our goose so artistically that we enjoyed it."

But soon Baker began showing signs of restlessness. He toured Europe and wrote of his experiences for the *New York Times.* While Baker was in Europe, Archduke Ferdinand, heir to the Austro-Hungarian throne, was assassinated, triggering World War I. Baker's buddies had a difficult time talking him out of enlisting in the British Army. He returned to New York to become a banker and play hockey, although his heart seemed to be only in the latter. But his sense of duty continued gnawing at him to the point that, by 1916, Baker was training to become a pilot. After only a short period, his zeal for flying through the air surpassed his desire to fly up the ice.

By all accounts, he had a flair for dogfighting, an innate sense of knowing when to make the right moves at the right times. He buzzed through the clouds like he was weaving through defenders on a Saturday afternoon at Princeton.

In 1917 Baker was sent over as a member of the 103rd Aero Squadron, formed from former members of the Lafayette Escadrille Squadron. He was among the first American pilots shipped to France, although much to his chagrin, he didn't enter the war zone immediately. His first assignment in France involved pushing papers, a duty that clearly bored someone who was accustomed to being in the center of the fray.

In April 1918 he was finally given a chance to fight in his single-seater Spad, painted in orange and black Princeton school colors. By May, he had recorded his first kill of a German aircraft—the first of three he would be credited with before war's end. He would receive the Croix de Guerre medal for his heroism. Transferred to the 13th Bomb Squadron, Baker led the first flight of that group to have a confirmed kill.

Baker enjoyed the thrill of aerial combat, probably because it provided him with the same adrenaline rush he knew from lugging the football in the open field and stick-handling through the men from Harvard. But Baker might have loved being a pilot more than he should have. He was clearly bothered by the thought that life after football and hockey might be somewhat anticlimactic. According to his biography by John Davies, Baker told friends after he departed Princeton: "I realize my life is finished. No matter how long I live, I will never equal the excitement of playing on the football field."

When the Great War was ending, Baker seemed more saddened than pleased, maybe concluding that he would not have an endeavor that would

After starring in both football and hockey at Princeton University, Hobey Baker fought for the United States in World War I, piloting a single-seater plane. One month after the war ended, Baker was killed in a plane crash in France. (Hockey Hall of Fame)

feed his passion the way sports and flying had. Perhaps he felt he hadn't fulfilled his duty or lived up to the measure of his own destiny. Why he needed to take one last flight over the French soil a month after the war ended is not known. He had been ordered stateside and was to leave that day. When he showed up at the airfield near Toul, France, on December 21, 1918, his subordinates protested his plans for a final flight, some of them undoubtedly believing the superstition that pilots shouldn't test fate by taking a "last flight." Too many stories existed about pilots crashing on their final trip into the sky. Pushing his luck further,

Hobey Baker's Final Game

Hobey Baker's last hockey appearance, on March 24, 1917, was a triple-overtime game played in front of 1,000 people who appreciated his talent to the point that they were willing to pay up to 75¢ for the privilege of seeing him play.

The Pittsburghhockey.net website shows a scan of the original advertisement that states that general admission was 35¢ and reserved ticket prices ranged from 50¢ to 75¢ to see Hobey Baker, calling him "America's greatest hockey star."

A sold-out crowd was at Winter Gardens to watch Baker lead the Philadelphia All-Stars to a 3–2 triple-overtime win against a previously undefeated Pittsburgh All-Star team. It was the lead story in Pittsburgh sports pages the next morning.

"So prominent with his spurts up the ice and his defense tactics," the *Pittsburgh Dispatch* wrote, "that [Baker] was the most conspicuous player on the ice."

The same reporter opined that the Pittsburgh team had outplayed Philadelphia, but Baker and strong goaltending had been the difference.

With an ice surface that was claimed to be 300 feet by 140 feet, the Winter Garden was reputed to have the world's largest ice rink. It was 100 feet longer and 55 feet wider than today's NHL standard rink.

"Even the large ice at the Winter Garden did not deter him," the *Pittsburgh Press* reported. "The extra space made him even more noticeable."

Given the speed and stick handling that Baker possessed, it seems impressive that the Pittsburgh All-Stars could even hold Baker to three goals.

According to the 94-year-old newspaper account, the two teams were unable to break the tie in two extra five-minute periods of overtime. At the 10-minute mark of the sudden-death overtime, Baker carried the puck end-to-end to score the game winner.

Pittsburgh was a fitting city for Baker's last game, because the Steel City had developed a strong affinity for hockey early in the 20th century. The area built an artificial ice rink before 1900, and a semiprofessional hockey league, called the Western Pennsylvania Hockey League, had been formed by 1902. Pittsburgh was a hockey city where fans appreciated seeing a hockey superstar. Fans there understood Baker's skill level.

When Baker played his last game, it was certainly not known that Baker would never play again, but America entered World War I 13 days after the game. One month later Baker was a lieutenant in the U.S. Air Corps serving in France. Within 19 months of his final game, Baker would be killed in a plane crash.

Baker decided to climb into a recently repaired plane.

Perhaps sentimentality ruled Baker that day. Perhaps he felt a nostalgic craving to say farewell to the skies where he had fought with honor and dignity. While training to become a pilot in 1916, he had chosen a football Saturday for a flight over the Princeton stadium. Fans recognized him instantly. They would remember that day as his goodbye to them.

Perhaps the same bravado and adventuresome spirit that helped him survive his combat experiences contributed to his death in the end. Baker was always confident in his ability to steer clear of danger. After all, he had avoided monstrous hits by big-chested linemen in football and dodged the high sticks that Canadian players always directed his way.

According to the Canadian wire service report of his death in the *Montreal Gazette*, eyewitnesses said Baker was trying a stunt at an altitude that was too low, when the Spad's 220-horsepower engine sputtered, then fell silent. But the *New York Times* report said the engine simply died 600 yards above the earth. Baker could have simply kept flying straight and crash-landed the plane a few miles away from the airfield. Many pilots, including Baker himself, had walked away from crash landings in the durable Spad. But Baker probably didn't want to scuttle his aircraft, which would have been an embarrassment, considering the flight didn't need to be taken. Maybe he had time to think all this, or maybe he merely acted instinctively, as had been his style in the athletic arena.

For a reason known only to him, Baker immediately engineered a difficult maneuver that instantly put him in peril because the nose of his plane was pushed further down. Though Baker struggled to keep the nose up, he ran out of sky before the task was completed. He died as his colleagues raced to take him to the field hospital. He was 26.

Hobey's relatives and friends were left to ponder his death. Had he been distraught over the prospect of entering a life where there would be no war or sports to test his mettle? Not even his closest friends knew for sure. The tragic circumstances of his death somehow fit the theatrical nature of his life. Baker's story reads like a Greek tragedy, with the noble hero slapped down by cruel fate. Neither Homer, nor Fitzgerald, nor even Hemingway could have written a more tragic climax to Baker's story.

Through the years, there has been debate about whether Baker might have taken his own life. In a 1991 article, *Sports Illustrated* raised the question again and offered that Baker's biographer Davies believed that Baker was "too proud to take his own life."

U.S. President Woodrow Wilson, the former Princeton president who chose to watch Baker practice on the day he was elected, was among those to issue condolences. Almost immediately, friends set about establishing a fund for an ice rink to be built at Princeton to carry Baker's name. It was put up in 1922 and still bears his name today. The 2,092-seat arena has been refurbished, but it is college hockey's second-oldest arena behind Northeastern's Matthews Arena.

Would Baker have returned to hockey had he arrived safely home from the war? Although professional hockey was garnering greater recognition, it probably would not have been palatable to Baker, who preferred more sportsmanship and less anger in his sports endeavors. Had he survived the war, he might have joined the 1920 U.S. Olympic Team. Moose Goheen was on that team, and that tandem would have been difficult to stop. If Baker had been a member of the team, the Americans might not have waited until 1960 to land an Olympic gold medal.

The following anonymous verse is inscribed on Baker's tombstone:

You seemed winged, even as a lad,
With that swift look of those who know the sky,
It was no blundering fate that stooped and bade
You break your wings, and fall to earth and die,
I think some day you may have flown too high,
So that immortals saw you and were glad,
Watching the beauty of your spirits flame,
Until they loved and called you, and you came. ■

After starring on the gold-medal 1980 Olympic team, the University of Minnesota's Neal Broten was awarded the first Hobey Baker Award in 1981.
(Mecca/Hockey Hall of Fame)

COLLEGIATE GREATNESS
Neal Broten and the Hobey Baker Award

In 1980 Chuck Bard, CEO of the Decathlon Club in Bloomington, Minnesota, suggested that his organization honor the best college hockey player each season with an award named after Hobey Baker. Since then, 31 players have won the award, all of them talented but none probably as dashing as Baker was when he graced the college ice.

The first player to win the Hobey Baker Award may have also been the best. Minnesota's Neal Broten was the inaugural winner in 1981, and it can be argued that no Hobey winner since has been a more accomplished player than Broten was.

"I don't think I ever saw an American player better than Neal," said Wisconsin coach Mike Eaves, who played with Broten on the Minnesota North Stars.

The list of winners includes such noteworthy NHL standouts as Brendan Morrison (1997), Chris Drury (1998), and Ryan Miller (2001), but the true debate of the best Hobey winner probably boils down to American Broten vs. Canadian Paul Kariya (1993).

Kariya was the better goal scorer, producing 402 career goals. Broten was the better playmaker, recording 634 assists. Kariya was a point-per-game player, and Broten was slightly below that pace. Both players have Olympic gold medals, with Broten earning his in 1980 and Kariya picking up his in 2002. Broten won a Stanley Cup (with New Jersey in 1995), and Kariya did not. But the greatest difference between the two players is Broten's reputation for being a two-way forward, a difference-maker in all three zones of the ice, and an expert in the faceoff circle.

"He played the way that Pavel Datsyuk plays today," said USA Hockey's assistant executive director Jim Johannson. "He could take the puck away from you the way Datsyuk can."

Broten—from Roseau, Minnesota—was only 5'9" and 175 pounds, and his NHL career was born in an era when NHL coaches were demanding bigger players. "But you never heard anyone say he couldn't play because of his size," said Lou Nanne, a former Minnesota North Stars general manager.

Trying to dislodge the puck from Broten's grasp was often an exercise in futility. "What people didn't realize about him was how strong he was on his skates," Nanne said. "He had excellent balance. When you watch great players you never really hit them hard. You didn't hit Wayne Gretzky hard and you didn't hit Broten hard."

It was Nanne who drafted Broten in 1979 after watching him dominate in the Minnesota High School Tournament for three seasons and in his first college season at Minnesota.

"Every time I saw him play he was compelling," Nanne said.

In real terms, Nanne traded famed NHL tough guy Dave Semenko to Edmonton to acquire Broten. The North Stars had drafted Semenko in the second round (25th overall) in the 1977 NHL draft only to have Semenko spurn their offer and jump to the Edmonton Oilers of the World Hockey Association. When the NHL annexed the WHA in 1979, Semenko's rights reverted to the North Stars. Again, Nanne couldn't sign him, but Semenko turned out to be a valuable asset. Nanne correctly surmised that he could turn Semenko's rights into Broten. At that time, NHL teams were still not completely comfortable drafting players from colleges, and Nanne figured Broten, being a smallish American center, was probably projected to be a third-round pick. Going into the 1979 draft, no true American player had ever been drafted in the first round, and only a handful of Americans had been drafted in the second round. Nanne wanted to draft Broten in the second round; the problem was that he didn't have a second-round pick because he had dealt his to the Montreal Canadiens for the rights to American-born defenseman Bill Nyrop. Knowing the Oilers wanted Semenko's fists back to protect Wayne Gretzky, Nanne was able to acquire a second- and third-round pick from Edmonton for Semenko's rights.

The Oilers' pick was the last pick in the second round, but Nanne was still confident that Broten would still be there. At that point, only a handful of teams were scouting aggressively in the U.S. The Semenko deal was finalized before the draft started, but it wasn't announced right away. Nanne recalls that the late Max McNab, then general manager of the Washington Capitals, called him late in the second round trying to deal him his pick early in the third round. McNab didn't know that Nanne had secured Edmonton's pick.

"I know you want Broten, and I'm taking him with that pick unless you make a deal with me now," McNab told Nanne.

"You can have him," Nanne said, not revealing that he had already made his move to land Broten.

The timing of Broten's draft year couldn't have been better for Nanne. Broten was eligible for the NHL draft after his first college season and before he played with the U.S. Olympic Team in 1980. Had Broten's draft eligibility been after the Olympics, he probably would have been a first-round pick.

The oddest aspect of the argument that Broten is the best Hobey Baker winner is that it wasn't a foregone conclusion that Broten was going to win—or even deserved to win—that year. That season, Neal had 17 goals and 54 assists for 71 points in 36 games for the Gophers. His brother, Aaron, 11 months younger than Neal, had 47 goals and 59 assists for 106 points in 45 games for

Minnesota that season. But voters seemed to factor in that Neal had missed nine games due to injury and that he was considered the more complete player. Although the Hobey Baker Award is given for the best performance of the season, it seems fair to wonder if voters were influenced by Neal Broten's history. By the time he was a finalist for the Hobey Baker Award, he had already scored the game-winning goal for Minnesota two years before in the 1979 NCAA Championship Game and then had been among Coach Herb Brooks' best players when Team USA won the gold medal at the 1980 Olympics at Lake Placid.

Although the Hobey Baker goes to the best college player regardless of citizenship, an American has won the award two-thirds of the time. In the first 31 years, there have been 21 American winners. Here is a look at what the Hobey Baker winners accomplished in their pro careers:

1981: Center Neal Broten* (Minnesota): Probably considered among the top five to ten players in American hockey history. Played in the NHL with Minnesota, Dallas, New Jersey, and Los Angeles.

1982: Left wing George McPhee (Bowling Green): Played 115 games in the NHL as a feisty forward but is more remembered as the longtime GM of the Washington Capitals.

1983: Defenseman Mark Fusco* (Harvard): After an outstanding

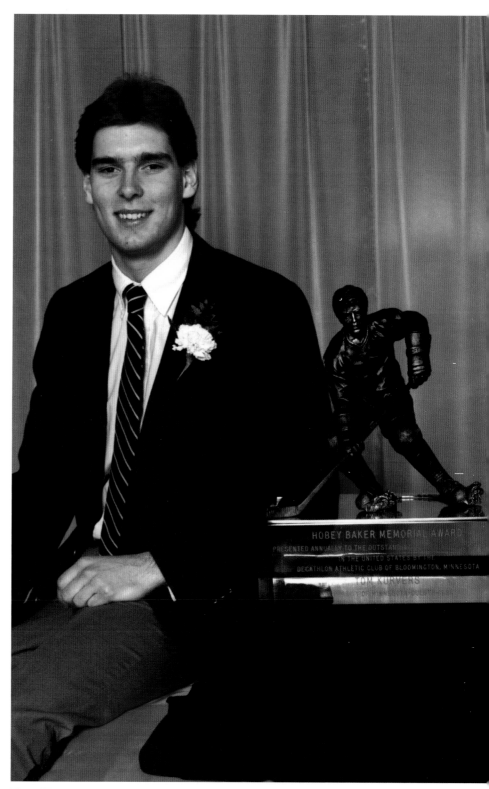

Tom Kurvers of Minnesota-Duluth won the Hobey Baker Award in 1984. Kurvers went on to play 11 seasons in the NHL.
(UMD Athletics)

career as a puck-moving defenseman at Harvard, he played for the 1984 U.S. Olympic Team and then spent two NHL seasons with Hartford.

1984: Defenseman Tom Kurvers* (Minnesota-Duluth): Enjoyed a lengthy career in the NHL, playing with seven different NHL teams. His best season was 1988–89, when he generated 16 goals and 50 assists for the New Jersey Devils.

1985: Right wing Bill Watson (Minnesota-Duluth): After scoring 49 goals in 46 games in his final season at Minnesota-Duluth, Watson turned pro with the Chicago Blackhawks. He played 115 NHL games.

1986: Center Scott Fusco* (Harvard): The Massachusetts-born Fuscos are the only brothers to win the Hobey Baker. Scott is the all-time leading scorer in Harvard history, with 107 goals and 240 points in 123 games. He played for the 1984 and 1988 U.S. Olympic Teams.

1987: Center Tony Hrkac (North Dakota): He netted 46 goals with 70 assists for 116 points in 48 games in his final collegiate season before turning pro with the St. Louis Blues. He played 758 NHL games.

1988: Goalie Robb Stauber* (Minnesota): The Duluth, Minnesota, native played 15 seasons of pro hockey, including 62 games in the NHL with Los Angeles and Buffalo.

1989: Left wing Lane McDonald* (Harvard): The speedy McDonald scored 68 goals in his final 66 games at Harvard and played for the 1988 U.S. Olympic Team. He retired from hockey in 1989.

1990: Center Kip Miller* (Michigan State): After scoring 48 goals in 45 games for the Spartans in his final college season, Miller played 17 years of pro hockey. He played 449 NHL games with eight different teams. He also had a 46-goal season for Denver in the IHL.

1991: Center David Emma* (Boston College): After scoring 112 goals in his college career, Emma had a nine-year pro career with stops in Austria, the AHL, the IHL, and 34 games in the NHL. He is the top scorer in Boston College history.

1992: Left wing Scott Pellerin (Maine): He was a 20-goal scorer one season for the St. Louis Blues and played 536 NHL games before retiring in 2004.

1993: Left wing Paul Kariya (Maine): In his lengthy NHL career, dynamic skater Kariya scored 30 or more goals seven times. He was a member of Canada's gold-medal Olympic team in 2002.

1994: Left wing Chris Marinucci* (Minnesota-Duluth): The Grand Rapids, Minnesota, native had a goal and four assists in his first 12 NHL games with the New York Islanders, but he never really received another NHL chance. He went on to be a top scorer in the IHL and scored 41 goals one season for the Chicago Wolves.

1995: Center Brian Holzinger* (Bowling Green): The Ohio native scored 102 goals in his career at Bowling Green and then played 547 games in his NHL career before retiring after the 2003–04 season. He played with Buffalo, Tampa Bay, Pittsburgh, and Columbus.

1996: Center Brian Bonin* (Minnesota): After scoring 34 goals with 37 assists in 42 games his senior season to win the Hobey, he had a 31-goal season for Syracuse in the American Hockey League. He played five NHL games with Pittsburgh and seven with Minnesota. He had two strong seasons in the Swiss League before retiring in 2005.

1997: Center Brendan Morrison (Michigan): At age 35, Morrison was still a key contributor for the Calgary Flames in the 2010–11 season. He had played in 895 career NHL games by the end of the season.

1998: Left wing Chris Drury* (Boston University): Drury won the NHL Rookie of the Year Award in 1998–99 and is currently playing for the New York Rangers. He was a member of the USA's silver-medal Olympic teams in 2002 and 2010.

1999: Center Jason Krog (New Hampshire): He was playing for the Chicago Wolves in the AHL in 2010–11, but he has played 202 NHL games in his career.

2000: Defenseman Mike Mottau* (Boston College): The Massachusetts native is currently playing for the New York Islanders.

2001: Goaltender Ryan Miller* (Michigan State): The East Lansing, Michigan, native was named the MVP goalie at the 2010 Olympics after leading the USA to the silver medal. Miller won the Vezina Trophy as the NHL's top goalie in 2009–10.

2002: Defenseman Jordan Leopold* (Minnesota): At 31, Jordan Leopold was playing for the Buffalo Sabres in 2010–11. It was perhaps his best NHL season.

2003: Peter Sejna (Colorado College): The Slovak native is the only European player to win the Hobey. He played 49 games for the St. Louis Blues before settling into a solid career in the Swiss League.

2004: Right wing Junior Lessard (Minnesota-Duluth): After scoring 32 goals in 45 games during his final college season, Lessard played briefly in the NHL with the Dallas Stars and Tampa Bay Lightning.

2005: Center Marty Sertich* (Colorado College): In the 2010–11 season, the 5'8" center is playing in the Swiss League. He is the son of Steve Sertich, who played for the 1976 U.S. Olympic Team.

2006: Defenseman Matt Carle* (Denver): The Alaska native reached the Stanley Cup Final as a 20-plus-minute defenseman for the Philadelphia Flyers in 2010.

2007: Left wing Ryan Duncan (North Dakota): The 5'6", 145-pound forward won the Hobey as a sophomore when he netted 31 goals in 43 games. He went to play in the Austrian League after finishing his college career with 85 goals over four seasons.

2008: Center Kevin Porter* (Michigan): A Michigan native, Porter had 33 goals his final season at Michigan and is now playing in the NHL for the Colorado Avalanche.

2009: Defenseman Matt Gilroy* (Boston University): He is now a mainstay of the New York Rangers' defense after four years as the rock of the Terriers' defense.

2010: Left wing Blake Geoffrion* (Wisconsin): On February 26, 2011, Geoffrion became the first native Tennessean to play for the Nashville Predators. He was Nashville's second-round pick in 2006.

2011: Center Andy Miele* (Miami): At 5'9", Miele racked up 71 points (24 goals), the most for a college player since the 2002–03 season. ∎

*American

Clarence "Taffy" Abel was probably America's first National Hockey League standout. Feared by opponents, Abel was a ferocious body checker who weighed as much as 245 pounds in an era when many forwards weighed about 150. Despite his size, he was reputed to be an accomplished skater.
(Hockey Hall of Fame)

HOCKEY IN THE 1920s
Taffy Abel and Friends

When 6'2", 245-pound defenseman Clarence "Taffy" Abel arrived in the National Hockey League in 1926, he was both a premium player and a center-ring attraction.

This was an era when forwards were small and sleek, many of them weighing less than 165 pounds. Abel's burly girth made him a curiosity. Fans were clearly intrigued by this bear-sized man who had no difficulty handling the speed of the game.

"He was a very good skater," his former Chicago Blackhawks teammate Art Coulter said in a 1996 interview. "When he would start up ice, the defense would just converge on him. They would be hanging all over him. He would be like a mother ape with five baby apes hanging off him."

Abel was not the first American-born and trained player in the NHL. That distinction belongs to former Dartmouth center/right wing George "Gerry" Geran of Holyoke, Massachusetts, who played four games for the Montreal Wanderers in 1917. But Abel, a member of the U.S. Hockey Hall of Fame, was the first true American standout, playing three seasons with the New York Rangers, starting in 1926–27, and five seasons with the Chicago Blackhawks, starting in 1929–30.

In the early 1930s the *Chicago American* stated of Abel, "Rated strictly on his defensive ability, there's no better left defenseman in the league."

U.S. Hockey Hall of Fame member Muzz Murray from Michigan was the first true American to reach the Stanley Cup Final when he played for the Seattle team that reached the 1918–19 Stanley Cup series that was cancelled due to the Spanish influenza epidemic. But Abel was the first American on an NHL team to *win* a Stanley Cup.

Coulter said Abel probably should have been elected to the Hall of Fame. Under the idea that he had been overlooked, Abel was nominated again in the mid-1990s, but his candidacy didn't receive any support by the selection committee.

Born in 1900, Abel was the grandson of the chief of the Cherokee tribe. He was a legend around the Soo until his hometown ice rink burned to the ground. To continue his hockey career, Abel moved to the St. Paul Athletic Club, where he started to draw the attention of the NHL and organizers of the 1924 U.S. Olympic Team. He made the Olympic team and was chosen to be the American flag bearer at the Winter Games in Chamonix, France.

In an era when it was considered blasphemy for defenders to stray from their own blue line, Abel managed to net 15 goals in five games as the USA won the silver medal in France. Word of his exploits reached Conn Smythe, then the manager of the New York Rangers. He had been interested in Abel prior to the Olympics because he had heard Abel was as big as a house but could still skate with reasonable quickness.

Abel's defensive ability and toughness made him attractive to professional coaches. But because he wasn't immediately enamored with the idea of an NHL career, he went back to St. Paul after the 1924 Olympics, resisting the idea of an NHL career with the same fierce stubbornness that made him one of the league's better defenders. Smythe's method for locking Abel into his first National Hockey League contract in 1926 was *literally* locking him in...or, at least that's what Smythe threatened to do.

Smythe had heard his hockey buddies gush about the 245-pound American defenseman for several years and was more than annoyed to discover Abel wasn't overly impressed by the NHL's offers and was as stubborn as Smythe when it came down to money.

Abel rejected several Rangers offers before Smythe convinced him to at least show up for a face-to-face meeting in the Pullman train car. Abel wouldn't budge on his stance, and when the conductor announced the train was about to roll, he began to head for the door. Smythe raced ahead of him and locked him in.

"The money's good, you won't do better, and the next stop is 250 miles away," Smythe said. "If you don't sign, you won't be getting off until then."

Abel, a powerful man with a quick temper, must have been amused by Smythe's style, because on another day he might have thrown Smythe through the window. Instead, he signed the contract, shook Smythe's hand, and jumped from the train as it was pulling out of the station.

The Rangers immediately proclaimed Abel to be the NHL's largest player, which would be both a curse and a blessing for Abel. Although opponents feared Abel's size, coaches felt he would have been more effective if he was better conditioned and 20 pounds lighter.

According to the media reports of that era, Abel was a gum-chewing, rough-and-tumble competitor whose body checks often sent opposing forwards airborne. He was also adept at pushing his opponents into the boards and draping over them until the referee whistled the play dead. His size and his willingness to use it made him an intimidating presence. When he was playing for the Blackhawks, the fans in New York, Boston, and Detroit loved to rain boos and insults down on him and razz him unmercifully about his girth.

Meal money didn't go to waste on Abel. At various points in his career, Abel weighed more than 260 pounds. When he played with the New York Rangers early in his career, he was paired with Ching Johnson, another beefy defenseman. At a combined 430 to 460 pounds—depending upon when they had last been fed—they were probably the heaviest defensive duo in the game. Johnson, although born in Winnipeg, actually had some American roots. He had come down to Eveleth, Minnesota, as a teenager to play senior hockey. He was still playing senior hockey in Marquette, Michigan, when he was in his forties.

In his rookie season, Abel's eight goals made him the Rangers' fourth-highest goal scorer and one of the league's top-scoring defensemen. That level of production put him in the company of Ottawa Senator King Clancy, New York American Lionel Conacher, and Boston Bruin Eddie Shore, all of whom were considered elite-level NHL defensemen.

Shore was considered among the best ever to play the position. But it certainly wasn't Abel's offensive touch that endeared him to fans; he never had more than three goals or six points in any future NHL season. He was known as an immovable object and quickly earned a reputation for doing whatever was required to achieve a win.

People in Abel's hometown understood his molten drive to win. According to local folklore, the legend of Abel's competitive spirit was established by a well-timed right cross. Abel's team, the Soo Indians, had just lost a 1–0 decision against a bitter rival when the team manager strolled into the dressing room and said, "Well, there's always the next game." The sentence was barely finished when Abel's fist caught the manager square on the jaw. It was a one-punch TKO, and Abel was suspended for the remainder of the season.

"He was two different personalities," says Bill Thorn, Abel's second cousin. "Off the ice, he was easygoing. But on the ice, you didn't want to meet him. He hated to lose." He also didn't like anyone taking advantage of him on or off the ice. A Canadian newspaper carried the story of Abel, then playing for the Rangers, being rolled for $100 by a Manhattan con artist who had convinced the kindhearted Abel to loan him $2. When Abel removed his money clip from his trousers, the thief snatched it and escaped into the streets before Abel could react.

Shocked and then enraged by the mugging, Abel returned to his room and plotted revenge. He pulled a gun from its hiding place in his room and set out to bring vigilante justice to his assailant. It didn't take long to locate him. The con man hadn't been smart enough to know he shouldn't be spending Abel's money within a few blocks of where the fleecing took place. It's not difficult to imagine the combination of fear and surprise the petty thief must have felt as he found himself staring at the business end of Abel's revolver. He immediately returned the ill-gotten cash to Abel. However, it was short the money he already had spent, so Abel escorted his new "friend" around town until he managed to borrow enough money to repay the original amount.

Thorn spent many hours listening to Abel's stories, and among those he enjoyed most was the tale of Abel's participation in one of the most famous games in Stanley Cup Finals history. Abel was on defense when 45-year-old coach and general manager Lester Patrick was forced into action as a New York Rangers goalie when starter Lorne Chabot was injured. In those days, NHL teams didn't carry a backup goaltender, and the Montreal Maroons, the Rangers' opponent, were rather unsympathetic to the Rangers' predicament. They saw the situation as assuring them a badly needed win.

"Taffy told me neither he or Ching Johnson was going to allow any shots to get through to the net," Thorn said. "He thought there was only a few [dangerous] shots on goal on Patrick."

Although Abel had served the Rangers well for three seasons and helped them win their first Stanley Cup in 1928, team management became concerned with the fluctuation of Abel's weight. When Abel refused to shed his excess pounds, the Rangers sold him to flamboyant Chicago Blackhawks owner Major McLaughlin for a whopping $15,000, a sizable sum in those days for a hockey transaction.

"He was comfortable the way he was, and he told them that," Thorn said. "At that weight, he could still skate very fast."

Abel's popularity was instantaneous in the Windy City. Fans loved the way Abel could use his massive body as a weapon of terror. Much of the time, the sight of Abel racing toward opponents like a charging rhino was enough to force a turnover. But those brave hearts who stood up to Abel found that he was willing to use his body as an instrument of destruction. In the 1932–33 season, Abel's seventh in the NHL, he registered more penalty minutes than he had since his rookie season with the Rangers.

In his fifth season with the Blackhawks, Abel showed up at training camp in the best shape of his career. Newspaper articles state Abel was 15 to 20 pounds lighter than during his previous seasons with the Hawks.

Sportswriter Jim Gallagher of the *Chicago American* newspaper wrote: "Montreal fans find it hard to understand why the Rangers even parted with Abel. Taff has trimmed his huge bulk a bit, although he still retains enough weight to render him a stone wall that is almost impervious to enemy attacks."

After Abel had been in the league a few years, not many opponents challenged him. "You would have had to be pretty stupid to do that," Art Coulter said. "And guys weren't that stupid."

At age 33, Abel helped the Blackhawks win their first Stanley Cup. That summer, he had a contract squabble with McLaughlin and decided to retire when it wasn't resolved.

"He told me it was only a matter of $100," Thorn said. "He had been promised more money if they won the Stanley Cup, and [if] McLaughlin wasn't going to give it to him, he was going home. And he did. He believed a promise was a promise."

The beefy defenseman returned home to Sault Sainte Marie. Today, the Lake Superior State University hockey team plays in Clarence "Taffy" Abel Arena, originally constructed in 1976.

Abel wasn't the only American in the NHL in that era. Geran did return to the NHL, although not as quickly as he would have liked. Eight years after the Wanderers went out of business, he signed with his hometown Boston Bruins. He scored five goals in 33 games in the 1925–26 season.

Geran had a reputation for being a character and highly adventurous. After playing for the 1920 U.S. Olympic Team, he returned to Boston for a year and then traveled abroad to play in the developing French League. The talent level in that league must have been inferior, because he scored 88 goals in eight games for the Paris Volants.

While in France, Geran grew to enjoy fine wine. That fact is known because the *Montreal Gazette* quoted NHL player Sprague Cleghorn telling a humorous story about how he pilfered Geran's wine.

Cleghorn lived above Geran in a Boston apartment building in 1925, and he noticed that Geran liked to park a bottle of wine outside on his window sill to chill before dinner. Hanging out his window, Cleghorn dropped a fishing line with a small noose attached and hooked the wine. He reeled up the bottle and enjoyed it himself. Geran apparently never discovered who was snatching his wine. Cleghorn said Geran "blamed it on neighborhood kids."

Years later, *Lewiston (Maine) Evening Journal* sports editor Norman S. Thomas reported that Geran was working as a bullfighter in Spain. At the time, Geran was Social Security age. "He's old enough to know better, but he loves the thrills," Thomas wrote.

In the 1925–26 season, Alphonse Lacroix, Team USA's 1924 Olympic goalie, became the first American to play in an NHL net. He signed to play five games for the Montreal Canadiens because regular goaltender George Vezina contracted tuberculosis. Lacroix was 1–4 with a 3.43 goals-against average and never played another NHL game.

Billy Burch and Ed Carpenter are sometimes mistakenly credited with being among the first Americans in the NHL because both were born in the U.S. Both, however, grew up in Canada, where their skills were developed. They considered themselves Canadian.

Defenseman Herb Drury, born in Midland, Ontario, is a more interesting case, although hockey historians clearly view him as Canadian. If you accept that Brett Hull was an American player when he played in the NHL, then an argument can be made that Drury was also an American. Like Hull, Drury was trained in Canada and then moved to the U.S. as a young man. But like Hull, Drury did embrace the U.S. as his adopted country. At age 21, Drury relocated south to play for the Pittsburgh Yellowjackets in the United States Amateur Hockey Association (USAHA), served in the military during World War I, and was a top player for both the 1920 and 1924 U.S. Olympic Teams. Starting in 1925–26, he played five NHL seasons with the Pittsburgh Pirates and another with the Philadelphia Quakers before retiring. Drury lived the rest of his life in Pittsburgh and is always mentioned prominently in any historical reports of Pittsburgh hockey.

Two members of the U.S. Hockey Hall of Fame did win a Stanley Cup with the Boston Bruins in 1929. Myles Lane was a former Dartmouth standout, and George Owen was a Harvard star, and both played defense for the Boston squad that

A member of the 1924 U.S. Olympic team, Herb Drury is often referred to as one of the first Americans to play in the National Hockey League. But Drury was a Canadian who moved to the United States to make money as a hockey player. Drury played six NHL seasons (1925–26 to 1930–31), scoring 24 goals in 207 games. (Bill Galloway/Hockey Hall of Fame)

defeated the New York Rangers in a three-game series to capture the Cup.

Born in Melrose, Massachusetts, Lane had started his NHL career as Abel's teammate on the New York Rangers in 1928–29. It could be said that Lane was the Hobey Baker of Dartmouth because he received national acclaim in both hockey and football. When he graduated, Lane owned the school record of 20 goals in a season and 50 in a

Arguably the best American hockey player in the 1920s, Francis "Moose" Goheen starred on the 1920 Olympic team but chose not to pursue an NHL career because he didn't want to give up his job at the Northern States Power Company. (Hockey Hall of Fame)

career by a defenseman. In those days, a college hockey season was eight games. Lane was also an All-American halfback for the Dartmouth football team, and one season Lane led the nation in scoring.

Lane went on to become a New York Supreme Court justice, and when he died in 1987, a *New York Times* obituary stated that in the 1920s "he was widely compared to Jim Thorpe and Hobey Baker as the ultimate all-around athlete."

In the same 1987 article written by Joseph Durso and famed *New York Times* obituary writer Robert McGill Thomas, Jr., former New York Rangers public relations director Stan Saplin was quoted as saying that the Rangers once tried to use Lane's popularity in Boston as a way to acquire Eddie Shore from Boston.

Col. John Hammond was the Rangers president at the time, and he was more of a promoter than a hockey guy. As soon as the Rangers signed Lane, Hammond, not known for his hockey knowledge, figured the Bruins would want their favorite son badly enough that they would give up Shore to have him. According to Saplin, Hammond ordered Rangers general manager and coach Lester Patrick to offer the Bruins $5,000 and Lane in exchange for Shore, who was already an established star.

Saplin said Patrick—who told him this story—knew when he sent the telegram that the Bruins had no interest in dealing Shore and certainly weren't going to trade him for an unproven rookie named Myles Lane.

But Boston president Charles F. Adams apparently had a sense of humor, because he sent a return telegram to Patrick that read: "Get a life preserver—you are Myles from Shore."

On January 21, 1929, the Bruins did acquire Lane, but Shore wasn't involved in the deal. The Bruins bought Lane's contract for $7,500, and Lane played sparingly on the 1929 Cup-winning team.

He ended up playing 71 NHL games before retiring after the 1933–34 season.

George Owen had a more noteworthy career with the Bruins. He was actually born in Hamilton, Ontario, but his parents moved to Boston shortly after his birth. He was a two-time captain of the Harvard team and ended up coaching one season at Harvard and playing four seasons of amateur hockey in Boston before signing with the Bruins at age 27.

He was a high-scoring defenseman for Boston for five seasons before retiring to coach at Michigan Tech. He ended up with 44 goals in 183 NHL regular-season games.

Arguably the best American hockey player in the 1920s was not in the NHL, nor did he aspire to be. Francis "Moose" Goheen was a rushing defenseman from White Bear Lake, Minnesota, known for his end-to-end dashes with the puck. He played football and baseball at Valparaiso University and then went on to play hockey for the St. Paul Athletic Club. He was a member of the St. Paul team that won the McNaughton Cup in the U.S. National Amateur Championship in 1916 and 1917. U.S. Hockey Hall of Fame member Nick Kahler, a high-scoring center, was also on that St. Paul squad. Goheen played for the 1920 U.S. Olympic Team but rejected an invitation to play for the 1924 squad. He also said no to contract offers from the Toronto Maple Leafs and Boston Bruins because he didn't want to give up his excellent job at the Northern States Power Company.

"Had he gone to Canada or other outposts in North America where the game flourished, Goheen would have been sainted years ago," Don Riley wrote in the *St. Paul Pioneer Press* in 1978.

Goheen wasn't the only standout American hockey player who didn't play in the NHL. Frank "Coddy" Winters, a speedy forward and defenseman, was a star in Cleveland-area hockey from about 1908 to 1925.

In his U.S. Hockey Hall of Fame biography, Joe Linder from Hancock, Michigan, has been described as the "first great American-born hockey player." He played from 1904 to 1920. Michigan's Upper Peninsula was heavily invested in hockey at the turn of the 20th century.

A February 1941 issue of *Esquire* magazine said of Linder, "Any list of the 30 best hockey players the whole world has had would have to include the American-born Linder."

Yet it is difficult to believe that Linder was superior to Goheen, who was six feet tall, weighed 200 pounds, and was not bashful about hurling himself at opponents. He was a wickedly fast skater with large, powerful thighs and sculpted shoulders. According to writings of the time, Goheen clearly had an advanced understanding of hockey tactics and puck movement. Goheen seemed to be a thoroughbred in a field of plow horses. Crowds would endure below-zero temperatures in the unheated Minnesota State Fairgrounds to see Goheen perform his hockey magic act.

"The team could be sluggish, and then Moose would make one of those rink-long trips, split the defense, leaving falling bodies behind, and pour in the goal," teammate Emy Garrett said years later. "From that point on, bedlam tore up the house, and his team would become unbeatable."

Although Goheen never played in the NHL, the U.S. Hockey Hall of Fame still inducted Goheen in 1952.

Minnesota-area sportswriter Halsey Hall once wrote about Goheen, "Nothing in sports could ever beat the sight of Moose Goheen taking the puck, circling behind his own net, and then taking off down that rink, leaping over sticks along the way." ■

After registering 10 goals and 9 assists in 48 games, Minneapolis native Cully Dahlstrom won the Calder Trophy as the NHL Rookie of the Year in 1937–38.
(Le Studio du Hockey/Hockey Hall of Fame)

USA HOCKEY

THE 1930s
Chicago's Yankees

The oddity of the Chicago Blackhawks' 1937–38 Stanley Cup championship season is that the first step toward that title came on a baseball diamond instead of a hockey rink.

Blackhawks owner Major Frederic McLaughlin was basking in the sun at Wrigley Field in the summer of 1937, enjoying a game between the Chicago Cubs and St. Louis Cardinals, when he realized the home plate umpire was American-born Bill "Stumpy" Stewart, who spent his winters as an NHL referee. McLaughlin was keenly interested when Cardinals manager Frankie Frisch started chirping at Stewart from the dugout. Frisch apparently didn't like Stewart's read on balls and strikes and wasn't timid about voicing that opinion.

Finally boiling over, Frisch, known as "the Fordham Flash," stormed from the dugout and made a charge toward home plate. The diminutive, barrel-chested Stewart peeled off his mask and pointed it at Frisch, as if it possessed the power to stop Frisch in his tracks.

"Franklin," Stewart growled. "Turn around and head back to that dugout, because I don't want to listen to you. I'll throw you right out of this game."

Frisch scowled for another moment or two before deciding retreat was his best course of action. He had scrapped with Stewart before and knew he didn't threaten unless he intended to follow through.

McLaughlin was clearly amused and impressed by what he had seen. "That's the man I need to run my hockey team," McLaughlin reportedly told folks who were with him. "Anyone who can handle Frankie Frisch is tough enough to handle my team."

A few days later, McLaughlin offered the 43-year-old Stewart a one-year contract for $6,500 to coach the Chicago Blackhawks, making him the only American coach in the NHL.

But Stewart, a sharp businessman from Jamaica Plain, Massachusetts, told McLaughlin he wouldn't do it unless McLaughlin gave him a two-year deal and a promise not to meddle in coaching decisions. He knew the major liked to tell coaches who should be playing and who shouldn't. McLaughlin was the George Steinbrenner of hockey in the 1930s. He agreed to both of Stewart's stipulations, although Stewart would discover later that those promises weren't made in full earnestness.

McLaughlin knew more about Stewart's toughness than he had witnessed at Wrigley. Stewart had been a highly respected NHL referee since 1928. In 1933 Stewart had awarded the only forfeit in NHL history after Blackhawks coach Tom Gorman hit him. Before awarding the forfeit, Stewart jumped over the boards and chased Gorman through the Boston Garden lobby.

But Stewart's toughness was only part of the lure to McLaughlin. Stewart was a well-respected American, and if anyone could help McLaughlin develop an all-American team and keep ridicule to a minimum, it was Stewart.

Always trying to bring more fans to Chicago Stadium, McLaughlin had been selling the fans on the idea of using more American players. When Taffy Abel retired to Sault Sainte Marie to launch a supper club in 1934, Chicago's Elwyn "Doc" Romnes was the only American standout left in the NHL. But Mike Karakas of Eveleth, Minnesota, became the Blackhawks goalie in 1935, and Cully Dahlstrom, from Minneapolis, signed with the Blackhawks in 1937. He had badly failed a tryout with the Boston Bruins in 1932, when he was 19. "Those guys were skating circles around me," he told writer Randy Schultz years later. "It was as if I was going in slow motion."

But his feistiness earned him a spot on McLaughlin's Blackhawks, although McLaughlin wasn't his biggest fan. However, McLaughlin was inexplicably becoming a fan of American hockey talent, maybe because he had witnessed the way fans worshiped Abel. Although never particularly liked by his players, McLaughlin certainly tried to

give American hockey a boost, even if it was simply a marketing idea to increase his profits.

The Major, as he was called, was a cantankerous businessman who frequently jousted at league meetings with Conn Smythe, Lester Patrick, and James Norris. He was an idea man, a mover and shaker, far more aggressive than the conservative men who sat in the governors' chairs for the other NHL teams. On some nights, he came across like the ringmaster at a Barnum & Bailey circus. That was especially true in 1937 when he announced he was planning to fill his roster entirely with American-born players, telling the New York Times he was going to create the "Chicago Yankees."

Since only a few American-born players had ever been thought worthy of NHL consideration, McLaughlin's idea was met with howls of laughter. Norris and Patrick filed protests with the league, claiming this practice would create an unfair advantage for the teams that were lucky enough to have the Blackhawks on their schedule late in the season.

The Blackhawks already boasted four American-born players on their roster, although only Karakas and winger Romnes had spent all of their lives in the U.S. The other two, Alex Levinsky and Louis Trudel, were born in the United States and then moved to Canada as youngsters.

For the final five games of the 1936–37 season, Blackhawks coach Clem Loughlin added defenseman Ernest "Ike" Klingbeil of Hancock, Michigan, and winger Ben "Bun" LaPrairie of Sault Sainte Marie, plus defenseman Paul "Butch" Schaeffer, center Milt Brink, and winger Al Suomi, all of Eveleth, Minnesota.

The all-American team had a 1–4 record during McLaughlin's experiment, recording the only win on a 4–3 decision against the New York Rangers.

Stewart was a well-respected American, and if anyone could help McLaughlin develop an all-American team and keep ridicule to a minimum, it was Stewart.

Patrick, who had plenty to say before the experiment, was strangely quiet after his team lost to the American squad. But overall, the American experiment hadn't been a success. The Hawks were outscored 27–13 over the five games, and Klingbeil was the only newcomer to register a point. He had a goal and two assists. None of the late-addition Americans played another NHL game.

"I think that since his team was in an American city he wanted American-born players," Dahlstrom told the *Hockey News* years later. "But he soon found out there weren't enough Americans to build one team around. I don't think it took him long to discover that."

But McLaughlin didn't surrender the idea immediately. Miffed that he had been subjected to ridicule, he made his experiment more interesting by hiring an American-born coach. That coach and several Americans, including Dahlstrom and Romnes, would help McLaughlin exact some revenge with one of the most unlikely Stanley Cup championship runs in NHL history.

Despite Stewart's background, he probably didn't like McLaughlin's "American-born player" concept all that much. "He believed if you could play, you could play, and it didn't matter where you were from," said Paul Stewart, his grandson, who would later play and officiate in the NHL.

Ironically, the first of several arguments Stewart had with the owner was over McLaughlin's desire to trade one of the American players. McLaughlin wanted to dump Dahlstrom because

he didn't believe he was talented enough. Stewart kept him anyway, and Dahlstrom went on to win the Calder Trophy as Rookie of the Year after netting 10 goals and 9 assists in 48 games. "My grandfather loved Cully Dahlstrom's grit," his grandson Paul Stewart said.

The McLaughlin-Stewart relationship was probably akin to the Steinbrenner–Billy Martin relationship in the 1970s in terms of their ability to push one another's hot buttons. McLaughlin had been a machine-gun battalion commander in World War I in the 86th Infantry Division. He certainly wasn't going to back down. As a professional umpire and NHL referee, Stewart was accustomed to having the final word. He wasn't going to bow to McLaughlin's authority. "When it came to final control over the players, it was stubborn versus stubborn," Stewart's son Bill II recalled.

Stewart undoubtedly knew what he was getting into when he took the job. But he was a tough man who believed correctly that he could handle anything McLaughlin could throw at him. Stewart viewed McLaughlin as having "a lot of dough and nothing to do with it."

Coping with McLaughlin's style was just part of being a member of the Chicago Blackhawks. Karakas once approached the Major with some suggestions about how to restructure the team to make it more competitive.

"We can be better organized," Karakas said.

"Organized? What are you, a communist?" McLaughlin replied.

Chicago Blackhawks players, from left, Jack Shill, Carl Voss, Carl "Cully"Dahlstrom, and Harold "Mush" March celebrate after the Blackhawks won the Stanley Cup in 1938. (Bruce Bennett Studios/Getty Images)

Stewart's arrival didn't instantly trigger any magical transformation of the Hawks into a championship-caliber team. Chicago's 14–25–9 record was only two points better than its mark the season before, and the Blackhawks had given up more goals than any team in the league except the Montreal Maroons.

No one anticipated what was to happen in the playoffs, least of all the players, who knew they had been outclassed in the regular season. The best-of-three quarterfinal against the Canadiens began as expected, with a 6–4 loss at Montreal. But then the Blackhawks' fortunes began to turn in Game 2 when Karakas posted a 4–0 shutout in Chicago Stadium, and again in Game 3 in Montreal when the Hawks won on Paul Thompson's overtime goal.

The semifinal series against the New York Americans followed a similar script. The Blackhawks lost the first game in New York, but then Karakas posted a 1–0 shutout in Game 2 in Chicago, and the Hawks rallied to beat New York 3–2 in the deciding game.

The Blackhawks' performance was a shocker, particularly to Levinsky. He had moved out of his place and sent his wife home to Toronto before the playoffs, thinking he would be joining her in a few days. He ended up living out of the backseat of his car for more than a month as the Blackhawks' roll continued.

Still, no one gave the Chicago team a chance in the final series against the heavily favored Toronto Maple Leafs, who had finished 20 points ahead of Chicago in the regular season. To make matters worse, Karakas had broken his toe against the New York Americans and couldn't start the series, although he kept telling folks he would like to try. Because these were still the days when teams didn't carry backup goaltenders, Stewart planned to seek NHL approval to use New York Rangers netminder David Kerr in Game 1. Kerr had led the NHL with eight shutouts that season and was second in goals-against average at 1.95. With today's sophisticated player-roster rules, Stewart's plan wouldn't have had much hope of league approval, but in those days, rules were sometimes made up as problems presented themselves.

But Leafs general manager Conn Smythe was not going to let Kerr play. Seeing an opportunity to give his team more of an advantage than it already owned, he insisted the Blackhawks had to use Karakas, with his broken toe, or 32-year-old Alfie Moore, a 12-year minor league veteran who Smythe allegedly had called in to play for Chicago. Moore had played for the Pittsburgh Hornets of the American Association League that season after failing in a brief trial with the New York Americans during the previous season. Karakas wanted to try to play, but the pain was unbearable.

Stewart was furious, because he had been under the assumption Kerr was going to play. "We get to the Gardens and Moore walks in to tell us that he's been ordered to play," Stewart told reporters later.

Legend has it that Moore, not known to be a stellar goaltender, wasn't greeted warmly in the Hawks dressing room. When Louis Trudel saw it was Moore who was going to be in the net, he reportedly said, "Why didn't you break your leg in Pittsburgh?"

Stewart didn't accept the incident without a fight. It infuriated him when Toronto Maple Leafs assistant general manager, Frank Selke, insisted that the Blackhawks had been told that Kerr might not be able to play. "You're a liar," Stewart shouted at Selke.

Smythe then stepped into the picture. "You can't call my pal Selke a liar and get away with it," Smythe said as he charged Stewart. Maple Leafs scout Baldy Cotton was also in the mix.

Newspaper reports aren't clear on who threw the first punch. "It was like the battle of Lexington and Concord; you don't really know who shot first," Paul Stewart said. "But I do know [my grandfather] said he went wild because he was really mad. He said, 'Conn Smythe screwed me.'"

Imagine the anger on the Hawks bench after the Maple Leafs scored on their first shot against Moore. But then, as it had during the entire play-offs, fortunes changed for the Blackhawks. Moore buckled down, and Chicago posted a 3–1 win. Once, when Moore thought the puck was behind him, it actually hit him in the seat of his pants; that's how dramatically the Blackhawks' fortunes had changed during the playoffs.

All the screaming started anew before Game 2, when NHL president Frank Calder ruled Moore was now ineligible because he had a contract with another team and the Hawks would have to use rookie Paul Goodman. The Maple Leafs hammered the rookie 5–1.

The Blackhawks had other problems heading into Game 3 in Chicago. Several players had been cut by high sticks in Game 2. Dahlstrom had injured his knee, and Toronto's Red Horner had broken Romnes' nose in three places with the butt end of his stick. Stewart told *Sports Illustrated* that when he went to visit his players at the hospital, "it was like a scene from a war movie."

Romnes would play Game 3 wearing a Purdue football helmet and face mask to protect the injury. Stewart asked the players not to take revenge on Horner, but he probably knew they wouldn't listen. The only good news for the Chicago Hawks heading into Game 3 was that Karakas was going to play, although his toe wasn't close to being healed.

"It was the roughest, wildest series I ever saw," Levinsky would say years later. "The games were completely out of the referee's control, and everybody skated around with his stick a mile in the air."

A record crowd of 18,402 showed up for Game 3 at Chicago Stadium. Fans were frisked at the door because it was expected they would bring in objects to hurl at the Maple Leafs, who had bruised their Blackhawks so badly in the previous game. The fact that McLaughlin had convinced the local newspaper to publish a photograph of all the injured players at the hospital helped rile Hawks fans even more. First and foremost, McLaughlin was a showman.

Romnes, who had won the Lady Byng trophy in 1936 as the league's most gentlemanly player, wasn't gentlemanly in Game 3. In the first minute, the 160-pound Romnes clubbed the 200-pound Horner and knocked him out, or at least that's what the Toronto media reported. The Chicago media said Romnes missed and Horner fainted. Stewart's son, Bill II, was at the game, however, and he would tell his family that Romnes "just tweaked his nose, kind of clipped him."

In a letter to sportswriter Jim Proudfoot almost 30 years later, former NHL president Clarence Campbell seemed to support the notion that Horner was overcome more by fear than the actual hit. "Without being touched, he fainted dead away and was only revived by a goodly supply of Tim Daly's smelling salts," Campbell wrote.

He also didn't seem to blame Romnes much for the incident. "In the second game, the Chicago team took a pretty good physical beating and poor Doc had his nose spread all over his face by Horner," Campbell added. "That night it was a mass of ugly green and purple and Doc was in no Lady Byng mood."

Also in that game, Romnes waylaid 200-pound Toronto defenseman Harvey Jackson. "He really laid into him," recalled Art Coulter, who watched the game. "He knew what he was doing."

Adding insult to Horner's alleged injury, Romnes ended up scoring the game-winning goal with 4:05 remaining to give the Hawks a 2–1 victory.

Two days later, the Chicago Blackhawks won 4–1 to finish off their improbable drive to the Stanley Cup championship. The players kissed Karakas and carried Stewart on their shoulders, but in keeping within the spirit of their season, they almost dropped him.

The Blackhawks weren't able to drink from the Stanley Cup because the Detroit Red Wings, who had won it the year before, had shipped it to Toronto, fully convinced the Maple Leafs would win easily. McLaughlin was beside himself, proud that he could thumb his nose at those who said he couldn't win with American players. Nobody was laughing at him now.

Stewart also felt a sense of pride because, as he would tell his family later, "They were laughing at us because of our mediocre year." He is recognized as the first true American coach to win the Cup. Though Hall of Famer Leo J. Dandurand—born in Bourbonnais, Illinois—was part-owner and coach of the Montreal Canadiens when they won the Stanley Cup in 1924, he wasn't considered a true American because he had moved to Canada as a youngster.

McLaughlin got his wish because technically the Blackhawks had eight Americans on their roster when they won the Cup, although half of them were players who were born in America and then moved to Canada in their youth.

The true American contributors in the playoffs were Karakas, Dahlstrom, Romnes, and defenseman Virgil Johnson from Minneapolis. Johnson played all 10 playoff games, won the Stanley Cup, and then returned to play for the St. Paul Saints in the American Hockey Association. He had another tour with the Blackhawks in 1943–44 and 1944–45.

Eveleth, Minnesota, native Tony Ahlin, a left wing, did play one game with the Blackhawks in 1937–38, the only NHL game he would ever play.

Famed University of Michigan coach Vic Heyliger, who guided the Wolverines to six NCAA championships in 13 seasons from 1944 to 1957, played seven games at center for the Blackhawks during that 1937–38 campaign.

Since the NHL counts birthplace in determining citizenship, the Blackhawks had more Americans on the roster than every league champion until 1995 when the Stanley Cup–winning New Jersey Devils legitimately had 11 Americans (Neal Broten, Jim Dowd, Shawn Chambers, Bill Guerin, Brian Rolston, Chris Terreri, Tom Chorske, Bob Carpenter, Danton Cole, Chris McAlpine, and Mike Peluso).

Winning the Cup didn't resolve the differences between Stewart and McLaughlin. Even while the Hawks were polishing off the Maple Leafs, there were rumors that McLaughlin was planning to fire Stewart. He had obviously decided he didn't like a man who had the courage to stand up to him as often as Stewart did.

The Major fired Stewart the following January. Stewart immediately headed for Florida to wait for the start of spring training. He used the $13,000 of pay to buy a beautiful home in Jamaica Plain. He came back to the NHL as a referee and worked until 1943.

Blackhawks management wanted to announce that Stewart had resigned to keep the team's image intact—after all, they were firing a guy who took them to the championship the year before. But Stewart told the *Boston Globe* he was fired for not following McLaughlin's orders about personnel. "I've never quit on the job," Stewart said, "and I'm sure not going to start now."

Stewart's accomplishment as the first true American coach to win the Stanley Cup is probably proven by the fact that it took 53 years for Bob Johnson (Pittsburgh Penguins, 1990–91) to be the second. Stewart was a trailblazer for other American coaches.

The Blackhawks played poorly the next season. McLaughlin found some other American players he liked, but he never found a collection quite as good as Dahlstrom, Romnes, and especially Karakas, whose importance to the Blackhawks' triumph is often overlooked. ∎

Frank Brimsek was named the NHL's Rookie of the Year in 1938–39 after posting a 1.58 goals against average and recording 10 shutouts.
(Le Studio du Hockey/Hockey Hall of Fame)

THE EVELETH MOTHER LODE
America's Hockey Capital in the 1930s

While the manufacturing community was busy extracting pure iron from the countryside surrounding Eveleth, Minnesota, in the 1930s, the NHL had started to mine a different mother lode.

Eveleth's production of elite-level hockey talent is one of the great stories, if not mysteries, of American hockey history. How could this immigrant community of 5,000 residents send 11 players to the NHL in an era when it seemed as if the league was an exclusive Canadians-only club? Crazier still, how in 1938, could Eveleth High School graduates Frank Brimsek and Mike Karakas own two of the NHL's six goaltending jobs? And how do we explain that when Karakas left the Blackhawks, his starting job went to another Eveleth resident, Sam LoPresti?

Today, Detroit claims the title of Hockeytown, but Eveleth was America's true hockey town in the 1920s, 1930s, and 1940s.

"We had two indoor ice rinks, and the city had tremendous interest in the sport," said Tommy Karakas, Mike's younger brother. "And baseball had a lot to do with the goaltenders. We played a lot of baseball, and [we] all had good glove hands."

In those years in Eveleth, the men, as a rule, worked in the mines, and their boys played hockey. In 2011 former Chicago Blackhawks left wing Al Suomi, then 97, was the NHL's oldest living player. In an interview with Hometownfocus.com website writer Brian Miller, Suomi recalled learning to play the game at age five, on what was called Fayal Pond: "You'd go out in the woods and chop a crooked branch to use as a stick," Suomi said. "For pucks we used rubber balls, tin cans, even frozen horse turds. If we were using [a horse turd], we used to say, 'Ya better keep your mouth shut.'"

Canadians didn't quite know what to make of Eveleth's prominence, given that the NHL was about 98 percent Canadian before the men from Eveleth began claiming roster spots.

"We just considered Eveleth a province of Canada," the late *Toronto Star* hockey writer Jim Proudfoot once said. "In terms of climate, it was very similar."

Eveleth was located about 100 miles from Canada and 60 miles from Duluth, where pure iron ore could be shipped around the world and molded into everything from automobile parts to steel casings. At one point, the Mesabi Iron Range in northern Minnesota was producing 80 percent of the world's iron ore. It also seemed like it was producing the vast majority of America's hockey talent.

Former Eveleth postmaster Gilbert Finnegan documented that in one season during the Depression, 147 Eveleth-born players were playing in various leagues and schools around the country. At a national Amateur Athletic Union tournament in Chicago in 1935, about 33 percent of the players on the eight teams were from Eveleth. One team at that tournament, St. Cloud Teachers College, used only Eveleth players to amass a record of 45–7–0 in three seasons from 1933 to 1936.

A key figure in frigid Eveleth's status as a hockey hotbed was Cliff Thompson, who was one of the original inductees into the U.S. Hall of Fame in 1973. He coached both the Eveleth High School and Eveleth Junior College hockey teams, and both teams were perennially dominant.

His career record at Eveleth Junior College was 171–28–7. His record at Eveleth High School was 534–26–9. If you add both records together, Thompson won 90.9 percent of all of his games behind the bench in Eveleth.

In 1927–28, the Eveleth Junior College team, along with Harvard, Minnesota, Augsburg College, and the University Club of Boston, were among those being considered to represent the United States at the 1928 Olympics. For financial and other reasons, every team except Augsburg pulled out, and the U.S. Olympic Committee decided not to have a representative.

In 1928–29, Eveleth Junior College was the No. 1-ranked college team in the country, ahead of No. 2 Yale and No. 3 Minnesota. Its toughest game that season was against Eveleth High School. Eveleth Junior College defeated the high schoolers 4–3, according to the research of the late U.S. hockey historian Donald Clark.

Thompson was at Eveleth High School from 1920 to 1958, and he won five state championships, including the inaugural state tournament in 1945. In one stretch, Eveleth won 78 consecutive games, including four consecutive state titles from 1948 to 1951. The overwhelming majority of Eveleth players who went on to play college or professional hockey were coached by Thompson.

Eveleth's hockey history could have easily begun earlier, but the first recorded game for the town was against Two Harbors on January 23, 1903. Fan response to the game led to the creation of four outdoor rinks by 1914.

By 1920 the Eveleth team was competing in the United States Amateur Hockey Association. Eveleth enjoyed some of the best amateur hockey in the country until 1926, when high operating costs and raids by professional teams forced teams such as Eveleth to take a lower profile.

But during the early 1920s, hockey thrived in Eveleth. The Eveleth Reds even attracted some future NHL players from outside of town, such as Manitoban Ching Johnson, who would eventually have a Hall of Fame NHL career with the New York Rangers, and Perk Galbraith, who would sign with the Boston Bruins in 1926. Sault Sainte Marie native Vic Desjardins, one of the first Americans to play in the NHL, was also on that team.

Eveleth won the USHA Group 3 title that season with a 13–1 record. Though Eveleth lost the national title to Cleveland, they did defeat the American Soo for the McNaughton Cup. Interest in hockey was so intense during that period that an estimated crowd of 1,000 stood in frigid temperatures outside the Western Union office to await results of the Eveleth playoff games in Pittsburgh and Cleveland.

The scene outside the Western Union office inspired the Eveleth mayor to push for the construction of the 3,000-seat hippodrome rink, which opened January 1, 1922. On game nights, the hippodrome would be jammed with spectators, many of the youngsters sneaking in through the coal chute, through windows, or through tunnels they had dug themselves.

"We'd tunnel under the frame of the building to get in and watch the game," Suomi recalled about his youthful days in Eveleth. "The ground was usually frozen, but we were able to do it. Then we'd spend the rest of the game avoiding the cops. If they came our way, we'd hide or move to the other side of the building."

An article by Chuck Muhich in the *State Sport News* in 1953 reminisced about how the hippodrome caretaker would sometimes turn on the lights to the building hours before game time only to find one section of the stands already filled with young boys. Frank Brimsek and Karakas could have been among those boys, watching the players who would one day make it to the NHL. America usually celebrates Jim Craig's brilliant performance at Lake Placid as the defining moment of U.S. goaltending history, but Karakas and Brimsek won Stanley Cup championships long before Craig was even born.

Frank Brimsek

Brimsek succeeded Karakas as goalie at Eveleth High School, where they had also been battery-mates on the baseball team. Brimsek was the pitcher, and Karakas was the catcher. "They were both quiet guys," Tommy Karakas said. "Neither one of them was a Dennis Rodman."

Brimsek's NHL debut would come with the Bruins in the 1938–39 season, but it was the Detroit Red Wings that first showed interest in him the season before. No draft existed in those days, and even if it had, it's doubtful Brimsek would have heard much about it in Eveleth, where people sometimes didn't pay much attention to what was going on outside their mining town. Brimsek later remembered he had been playing in the NHL for several years when a couple of townsfolk stopped him to ask, "Frankie, we haven't seen much of you lately. What have you been up to?"

"Not much, just keeping busy," Brimsek had replied.

When the Red Wings informed Brimsek that he was on their protected list, Brimsek had no idea what that meant. He showed up for their training camp but quickly decided he wouldn't sign with them "because I didn't like Jack Adams."

Adams was the Red Wings' irascible general manager who controlled his hockey team like a bully might control the neighborhood schoolyard. Adams liked to rule through intimidation. "Adams had a bad habit of favoritism, and I wanted no part of that," Brimsek said.

After spurning the Red Wings, Brimsek decided to play for Pittsburgh in the Eastern Hockey League. In the Steel City, Brimsek first earned his reputation as a man of few words and bushels of toughness. Brimsek once played in Pittsburgh with an eyelid that had been sliced so severely that "I could see through it even when I closed my eyes."

His decision to sign with the Boston Bruins wasn't difficult. He liked Bruins general manager Art Ross, who was the first to sense greatness in Brimsek. But Ross still needed proof, as did the players on the team. Brimsek had an impressive athletic build and a ruggedly handsome Errol Flynn look about him, but he seemed too shy to be an NHL goaltender. He was too low-key, too sensitive, too quiet, too much of a brooder and worrier to survive in a world where manhood was tested nightly. How was this shy man going to replace the great Tiny Thompson, who had won 252 games, posted 74 shutouts, and won four Vezina Trophies in a decade with the Bruins?

But Ross had run a test before he decided to fire Thompson and replace him with Brimsek. He shot 25 pucks at Thompson from 10 feet, and Thompson nailed 19 of them. He did the same with Brimsek, who snagged every puck like he was grabbing apples off a tree limb. After that display, Ross decided to trade Thompson to the Detroit Red Wings for the rights to goalie Normie Smith and $15,000 and insert Brimsek as the Bruins' new guardian of the corded cottage.

Even though Brimsek had performed well in the test, no one anticipated the impact he would have on the game. In his rookie season, he had a record of 33–9–1 with a 1.56 goals-against average and 10 shutouts. He also won the Calder, plus the first of his two Vezina trophies. He was tagged with the nickname "Mr. Zero" because he recorded six shutouts in his first eight NHL starts. His teammates later shortened the moniker to "Zee."

His performance shocked teammates, most of whom had never heard of Brimsek before he arrived in Boston. "His hands were like lightning—the fastest I ever saw," Ross said later.

Brimsek played his first NHL game on December 1, 1938, at the Montreal Forum and lost to the Canadiens 2–0. He beat the Chicago Blackhawks on December 4 to start a string of three consecutive shutouts. The Montreal Canadiens finally fired two pucks past him in his fifth game, but the Bruins still won 3–2. He then followed with three more shutouts in a row. Brimsek later recalled the feeling of tension he had in his first game in the Boston Garden after replacing Hall of Famer Thompson. "The crowd was so quiet that first night," he said. "I could hear them breathe and could feel their cold eyes on my back."

His teammates quickly became fond of their quiet colleague and eventually learned to be amused by his idiosyncrasies, especially his frequent medical maladies. Brimsek's pregame health was usually a barometer for how well he would play. "When Frankie said he wasn't feeling well, we knew he was going to have a good night in goal," said Hall of Famer Milt Schmidt.

Fifty years after the fact, Brimsek recalled that gamblers would ask him how he felt as he entered Boston Garden.

On more days than not, Brimsek would complain of scratchiness in his throat, sinus trouble, achiness in his body, or a throbbing headache and predict he was just hours away from coming down with the grippe. One by one, Bruins would stop by Brimsek's locker and inquire of his health. Coach Dit Clapper had the honor of doing the final Brimsek medical update.

"How you feeling tonight, Frankie?" Clapper would ask. "Rotten," Brimsek would reply, which meant his teammates would wink at each other and congratulate one another on their good fortune.

Brimsek had many nights of feeling poorly and playing well en route to 252 career wins and a lifetime 2.70 goals-against average. "Goaltending is mostly luck," the humble Brimsek would say often.

Maurice "Rocket" Richard said Brimsek was the toughest goaltender he ever faced. "I had a lot of trouble against him," he said. "He was a stand-up goaltender, and there didn't seem to be any room to shoot the puck."

Players from that era described Brimsek as being technically flawless. "You had to beat Brimsek, because he never beat himself," said Emile Francis, who played in goal for the Chicago Blackhawks and New York Rangers.

Francis admired Brimsek enough to seek his counsel when he was struggling to keep the puck out of his net early in his career. Fraternization with opposing players was considered sinful in those days; players could be fined $100 for talking to rivals, a sizable sum in the 1930s. But there were also no goaltending coaches, and Francis was concerned about his slump. He decided to take a chance, and when the two goalies passed each other in Boston Garden one night, he quietly asked Brimsek to meet him after the game.

Brimsek picked the Ironhead, a bar near the Boston Garden. When Francis arrived, he found Brimsek sitting alone in a booth near the back of the bar. The conversation went like this:

"What do you need?"

"I'm getting beat to my glove side."

"Did you play baseball?"

"Yeah, I played shortstop."

"I thought so. You're charging the puck like you're playing the infield. You have to slow down. What lie stick are you using?"

"An 11."

"Use a 13. It will stand you straighter."

Francis and Brimsek chatted briefly after that but then quickly departed, not wanting to risk being seen. Francis said he never spoke to Brimsek again, but he appreciated the advice. "That was the answer," he said. "I started playing better right after that."

As was the case with many NHL players, Brimsek lost some time to the service during World War II. He missed the 1943–44 and 1944–45 seasons while in the U.S. Coast Guard. During his ninth NHL season in 1948–49, he began to hear some boo birds in the Garden even though he had a 2.72 goals-against average that season. The boos mostly reflected the fact that the Bruins weren't playing as well as they had at the beginning of his career. That season the *New York Times* carried a story suggesting Brimsek, called "the best goaltender in NHL history," by *Sport Magazine*, might be slipping as he headed toward his 34th birthday. That kind of criticism was insensitive, given that Brimsek was coping with the death of his one-year-old son.

When Clapper resigned at the end of the 1948–49 season, Brimsek surprised the hockey world when he sent a telegram to *Boston Herald* sportswriter Henry McKenna in which he expressed hope that the Bruins would move him to another club.

"I was stunned to hear of Dit Clapper's resignation," Brimsek said in the telegram. "You know my high personal regard for him. Now with Dit gone, I sincerely hope management will let me go."

In a 1996 interview, Brimsek said the Bruins weren't really surprised by his request for a trade. He had told them two years before that he wanted to go to Chicago, where his brother John had a blueprint business.

After serving on a supply ship in the South Pacific during the war, Brimsek found that he didn't enjoy playing as much as he had before the war. "When Art Ross told me when to report after I got back, I told him [I was] going deer hunting," Brimsek said.

Brimsek had occasionally talked of trying to get closer to Eveleth, and sportswriter McKenna speculated correctly that Brimsek would be sent to the

Chicago Blackhawks. The Bruins wanted to trade Brimsek, not sell him, but the Hawks' general manager wouldn't part with any top player, so the two sides settled on a cash payment that was said to be the largest since the Toronto Maple Leafs paid $35,000 to get King Clancy from Ottawa in 1930.

Brimsek played one season with the Blackhawks and posted a 3.49 goals-against average before heading back to Eveleth. He was elected to the Hockey Hall of Fame in 1966.

Mike Karakas

Mike Karakas, born in 1911, was one of six brothers, five of them hockey players (four of them goaltenders). His older brother George, born in 1908, played for Eveleth in senior-league competition. But at 24 he suffered an appendicitis attack. It ruptured while the family was taking him to the hospital in Duluth. He died shortly thereafter. "We thought he was even better than Mike," said younger brother Tommy.

Luke, born in 1916, played minor league hockey in Muskegon, Michigan, and Omaha. The only winger, John, born in 1919, played for the Baltimore Blades in the American League and the Los Angeles Monarchs of the Pacific Coast League. Tommy, born in 1925, played minor league hockey for five years, primarily in Minneapolis, Milwaukee, and Portland, Oregon. His career was interrupted by World War II. While he could have been sharpening his skills for a shot at the NHL, he was analyzing the movements of the Imperial Japanese Army as a member of the U.S. Army's military intelligence. When the U.S. Marines hit the beach at Okinawa, Tommy Karakas was there with them.

Mike Karakas was signed by the Blackhawks for the 1935–36 season. He posted nine shutouts and boasted a 1.85 goals-against average. As the NHL's first No. 1 American goaltender, his sphere of recognition expanded beyond the normal bounds of hockey. Several media outlets, including the uppity *Colliers* magazine, took notice of his

Mike Karakas was known as "Iron Mike" long before Mike Ditka came to Chicago. A product of Eveleth, Minnesota, Karakas posted a 1.88 goals-against average and had two shutouts to help the Blackhawks win the Stanley Cup in the 1937–38 season. The 147-pound netminder had catlike agility around the crease. (Le Studio du Hockey/ Hockey Hall of Fame)

arrival. *Colliers* did a four-page spread on Karakas entitled "Yankee Invasion." His notoriety also prompted General Mills to put his face on a Wheaties box. "It wasn't like today, getting a deal with Nike," brother Tommy said. "I think we just got to eat a lot of Wheaties."

The highlight of Karakas' hockey career was the 1937–38 championship, when he helped the Blackhawks win the Stanley Cup after a disastrous regular season. Karakas didn't enjoy his finest regular season either. He had a 1.71 goals-against average in the playoffs and a 1.00 goals-against average in the finals. He might have been the play-offs' most valuable player had an award been given (awarding the Conn Smythe Trophy didn't begin until 1966.) "I think they had to be the worst team in NHL history to win the Stanley Cup," Tommy Karakas said.

Neither Brimsek nor Karakas were large goalies. Brimsek was 5'9" and weighed 170 pounds, and Karakas was probably an inch taller and weighed 15 to 20 pounds less. They came from the same program, but their styles were different. Brimsek relied on his positional play and the excellent glove hand he had developed on the Eveleth diamond.

"Mike was a little more adventurous," Tommy Karakas said. "He would go halfway to the blue line to get the puck, and he had a tremendous glove hand. When it came to crunch time, he could always do it."

During the 1936–37 season, Boston Bruins great Eddie Shore said Karakas was the NHL's best goaltender. Karakas had 28 career shutouts for the Blackhawks in an era when the team's talent level was not impressive. Chicago sportswriters nick-named him "Iron Mike," presumably because he didn't miss a regular-season game in his first four seasons.

Karakas took his NHL life in stride until the Blackhawks sent him first to Montreal and then to the minors in Providence. When he was first sent to the minors, they asked him to play for $75 a week. He had been making five times that in the NHL for the abbreviated work year. He knew he was paying the price for the Hawks' poor perfor-mance because it was easier to move him than the other 15 guys. "He was ticked," his brother Tommy remembered.

While playing in Providence, Mike Karakas' legend extended well beyond the rink. In the middle of the night, a fire broke out in his apart-ment building, and Karakas awakened in time to haul out his wife, two kids, a minister, and the rest of his family. "Those were the biggest saves of his career," Tommy said.

For the 1943–44 season, Karakas was brought back to Chicago and helped the team reach the Stanley Cup Finals, where they lost to the Montreal Canadiens. When he retired, Karakas had played about 20 seasons in the minors and the NHL.

Sam LoPresti and John Mariucci

After trading Karakas in 1940, the Blackhawks replaced him with another Eveleth goaltender, Sam LoPresti. That same season, the Blackhawks also brought in John Mariucci, a left-winger who would instantly became one of the league's tough-est players.

Physically, the 215-pound LoPresti was a sharp contrast to the spindle-legged Karakas. LoPresti, who was built like a fullback, had actually played football at Eveleth Junior College. His wrists were mammoth, so large that no normal watchband would fit around them.

When Mariucci was playing at the University of Minnesota, he told the Minnesota football coach, Bernie Bierman, he had a player who could play "goalie on the hockey team, fullback on the football team, and catcher on the baseball team." Mariucci gave Bierman a complete scouting report of LoPresti's prowess, and when he was done, he told Bierman that LoPresti was also from Eveleth.

"Eveleth," Bierman supposedly growled at Mariucci. "I'm not taking any more players from Eveleth. Working with you is difficult enough."

In 1940, Chicago Blackhawks goaltender Sam LoPresti set an NHL record when he made 80 saves in a game against the Boston Bruins. His NHL career was cut short by World War II. (Le Studio du Hockey/ Hockey Hall of Fame)

As a 24-year-old rookie with the Blackhawks, LoPresti was 9–15 with a 3.02 goals-against average. But he impressed the Hawks management, particularly when he made 80 saves on the road against the Boston Bruins. In one game, LoPresti faced 27 shots in the first period, 31 in the second, and 22 in the third. (The Bruins must have gotten tired in the third period.) LoPresti lost the game 3–2 when Eddie Wiseman beat him for the game-winner with 2:31 left. The Blackhawks had managed just 18 shots against Brimsek in that game.

LoPresti, who died in 1984, was a modest man; never one to dwell much on what happened in the past. His son, Pete, who also played goal in the NHL, said his father only mentioned that game once. When Sam was visiting his son in the Minnesota North Stars dressing room, he noticed how big his son's new catching glove was. "If I had had a glove that big, I wouldn't have missed that third," he told his son. "I probably would have stopped the first two too." He then described how the third goal had hit him and then "flip-flopped" into the net.

In 1942 he was 21–23 with a 3.19 goals-against average and might have been headed for a lengthy career if Uncle Sam hadn't beckoned him to help with the war effort. He joined the U.S. Navy and was assigned duty on a supply ship. On one cruise near the coast of Africa, LoPresti's vessel was torpedoed by a German U-boat. LoPresti and some of his shipmates scrambled into a lifeboat before their ship sank.

Pete LoPresti said his father only gave him details of the sinking once. Sam LoPresti said the German submarine surfaced near their lifeboat, and he and the other 20 men in the boat feared the Germans planned to finish them off. "That's when we were the most scared," his father had said.

But the German captain merely inquired whether the surviving crew members had suffered any injuries that needed treatment. Told the U.S. crew had no injuries, the captain closed his hatch, submerged, and sailed away. LoPresti told his son they had enough provisions on the boat to last two weeks. They bobbed in the water for 41 days. "I remember him telling me how they had to ration malted milk balls in the last few days," Pete LoPresti said.

Currents carried them toward South America, where they were picked up by a ship and transported to Brazil. Sam LoPresti, about 230 pounds when the trip began, weighed about 175 when it was over.

LoPresti didn't attempt to return to the NHL after he was discharged from the service. Having known enough adventure for one lifetime, he returned to Eveleth to operate a small tavern.

Mariucci, meanwhile, did return to the Blackhawks after the war, and the Blackhawks were thankful.

Writings of that era suggest the 205-pound Mariucci was among the league's roughest defenders. Mariucci had been a ferocious defensive end on Minnesota's football team, once shutting down University of Michigan All-American Tom Harmon for zero yards. The Chicago Cardinals reportedly wanted Mariucci, but hockey actually paid better.

Legend has it that Mariucci didn't actually begin playing hockey seriously until he was 17. Chicago reports said his first game with the Blackhawks was only the 125th game of his hockey career. Today, that's about a season and a half for a Bantam AAA player. Mariucci played hockey in much the same manner as he performed on the gridiron: he smacked centers with the same force he used against Harmon. After his first 13 games

with the Blackhawks, Mariucci had just under 50 stitches from his forehead to chin.

"I'm tired of sewing you up," Chicago trainer Eddie Froelich growled.

"Imagine how I feel," Mariucci replied.

After the war, Mariucci became the Blackhawks' captain. He always considered it part of his job to protect the Blackhawks' Pony Line of Bill Mosienko and Max and Doug Bentley. "If you touched those guys, you had to face Mariucci," Emile Francis said.

During the 1946–47 season, Mariucci infuriated the Montreal Canadiens with an open-ice decking of Punch Line member Elmer Lach, who suffered a broken cheekbone and had to be placed on the disabled list.

Mariucci and the Detroit Red Wings' Black Jack Stewart were the combatants in one of the wildest NHL fights, according to Francis, who played on the Blackhawks with Mariucci in the 1946–47 and 1947–48 seasons. "It lasted 10 to 12 minutes, and neither one wanted to quit," Francis said.

Mariucci may have been particularly incensed that game because Gordie Howe had checked Doug Bentley into the boards after the whistle. Max Bentley went after Howe, and Red Wings captain Sid Abel had gone after Max. That scenario probably didn't sit well with Mariucci, who was very protective of his teammates.

His fight with Stewart resumed in the penalty box and spilled into the players' corridor. When it was over, Mariucci had to pass the Red Wings' bench to get to the Chicago Stadium dressing room. Detroit coach Jack Adams cussed him out every inch of the way, but when Adams' assistant, Johnny Mowers, started riding him, Mariucci had heard enough.

"He had one punch left, and he landed it on Mowers," Francis said.

Not many in his era were tougher or as loyal to teammates as Mariucci. After he left the NHL, he ended up playing for St. Louis in the American Hockey League, where every young tough guy wanted to prove himself against Mariucci. One incident occurred during an exhibition game in Barrie, Ontario. A rookie rapped him on the head with his stick, but Mariucci, probably growing weary of having to whip every gunslinger on the planet, didn't respond. When the young pup smacked him again, Mariucci dropped his stick and went after him. Mariucci was in such a rage that the rookie fled for his life. Sugar Jim Henry opened the door to the bench to offer the kid safety, and the guys kept Mariucci at bay until he was cooled off.

After the game, Mariucci told Springfield coach Earl Seibert, whom he knew from his days with the Hawks, "Do me a favor and don't play that kid against us tomorrow, or there will be a dead pigeon on your hands."

Shortly thereafter, there was a knock at Mariucci's door, and Mariucci found the rookie standing before him. "I want to apologize for my actions, Mr. Mariucci," he said. "And my coach said I should ask you if it would be all right for me to play against your club tomorrow. I promise to behave myself."

Mariucci retired after the 1951–52 season and went on to leave a more significant imprint on the game as a coach than he did as a player. He fought for the advancement of the American player just as ferociously as he fought Stewart that day.

Other players from Eveleth include Joe Papike, who played parts of three seasons with the Blackhawks but never quite earned the status of full-time player. In the 1940–41 season, he managed two goals and two assists in nine games with Chicago.

Eveleth-born Aldo Palazzari's career ended prematurely and tragically when the speedy left-winger lost his left eye as a result of an injury suffered at the New York Rangers' training camp in Winnipeg just prior to the 1944–45 season.

Defenseman Manny Cotlow, a Minnesota native who was trying out for the Rangers, was on the ice when the accident occurred. "Hank Goldup went around him, and his stick came up and got him," Cotlow said. Palazzari's eyeball had ruptured.

Cotlow said he turned away. "I couldn't stand to look at something like that," he said.

In Palazzari's one NHL season, split between the Bruins and Rangers, he had eight goals in 36 games, a respectable total for a first-year player. His son, Doug, would carry on the Eveleth tradition by making the St. Louis Blues roster in 1974.

Eveleth was also the home to John Mayasich, a member of the gold-medal 1960 U.S. Olympic Team, and Mark Pavelich, who played for the 1980 gold-medal team and then enjoyed a 355-game NHL career.

Goaltender Willard Ikola, a star at the University of Michigan and goaltender on the silver medal–winning 1956 U.S. Olympic Team, was also from Eveleth. Suomi, Milt Brink, Rudy Ahlin, and Paul "Butch" Schaeffer had brief tours of duty with the Blackhawks.

In his historically important interview with hometownfocus.us, Suomi provided an interesting account of Eveleth boys turning pro with the Chicago Baby Ruths, a team created simply to market the famous candy bar. In 1934 Eveleth's Suomi, Leonard Saari, and Johnny Rosinka were paid $25 per week to play for the Baby Ruths, then coached by Eveleth's Connie Pleban.

"You have to understand that this was in the middle of the Depression, and $25 was a lot of money at the time," Suomi told the website. "We

Up against the NHL's pro-Canadian sentiment of the 1930s and 1940s, no American player was more prepared to fight his way into an NHL job than John Mariucci of Eveleth, Minnesota. Mariucci played for the Chicago Blackhawks from 1940 to 1948, with time off for military service during World War II. Retiring with 308 penalty minutes in 223 games, he may have been one of the toughest players of his era. (Le Studio du Hockey/Hockey Hall of Fame)

looked at each other and said, 'What do we got to lose? Let's go.' I went home and told mother and dad. My mother looked at me and said, 'You're going to where all the gangsters are?'"

In 1935 the Baby Ruths, with nine players from Eveleth, won the national title by defeating the Boston Olympics in the finals of the National Amateur Athletic Union Tournament. It was reported at the time that one-third of the players in the tournament were from Eveleth. The winner of the tournament was supposed to represent the United States in the 1936 Olympics in Garmisch-Partenkirchen, Germany. But the Baby Ruths were not allowed to go because they were considered a professional team.

But Suomi's participation on the Baby Ruths caught the attention of the Chicago Blackhawks,

who offered him a roster spot when Major Frederic McLaughlin was toying with his idea of using more American players. The experiment lasted only five games, and Suomi had no points and one close call. "I picked up a loose puck in Boston and had a breakaway," Suomi said in the same interview. "But I got tripped from behind just as I got close to the net."

Given the importance of Eveleth to American hockey history, it seems fitting that the U.S. Hockey Hall of Fame Museum is located in Eveleth. American hockey talent today comes from every corner of the United States. But in the 1920s and 1930s, there was no question that Eveleth, Minnesota, was the hockey capital of America. ∎

Team USA Head Coach Ron Wilson looks on in disappointment after the United States lost in the bronze-medal game at the 2009 IIHF World Championship in Switzerland. The Toronto Maple Leafs coach is the only American to record 600 NHL wins. (Matthew Murnaghan/HHOF-IIHF Images)

AMERICAN COACHES
Six for the Ages

Ron Wilson

When Brian Burke was first introduced to Ron Wilson during their freshman year at Providence College in 1975, he expected Superman and got Clark Kent. Wilson had been the subject of a heavy recruiting buzz because he had produced 100 points in his final season of high school hockey. Burke was underwhelmed when he saw that Wilson was 5'9" and weighed 160 pounds. "If he had 100 points, I figured it must not have been much of a league," Burke said. "But when he hit the ice, you could see what kind of player he was."

When Wilson completed his college career in 1979, he had accumulated 78 goals and 172 assists for 250 points in 111 collegiate games. He had established an NCAA record for career points by a defenseman that is still standing in 2011.

"You can argue he was the best college player ever," said Burke, who played four seasons with Wilson.

Based on the way Wilson analyzed his sport as a young man, Burke isn't the least bit surprised that Wilson has become one of the most accomplished American coaches in hockey history. "He was a thinking player," Burke said. "You would see him diagramming plays with a salt and pepper shaker at a pregame meal."

Thirty-plus years later, Wilson, now coach of the Toronto Maple Leafs, became the seventh coach—and the only American—in NHL history to record 600 or more wins behind the bench. He reached that 600-win milestone on January 11, 2011, with Toronto's 4–2 win against San Jose. He earned himself a small league fine by offering a $600 bounty if a player should net the winning goal and earn him the 600th against his former San Jose team.

After the historic win, Wilson didn't receive a call from the president, but he did receive one from USA Hockey consultant Art Berglund, who had helped nurture Wilson's career. Although Wilson was born in Canada, he had moved to Rhode Island as a young man. No one is a prouder American, having played for U.S. National Teams in 1975, 1981, 1983, and 1987. Berglund helped him land the job as an assistant coach for Team USA when it finished second at the 1990 Goodwill Games.

With a gold medal at the 1996 World Cup, a silver at the 2010 Olympics, and a bronze at the 1996 World Championship, Wilson owns an impressive international résumé. "He comes from coaching genes," Berglund would say. "And he proves himself at every level he reaches."

Wilson grew up in NHL arenas. His late father, Larry, and his uncle Johnny were both NHL players and coaches. Larry had played six seasons in the NHL and coached one season with the Detroit Red Wings, while Johnny had played 12 seasons and had a lengthy coaching career, with tours of duty in Detroit, Los Angeles, Colorado, and Pittsburgh.

Smart and self-assured, Wilson knew how to explore his options when the NHL wasn't yet ready to fully embrace a smallish defenseman. He went to Switzerland to play where he became a megastar, complete with endorsements for sticks and gloves. "He was huge over there," said Atlanta Thrashers president Don Waddell. "His recommendation got me a job to play over there."

As a coach, Wilson is known for his modern approach—he was using laptops in preparation long before it was fashionable—and biting humor. Verbal jousting with the media and his players is part of his shtick. "That has worked for him his entire career," Burke said. "That's when he is most comfortable, when he can take shots at his players and they can take shots at him. That's how it was in our dressing room in Providence, and that's the way he still likes it."

Eddie Jeremiah

Eddie Jeremiah once joked that he had been inspired to become a coach because he feared the alternative was a career doing inventory on women's intimate apparel. Right after leaving Somerville High School in Massachusetts, he had a job offer to become a bookkeeper for a company that sold female undergarments. The thought of spending his life tracking the sales of bras and panties caused him more fear than he had ever known as a three-sport star at Somerville.

"In that instant," Jeremiah would tell *Sunrise* magazine years later, "my future whirled before me.... I ran to my high school coach, Dutch Ayer, and told him I wanted to go to college."

His decision to attend Dartmouth College changed his life and the lives of the many who knew him as one of the top coaches in U.S. sports history. Instead of checking his math on the bra accounts, Jeremiah not only spent 29 years as Dartmouth's coach, but he also championed the cause of the American player most of his adult life. He was the first of the big-time American hockey coaches, setting a professional example for others like Snooks Kelley, Jack Kelley, John MacInnes, Jack Riley, Amo Bessone, Bob Johnson, Herb Brooks, and the many other coaches who have left their fingerprints on coaching game plans through the years.

Jeremiah's Dartmouth teams controlled college hockey in the early 1940s the way the Edmonton Oilers dominated the NHL in the mid-1980s. Dartmouth's 46-game winning streak, lasting from 1942 to 1946, is still the longest in college hockey history.

Called "Jerry" by most who knew him, Jeremiah was known as a player's coach. He managed to walk the tight line between being both a friend and mentor to his players.

"Jerry wasn't tough," said former U.S. Olympian Crawford "Whitey" Campbell, who played for Jeremiah in the 1940s. "He didn't have to be. He had more talent than anybody. He loved the fundamentals."

Jeremiah was methodical in his approach, going over every possible scenario that a player

Eddie Jeremiah coached Dartmouth College for 29 seasons. His teams dominated college hockey in the 1940s. Jeremiah's detail-oriented, methodical approach set standards for other American coaches to follow. Throughout his career, he championed the cause of American players seeking credibility and respect in the world of collegiate hockey. (Dartmouth Athletics)

might face. If he was teaching a three-on-two drill, he would anticipate every possible move a defender could make and provide his players with options for dealing with those moves. He was so detail-oriented that he would drill his players on the most obvious of tactics.

One of his captains at Dartmouth was Jack Riley, who later coached the gold-medal team in the 1960 Olympics and enjoyed a long coaching

career at West Point. His admiration for Jeremiah couldn't have been higher. But one day on the team bus, he couldn't resist parodying his lovable coach.

"Boys," Riley said, doing his best Jeremiah imitation, "we are going to play a team today, and they are all going to be wearing skates."

He hadn't quite finished his routine when Jeremiah boarded the bus. Riley would have gladly taken several cross-checks to the back rather than have Jeremiah as mad at him as he was that night.

Everyone in hockey respected Jeremiah. He joined John Mariucci in the fight for NCAA legislation to prevent older Canadian players from filling college roster spots. Jeremiah was a principled man who endured the harsh wrath of Boston College and Boston University fans in 1952 when, as chairman of the Eastern Conference Selection Committee for the NCAA tournament, he ordered a playoff to determine whether Boston University, Boston College, Yale, or St. Lawrence could go to the NCAA tournament. Boston University and Boston College officials believed they should go because their teams had more wins. But Jeremiah noted that all four teams had similar loss totals and ordered the playoff. Boston University and Boston College refused to participate.

"[Jeremiah] held to this honest, courageous stand despite some violent opposition," Princeton coach Dick Vaughn said at the time.

Snooks Kelley, coach at Boston College, was overcome with emotion the night he and Jeremiah faced each other for the final time as adversaries during the 1966–67 season. Jeremiah was dying from cancer in his final season at Dartmouth.

"I really feel badly about Jerry leaving the game," Kelley told Boston reporters. "When they made him, they threw the mold away. He's to college hockey as Ted Williams was to baseball. I call him Mr. Dartmouth."

John Mariucci

Mariucci's fighting days weren't over when he hung up his skates for the last time. He began using words instead of his fists.

Mariucci became coach at the University of Minnesota in 1952 and won 215 games there before leaving 15 years later. He then took a job with the Minnesota North Stars. His rough-and-tumble demeanor often masked what his friends considered his gentle soul and kind heart. He was a strange blend of intellect and toughness, a man who could speak four languages, yet still seemed to enjoy a good scrap now and then.

"He loved art and knew a lot of history," remembered Jack McCartan, who played for him at Minnesota and on national teams. "We would be in Europe, riding on the bus, and he would be lecturing us on the history of the area, just like he was a teacher."

But Mariucci's lifelong fight, the crusade that consumed the last 38 years of life, was the battle to gain respect for the American hockey player. No coach in America fought that battle with more passion and ferocity than Mariucci. He brought a missionary zeal to his work, whether he was preaching the importance of the Minnesota high school program or explaining yet again why he primarily recruited Americans.

"People thought he was anti-Canadian," said Herb Brooks, who played and coached under Mariucci. "But he wasn't. He was a visionary. He believed in the American player."

His close friend Bob Ridder called Mariucci "the noblest Roman of them all," a line borrowed from Shakespeare's "Julius Caesar." And yet, Mariucci didn't mind poking fun at himself. He would talk about how many of his ex-players were all making plenty of money in the real world.

"Why don't I make any of the money?" he would muse. "I should have listened to myself."

One of his players' favorite memories of Mariucci came when he coached the 1956 U.S. Olympic Team. Before the team landed in Europe, Mariucci spent an inordinate amount of time preaching the importance of keeping track of one's own luggage. Mariucci said he didn't want to have to wet-nurse anyone on this trip. Every man should keep track of his own belongings. He didn't want to wait for someone who couldn't keep track of his own stuff. "Of course, when all of the bags came down," player John Mayasich remembered, "the bag that was missing belonged to Mariucci."

As a coach, Mariucci was more of a motivator than a strategist. His temper would sometimes get the best of him on the bench. If a player made a mistake, he would bench him, putting him in the back row.

Former Minnesota player Lou Nanne recalled a game against Michigan when Mariucci called for the next pair of defensemen, and nobody jumped on the ice.

"Where are my defensemen?" Mariucci bellowed.

"We are all here in the back row," Nanne replied. Mariucci had forgotten that he had benched all of his remaining defensemen.

Nanne said many times that Mariucci influenced his life more than anyone else except his parents. He loved Mariucci like a father, which meant they did not always agree.

At the 1975 World Championship in Vienna, the two men fought on the bench during the game. Mariucci didn't like the way Nanne was playing, and for some inexplicable reason, he began swatting him on the back of the head. Nanne took it for several seconds before he began wrestling with his mentor. While the game went on around them, the players pulled them apart. Realizing the press was going to quiz him about it, Nanne called Mariucci and asked him what he should tell the media.

"Tell them the truth," Mariucci said. "Tell them that's just the way our relationship works."

John Mariucci was known as the "godfather" of Minnesota hockey. He is a member of both the U.S. Hockey Hall of Fame and the Hockey Hall of Fame. (Graphic Artists/Hockey Hall of Fame)

Nanne also remembered when Mariucci was an assistant coach with the North Stars and Wren Blair was coach. After the team had arrived home from a long West Coast road trip, Blair ordered a practice for 9:00 AM. That morning, Mariucci put all of his players on the bench and launched into a round of storytelling, interrupting himself with a whistle he blew every minute. Finally one of his players asked him why he was blowing the whistle. "In case Wren is listening, I want him to think I'm putting you guys through stops and starts," Mariucci said.

Mariucci was most proud of his allegiance to the Minnesota high school hockey program. He's considered the "godfather" of Minnesota hockey. In 1952, when Mariucci started trumpeting the state's high school tournament, it was drawing 15,000 fans. At the time of his death in 1988, the state tournament attendance had topped more than 100,000.

During his tenure with the Minnesota Gophers, he brought in only a handful of Canadian players, insisting it would destroy high school hockey if he didn't give the vast majority of scholarships to Minnesotans. "If I didn't give scholarships to Minnesota kids, where would they go to play?" Mariucci would say.

At Mariucci's funeral, Nanne said, "You can talk about Clarence Campbell, Rocket Richard, Gordie Howe, and Walter Brown. Mariucci is right up there with them when it comes to having an influence on the game."

In nominating Mariucci for the Hall of Fame, USA Hockey president Walter Bush said, "In 1952, if we had gone to Madison Avenue to find a way to spread the growth of hockey in the United States, we would have hired John. But we were lucky. He did it all for the love of the game."

Jack Kelley

Jack Kelley was to college hockey in the 1960s what Vince Lombardi was to the NFL. Kelley was probably the toughest, most competitive, and most successful coach in college hockey. He ran his practices like a drill sergeant preparing troops for combat. In fact, Pittsburgh Penguins owner Howard Baldwin, an ex-Marine who had tried unsuccessfully to play for the Boston University team, said of his first Kelley practice: "I felt like I was back in basic training on Parris Island."

Most players started out detesting Kelley and his marathon practices, but gradually they learned to respect his methods. He was profes-

Jack Kelley coached Boston University to NCAA titles in 1971 and 1972. In 10 seasons, his record was 208–80–8. (Courtesy of Boston University)

sional in his preparation and relentless in his dedication. "He was tougher than anyone imagined," said Boston University coach Jack Parker, who played for Kelley from 1965 to 1968. "The all-out work ethic, the duration of practices, the number of wind sprints. He was a pain, but most of us understood we weren't going to get better coaching."

In 10 seasons at Boston University, starting in 1962, Kelley had a record of 208–80–8. Of those 80 losses, 29 came in the first two seasons, when Kelley was implementing his program.

"When he came on the ice, the jabber, the noise, it all stopped," said his son David E. Kelley, a Hollywood writer and producer. "A hush fell over everyone."

Kelley and Cornell's Ned Harkness are credited with ending the western teams' dominance of college hockey. Kelley finished his career at Boston University by winning NCAA titles in 1971 and 1972.

At the time Kelley was winning his second title, 28-year-old Baldwin, whom Kelley jokingly insists "cut himself" at Boston University years earlier, was financing a new team called the New England Whalers in the World Hockey Association. He brazenly asked one of college hockey's most successful coaches to join this new league that NHL executives were arrogantly predicting would drown in a sea of red ink.

"He was a big name in Boston," Baldwin said. "I felt he was a very innovative coach. He was the kind of man I wanted."

The WHA was turning to many college coaches. Bob Johnson had said no thanks to the New York Raiders. The Philadelphia Blazers had offered 1972 U.S. Olympic coach Murray Williamson $60,000 to coach, but Williamson thought the situation was too unstable. But Kelley, who really had nothing left to prove at the college level, agreed to a two-year contract with Baldwin and the Whalers.

"I remember the only argument was I wanted the payroll to be $650,000 and he wanted it to be $700,000. Now you couldn't get a second-rate defenseman for that," Baldwin said.

Kelley did bring along his Boston University captain, John Darby, but he didn't load up on college players the first year. He had some NHL veterans, including Boston Bruins standout Teddy Green. By his own admission, Kelley needed to adjust his style for the pros. He tells the story of the Whalers making their first road trip, and he gathered the players all around him and gave every one a rundown of what time the buses would be leaving, when meals would be served, and when curfew would be.

As he was wrapping up his itinerary, Rick Ley, who had already played four seasons in the NHL, raised his hand with a question. "Coach," he deadpanned, "what kind of pajamas should we wear?"

Kelley always enjoyed that story. "They let me know quickly that pros expected to be treated differently than college players," he says.

In his first season of professional hockey, Kelley guided his team to the WHA championship. But the following season, he turned the team over to Ron Ryan and went to Colby College to coach because he liked the college game better than the pro game.

"My father loved to teach as much as he loved to coach," David Kelley said. "His frustration was that he never got to teach enough. He could never get his power play to be as effective as he wanted it, because he couldn't have enough practices. There were too many games."

Herb Brooks

While Kelley was making his pro debut in the WHA, the late Herb Brooks was establishing himself as a rising star among American hockey coaches.

After succeeding Glen Sonmor as head coach of the high-profile Minnesota program at the start of the 1972–73 season, Brooks led the Gophers to NCAA championships in 1974, 1976, and 1979. Along the way, he earned a reputation as an innovative coach whose style seemed to combine the best of North American and European hockey.

Herb Brooks led the University of Minnesota to three NCAA championships before being named the head coach of the 1980 U.S. Olympic Team. (USA Hockey)

But even with his impressive credentials, Brooks wasn't the first choice to coach the 1980 U.S. Olympic squad. At best, he was the third choice, and even that is open to debate. First, Harvard's Bill Cleary turned down the job, then Michigan Tech's John MacInnes declined for health reasons. But even then, it was no "lock" that members of the selection committee would appoint Brooks, even if he did have impressive credentials.

Brooks never liked the politics of hockey and had battled with the Amateur Hockey Association

of the United States over how to develop players. Brooks always liked to set his own brisk cadence, figuring correctly that success was the best defense of his methods. Former USA Hockey president Walter Bush, who had debated with Brooks about the direction of American hockey, was among those who supported Brooks. Having watched Brooks win the three national titles at Minnesota, Bush was confident Brooks was the man for the job. He certainly hadn't seen a more organized coach.

"When Herb came in for an interview, he already had a folder an inch thick full of information he had compiled," Bush said.

What Brooks would accomplish for the United States over the next year—culminating in the gold-medal triumph at Lake Placid—was clearly the most high-profile coaching achievement in American hockey history. He molded a team of college players into a unit that would beat the world's best team. His 1980 Olympic team beat the Soviets, who may have been as talented as any NHL team with the exception of the New York Islanders.

Brooks bullied his players, cajoled them, dazzled them, and occasionally even made them laugh. But what he did primarily was prepare them to play the best game of their lives at precisely the right time. The Soviets were known for their conditioning, but Brooks skated his players to the point where they could have skated from Lake Placid to Moscow if the earth had frozen. In fact, if all the skating done during the pre-Olympic practices was added together, the American players may have actually skated that far. Brooks also developed a style of hockey that was designed to counter whatever the Soviets threw at the Americans.

"It was a hybrid," Brooks said. "It was the best of the Europeans and the best of the Canadians. In the worst-case scenario, you always had the North American style in your back pocket. If it all unraveled, we could still play dump and chase."

Sometimes players hated Brooks for the mind games he played with the team. But in the end, they realized that he had mentally hardened them for the impending battle. Brooks always had a reason for doing what he did, whether it was threatening to cut Mike Eruzione or riding Rob McClanahan. Mostly, he was looking for ways to unify the team, even if that unification came at the expense of liking him as a coach. "I was always looking for the moment to solidify this team," Brooks said.

When the United States defeated the Soviets, he showed a brief moment of emotion and then left the ice, saying later that the moment belonged to his players.

After the U.S. defeated the Finns to win the gold medal, it was presumed that Brooks would end up in the NHL. Rumors circulated that he would replace Fred Shero in New York, but instead Brooks went to Switzerland to coach where the pace would be less strenuous. "I was dead tired, out of gas," Brooks said. "I needed to recharge my batteries."

In 1981 Rangers general manager Craig Patrick, who had been Brooks' assistant in Lake Placid, hired Brooks as head coach. Even though this ascension was expected, it was still noteworthy. The NHL still hadn't embraced the idea of a coach stepping directly from college to the big leagues. Jack Kelley had enjoyed some success in the World Hockey Association, but Ned Harkness' move from Cornell to become the Detroit Red Wings' coach and general manager hadn't worked as well.

Rangers veterans were certainly skeptical about the move, especially since Brooks brought in a style that was completely foreign to most of them. With Shero, practices had been short and conditioning had been lax. With Brooks, practices were long and conditioning was torturous.

Rangers players didn't initially accept Brooks' ideas on conditioning and offense. One of his favorite practice exercises was to get his players to skate three laps around the rink in 45 seconds. "Reijo Ruotsalainen would lap me," former NHL player Tom Laidlaw recalled. Players, especially veterans such as Carol Vadnais and Eddie Johnstone, had trouble adjusting to Brooks' offensive style, which required players to circle back to get the puck.

Laidlaw, who was in his second season with the Rangers in 1981, was quickly singled out for special abuse by Brooks. When Laidlaw arrived at training camp 15 pounds overweight, Brooks skated him mercilessly.

Laidlaw's attempts to lose weight to please Brooks became a source of team humor. Once he opened his door to find a room-service meal with one slice of white bread and a glass of water. His teammates, who sent him the meal, were laughing hysterically down the hall.

Brooks wanted to transform Laidlaw into one of the NHL's best stay-at-home defensemen. "Tommy," Brooks said at one practice, "if you ever have the puck, give it to someone else, because you shouldn't have it."

Brooks had plenty of rules that were difficult for some of the veterans. For example, he liked his players to be in the dressing room 45 minutes before a practice was to begin. That rule, in particular, drove Ron Duguay batty. Even though he would arrive 45 minutes before practice, he would wait in his car until he was officially late. That was his form of protest.

Early in the season, Duguay had written a check for $1,000 and given it to Brooks. "This is for the fines I know I'm going to get," Duguay said. "When I use that all up, let me know, and I'll write you another check."

Brooks also liked to conduct a 45-minute meeting after practice. He knew darn well he didn't always have an attentive audience. Privately, he joked about the players' complaints that he used 45 minutes to say what should take two minutes.

"When someone asks me what time it is," Brooks said, "I usually tell them how to build a watch."

Brooks lasted until his fourth season with the Rangers before Patrick went behind the bench to replace him. But Brooks left a mark on the game, and other coaches paid attention to what he was doing with his offensive game plan.

"I hated him when he first got there," Laidlaw said. "But I realize now how much he helped me become a better player. He was just ahead of his time. If he came along today, he would be a great NHL coach."

Bob Johnson

The season after Brooks started in New York, his archrival, Bob Johnson, left the University of Wisconsin to become coach of the Calgary Flames. The hiring raised some eyebrows because this was a Canadian team hiring an American coach. And Johnson wasn't like Brooks who, for all of his modern approaches to the game, didn't spare the rod when dealing with the players. Instead, Johnson was a rah-rah guy who tried to get the most out of his players by making practices fun and entertaining. "He was the most positive man I ever met," said Cliff Fletcher, who made the decision to hire Johnson.

Like Brooks, Johnson came to the NHL with three NCAA championships to his credit. He had won in 1973, 1977, and 1981, endearing himself to

Wisconsin fans forever. They called him "Badger Bob," which through the years was shortened to just "Badger." He had also coached the U.S. Olympic Team at Innsbruck in 1976, losing the bronze medal in a loss to the West Germans.

When he arrived at Calgary, his players didn't know what to think of a coach who looked at each practice session as if it were one of life's great adventures. Was he for real? Could anyone be this infatuated with hockey? What they discovered was that Johnson adored being at the rink. His passion for hockey was second to none, and his meticulous notes scribbled on legal pads were as much a part of his coaching look as a coat and tie.

"He loved the game," said Ken Johannson, a close friend of Johnson's for 35 years. "If there was as much written about hockey as other sports, Bob would be listed with John Wooden or Bobby Knight or Don Shula—coaches of that ilk."

Johnson was a master motivator. He dressed up practice goaltenders in Oilers attire so the players could visualize knocking the puck past Edmonton nemesis Grant Fuhr. He took them to see *The Karate Kid* to show them someone overcoming adversity to succeed. He planned bowling tournaments and used animal parables to explain the importance of conditioning. "The lion is king of the beast," Johnson would say. "But if you go to the zoo, you see when he wakes up, the first thing he does is stretch. We can learn from the animals."

When the Flames were having difficulty containing the jet-propelled rushes of Oilers defenseman Paul Coffey, Johnson surprised the team at practice by commanding his players to leave the ice and take off their skates. With three players left on the ice ready to simulate how Coffey and his teammates were breaking out of their zone, he led the group on a forced march to the upper reaches of the Saddledome so they could get a better perspective on Coffey's breakout rushes. Johnson figured that from 100 feet up, the Flames could see what Coffey was doing.

Johnson also liked to take his team to movies on the day before a game. "It was like a big field trip to him," said *Toronto Sun* writer Steve Simmons, who knew Johnson as well as any member of the media. "That's when I think he was happiest. He always considered himself a teacher."

He brought players together frequently for meetings, often to talk about the power play, which he considered the difference between winning and losing. "I wore out two sets of goalie pads just going to all of his meetings," said Don Edwards, who played for the Flames from 1982 to 1985.

Toronto Globe and Mail sportswriter Eric Duhatschek recalled that Johnson always said there were two approaches to coaching—you either appealed to a player's pride or his fear. Johnson could see that Scotty Bowman and Mike Keenan were highly successful by coaching through fear. Their athletes responded because they were afraid of losing their playing time or their place on the team.

"[Johnson] said he could never do it that way," Duhatschek recalled. "He talked about coaching from the point of pride—pride in the jersey, pride in what you accomplish as a team, pride in getting better."

Johnson constantly preached improved nutrition and fitness, and players initially didn't like his approach. When Gary Roberts attended his first NHL training camp, he thought he was in good shape. He had an asthma attack in the two-mile run and failed every physical test. While addressing the team, Johnson pointed out that Roberts, a first-round pick, had been the worst-conditioned player at camp.

The hockey community was stunned when the Calgary Flames hired American college coach Bob Johnson to be their new coach in 1982–83. Before Johnson and Herb Brooks landed NHL coaching jobs a year apart, the league had rarely given college coaches a chance at the professional level.
(USA Hockey)

"It definitely embarrassed me to the point where I never let it happen again," Roberts told Duhatschek. "And when I saw him in his wheelchair, in his last days, he looked at me, hadn't seen me in a while, and said, 'Roberts, I knew you could do it. I knew you'd make it.' That's when it hit me—that he was trying to help me. In his own way, he helped me a great deal."

Johnson actually had a chance to join the professional ranks 10 years before he signed with the Flames. In 1972 the New York Raiders of the World Hockey Association tried to coax him away from Wisconsin with a lucrative contract. Johnson opted for the security over the quick hit. "My lawyer advised me that it was a shaky situation," Johnson told a *Calgary Herald* hockey writer in 1982. "I had no desire to coach pro then and I guess I didn't miss anything. I understand the Raiders moved three times in one year."

Johnson hadn't actually set out to be a hockey coach. He had been an excellent baseball prospect in Minneapolis, signing with the Chicago White Sox organization. When he didn't make it in baseball, he turned to hockey. He never lost his love for the sport. "Truth is, Bob may have been an even better baseball coach than he was a hockey coach," said two-time Olympic hockey coach Dave Peterson.

If that's true, Johnson probably could have been another Tommy Lasorda or Sparky Anderson. People enjoyed hearing him talk and appreciated his optimism.

At one point, in 1986, the Flames had just lost their 11th consecutive game on a 9–1 decision. Chins were on the floor, faces were glum, and attitudes stunk. Lanny McDonald said it seemed as if the weight of the world was on every player's shoulders when Johnson bounded into the dressing room like he had just won the lottery.

"Boys," he said, "the slump is over because Jim Peplinski scored our goal tonight. That's our breakthrough." The next game, Peplinski scored the winning goal, and the slump was broken.

In 1987 Johnson was faced with a difficult choice. He was 55 years old, and AHAUS had offered him a chance to be the organization's executive director. Though he wasn't ready to stop coaching, he knew the job probably wouldn't be open when he was ready.

Johnson resigned in Calgary and threw himself into the office work, just as he had the coaching. He waved the U.S. flag proudly, often pontificating about how hockey would be changed if the sport could attract more premium athletes. He would watch a *Monday Night Football* game and wonder how the football players would fit into an NHL team's hockey lineup.

"What kind of hockey player would Bo Jackson make?" Johnson would ask. "Probably, a tough, high-scoring center. Three out of four kids who try hockey like it. But most of them never get exposed. We need more rinks in this country."

But Johnson really didn't enjoy being strapped to a desk, and more important, he wasn't done coaching. "He was like a caged lion in an office," said Brad Buetow, who was coaching at Colorado College at the time.

When Craig Patrick offered Johnson the job as Pittsburgh Penguins coach, he jumped at the opportunity. He thought from the beginning that this Mario Lemieux–led team could win the Stanley Cup quickly. The Penguins were a veteran team, but they instantly took a liking to Johnson, who knew how to handle stars as well as how to teach young players.

He would walk into the dressing room before a game, spot Lemieux, and commence his speech. "Here's my guy getting a rubdown, getting his back ready to go, he'll be banging along the boards, his legs will be going," Johnson would say.

Assistant coach Barry Smith said he sometimes would get frustrated because Johnson always saw the silver lining and never entertained the idea that something was going wrong.

"We're not working that hard today," Smith would say.

"Barry, the ice is bad," Johnson would say. "Bad ice. We can't handle the puck. We can't move the biscuit the way we want to."

Detroit Red Wings coach Scotty Bowman, the winningest coach in NHL history, said he admired the way Johnson believed that he could turn average or below-average players into good players. Bowman was the director of player development in Pittsburgh when Johnson arrived.

"He loved [Penguins right-winger] Jay Caufield, even though Jay wasn't a great hockey player," Bowman remembered. "He thought if he could have gotten Jay Caufield earlier in his career, he could have made him into a good player. And maybe he could have."

Johnson made no secret of being pro-American, although it didn't seem to color his coaching, except that he liked to bring in players he knew, and he knew plenty of Americans.

"We took a lot of heat for having American players," Barry Smith said. "Every time we would get another player, everyone would say, 'Here comes the American flag.' But really, he was like most coaches in that he liked good players who could handle the puck."

Johnson liked coaching in a working-class city where the media and fans adored him and his ideas. Often he and Smith would stay late to watch an NHL game on the satellite dish, and then Johnson would drag his assistant out for a late snack. He would always pick a working-class bar where he could get an Iron City beer and a sausage. "This is a steel town, and we have to go to a steel town bar," Badger would say.

"He would walk in, and they would all cheer him," Smith said. "He would sit with all the guys in hard hats and say, 'Let's talk hockey.'"

Johnson loved golf analogies. Home wins were pars, home losses were bogeys, and road wins were birdies. "[He believed] if you shot par over the course of the season you'd make the playoffs," Duhatschek recalled.

When Johnson ended up taking a coaching job in Pittsburgh, Duhatschek and *Calgary Herald* writer George Johnson warned the Pittsburgh writers that the golf talk was coming.

Late in the season, the Penguins finally came to Calgary, and Pittsburgh writers Dave Molinari and Tom McMillan told Duhatschek and Johnson that Badger Bob had not made a single golf reference the entire season. Minutes later, Johnson saw the four sportswriters gathered and offered, "The playoff race is like going into the final round at Pebble Beach..."

"All four of us, on the floor, erupted with laughter," Duhatschek said.

Bob Johnson, of course, had no idea why his words were so funny.

Badger's style played well in Pittsburgh. He was adored. In the 1990–91 season, Johnson led the Penguins to the Stanley Cup Championship, becoming the first American coach to win the trophy since Bill Stewart won in 1938. Johnson was pumped up by the experience and was looking forward to coaching the U.S. squad at the Canada Cup. That August, while with the team, he became ill. The diagnosis was a malignant brain tumor.

He never stopped being positive. Less than 36 hours after surgery for a brain tumor in August 1991, he sketched out a strategy for the U.S. team to deal with the Swedish forechecking system in the opening game of the Canada Cup hockey tournament.

A few months later, he died in Colorado Springs. His motto had always been: "It's a great day for hockey." That certainly wasn't true on the day Bob Johnson passed away. ∎

A member of the American team gives a Swiss player a sweater and a friendly handshake before the two teams faced off in St. Moritz. (Mark Kauffman//Time Life Pictures/Getty Images)

THE 1948 OLYMPICS
Brown vs. Brundage

The hockey competition on the ice at the 1948 Olympic Games in St. Moritz, Switzerland, probably wasn't as fractious as the hockey war being waged in the boardroom. History books say Canada vs. Czechoslovakia was the 1948 Olympic hockey story.

But the true story in St. Moritz was Walter Brown vs. Avery Brundage.

Behind closed doors, Brown, vice president of the American Hockey Association of the United States (AHAUS), had locked horns with International Olympic Committee (IOC) president Avery Brundage. The issue: which hockey squad would represent the U.S. in St. Moritz. In a calculated move, Brundage had knowingly allowed two American teams to show up in St. Moritz, believing it was time for him to battle the AHAUS, a fight he expected to win.

Brundage was a pompous administrator who was often accused of trying to run the International Olympic Committee like a dictatorship. He had resented the International Ice Hockey Federation's decision to recognize AHAUS as the controlling body for the U.S. Olympic hockey team. In Brundage's opinion, AHAUS's registration of senior men's teams smacked of professionalism. He loathed that senior players were often paid, even if the money was shelled out under the guise of reimbursing players for wages they lost by playing hockey. He wanted the Amateur Athletic Union (AAU) to run the American hockey show, even though some players on the AAU team had also played under the same reimbursement plan.

"Some of the players on the AAU team can't in good conscience take the Olympic oath, not as we see it," Brown told Brundage.

Brundage was never timid about initiating a scrap, but Brown was a worthy adversary. Brown was the president of the Boston Bruins, Boston Celtics, and the Boston Garden, and more important, he had done plenty of business deals with European arena owners. He was well known and admired abroad. In 1931 he had handpicked players to tour Europe. The trip would include playing in the World Championship.

Brown's Boston Olympics squad, or the Massachusetts Rangers as they were known in Europe, won the 1933 tournament in Prague. Brown continued to personally select players for a European tour through 1936, when he was manager of the Olympic team in Garmisch, Germany. In 1947 Brown came back to manage the U.S. entry for the 1947 World Championship in Prague. IIHF members had voted overwhelmingly that AHAUS, not the AAU, be recognized as the master of USA's Olympic hockey program. Brundage seethed over the vote and sent out word that he didn't intend to accept the IIHF decision.

Controlling the Olympic team was an important issue for AHAUS officials, who were finally starting to feel their clout expanding. Starting in 1920, hockey had been controlled by the United States Amateur Hockey Association, but that group was disbanded in 1926. No organization had seized control until the AAU took over in 1930. In the interim, the United States didn't participate in the 1928 Olympics and 1930 World Championship.

The AHAUS organization was founded on October 29, 1937, at Madison Square Garden in New York, when representatives from 14 teams in the New York Metropolitan, Michigan-Ontario, Eastern Amateur, and International Leagues agreed to a national affiliation. AHAUS's first president was Thomas F. Lockhart, who had been coaching the New York Rovers in the Eastern League. During his AHAUS career, Lockhart also served as business manager for the New York Rangers.

Lockhart's vision of a formal national youth program really didn't occur until 1947, when Minnesota formed its own association and joined AHAUS. The addition of Minnesota added credibility to AHAUS and significantly increased membership. (Of the 131 teams AHAUS registered in 1947 and 1948, 36 percent were located in Minnesota.) After Minnesota joined AHAUS, Bob Ridder, who was a radio executive and the Minnesota Hockey Association's first president, quickly became an important figure on the national level.

The Olympic controversy took shape the year before the Games. In 1947 Dartmouth standout Jack Riley read an article in a newspaper stating the winner of the AAU tournament would represent the United States at the 1948 Olympics. He asked his coach Eddie Jeremiah to enter the Dartmouth team, but Jeremiah declined. Riley took matters in his own hands and convinced several Dartmouth players to enter the tournament as the Hanover Indians. They won the tournament and expected to be the Olympic team.

The following year, Riley talked to Brown, who told him to put together an AHAUS team to compete in the Olympic Games.

"If you get the players, I guarantee you will play," Brown told Riley.

Riley wanted to bring along his brothers, Billy and Joey, but Brown said he didn't want players with college eligibility remaining. That didn't make Riley happy, because he considered his brothers to be two of the best players in the country. His brother Billy is still Dartmouth's all-time leading scorer with 228 points, and Joey totaled 116 points in two seasons. In one game against Princeton, he had six goals and four assists.

Riley's team set sail for Europe three weeks before the Olympics in order to have time to play exhibition games. When Riley arrived, an Associated Press reporter, Ted Smith, informed him there was another U.S. team representing the AAU already there and that his brothers were on the roster.

That was not accurate. Billy Riley wasn't there because his wife, knowing Jack's AHAUS team would probably play, wouldn't let him go on what she called "a three-week soiree."

"We were still sure we were going to play, because there was no way the Europeans were going to go against Walter Brown," Riley said.

Although Brundage had assured the AAU players that they would be playing, he began saying that maybe both teams should be barred. According to Olympic rules, a team was supposed to play only when it was recognized by its national governing body and its international federation. Each team had only one of the required stamps of approval.

Moreover, because the Swiss organizers also backed the AHAUS team, Brundage threatened to pull the entire American delegation out of the Olympic Games if the AHAUS team played. That infuriated the Swiss, who had sided with AHAUS because they badly needed the hockey gate receipts and knew Brown was Pied Piper to the European hockey federations. Brundage's threat to turn the Olympics into a shambles over one team must have seemed ludicrous to the Swiss.

But Brundage's entrenched stand didn't surprise AHAUS officials. "He didn't seem to like hockey, or the Winter Games," Ridder said. "But he didn't hate us as much as he hated the skiers. He considered them an abomination."

Dartmouth player Whitey Campbell, a member of the AAU team, had seen plenty of action as a tailgunner in World War II, but he had never seen anything quite as bizarre as this political cesspool. "It was embarrassing," Campbell said. "The whole

Walter Brown was a kingpin in American hockey from the 1930s into the 1960s. In 1948, Brown was vice president of the Amateur Hockey Association of the United States (AHAUS). He was instrumental in convincing the International Olympic Committee to permit the AHAUS team to play in the 1948 Olympics. (Hockey Hall of Fame)

world was mad because we were doing our laundry internationally."

Brown, an important friend of European rink owners, asked local rinks to deny practice time to the AAU team. Campbell's team was able to secure some practice time on some natural ice, but they were allowed on the ice only after figure skater Dick Button had finished his practice routine. Meanwhile, Brundage was doing all that he could to make sure the AAU team was recognized as the official Olympic team. Although the AAU team

The United States takes on Switzerland during the 1948 Olympics in St. Moritz. Though the United States did not medal, the Americans posted wins over Poland, Italy, and Sweden.
(Mark Kauffman//Time Life Pictures/Getty Images)

had received shoddy equipment before the trip, they did receive the official Olympic pins and the fine white USA team jackets.

Riley, a U.S. Navy bomber pilot during the war, didn't appreciate the treatment he was receiving. "They are acting as if we are the Japanese Navy invading them," he growled.

Ever confident, Riley suggested that the two American teams could play each other, with the winner going to the Olympics. Nobody liked that idea, and the bickering continued until the International Olympic Committee decided two days before the Games that both teams would be banned. That didn't stop the debate. Brown pushed hard against the committee's decision. Just past midnight on the eve of the opening ceremony, the IOC officials finally accepted that the AHAUS team was going to play.

AAU players awakened the next morning not knowing what happened in the middle of the night. They still believed they might compete and were told to march in the athletes' parade.

"We marched to the outside ice arena, and there before our eyes was the other [U.S.] team getting ready to play Switzerland," Campbell said. "That's when it dawned on us that we probably weren't going to get to play."

Campbell was one of three Dartmouth players on the AAU team. Four other Dartmouth players were members of the AHAUS team. When the controversy finally ended, Campbell went up into the stands and cheered for the AHAUS squad. "There was no bad feeling because they were all our buddies," Campbell said.

The soiree that Billy Riley's wife feared then came to pass. AAU players immediately began to ski and party in the beautiful Swiss Alps. Campbell was there about a week until the Dartmouth athletic department notified his coach that Campbell and his teammates should report back to school.

The AAU players had an easier time on the slopes than the AHAUS team had on the ice. After the first game, the International Olympic Committee decreed that the 1948 hockey games wouldn't be considered an Olympic event. No medals would be awarded. The AAU players were told they would be considered Olympians. But the news didn't surprise or overwhelm the AHAUS players. "What the hell was a gold medal," Riley said. "None of us knew anything about medals. We just wanted to play."

Amid the turmoil, the U.S. team played poorly in their opening game and lost 5–4 to an inferior Swiss team. Back in sync, they won over Poland, Italy, and Sweden. By then, emotions had cooled, and the politicians agreed to a compromise that allowed the Olympic results to be counted if the Americans didn't win a medal. On the final day of the hockey competition, the Americans lost 4–3 to the Czechs in a game that decided the bronze medal. The Americans unofficially finished fourth.

"I still think if we would have sent out the Dartmouth team we would have won the tournament," Campbell said.

The Americans have won eight medals in Olympic hockey competition. Here is a rundown of the U.S. results through the years:

Antwerp, Belgium (1920): The Winter Games weren't officially added to the Olympic docket until 1924, but the United States did compete in the unofficial Olympic Games in Antwerp. Canada and the United States were by far the most dominant teams. The Americans defeated Switzerland 29–0 in one game. At one point, the Americans had hoped to send only players born in the United States. But realizing their talent level wasn't all that strong, they decided to send some Canadians who were playing for U.S. teams. That's why some talented Canadians like Herb Drury and Frank A. Synott appeared on the U.S. roster. Drury would end up playing in the NHL. The USA's best player was Moose Goheen, who might have been the best player in the tournament. Canada defeated the USA 2–0 in the semifinals en route to the gold. The Americans won the silver.

Chamonix, France (1924): Future NHL player Clarence "Taffy" Abel would help the Americans win the silver medal by scoring 15 goals as a defenseman. But Drury, whose Pittsburgh team would join the National Hockey League the following year, led the Americans in scoring with 22 goals in five games.

St. Moritz, Switzerland (1928): General Douglas MacArthur, then chairman of the United States Olympic Committee, made the final decision not to send an American hockey team to the Games. The University Club of Boston had a very strong team, with future NHL standouts such as George Owen and Myles Lane on the roster. But the team couldn't scrape together the cash needed to make the trip. Several college teams were approached, but only Augsburg College of Minneapolis seemed willing to go. According to research by hockey historian Donald Clark, MacArthur decided that Augsburg, led by five Hanson brothers, "was not representative of American hockey."

Lake Placid (1932): By this time, the Americans had enough talent to discontinue the practice of supplementing their roster with Canadians. The Americans sent a team of Eastern All-Stars and won the silver medal in a very weak field of entrants. Only Poland and Germany sent teams to be whipped by the Canadians and Americans. Some interesting politics did occur in 1932 because the U.S. Olympic Committee had asked the Amateur Athletic Union (AAU) to take charge of ice hockey. The committee believed the U.S. Amateur Hockey Association had evolved into a weak functioning body. This development would be important in years to come. The 1932 team was coached by former Harvard coach Alfred Winsor, who had left his mark on hockey in another way. Winsor has been credited with being the first coach to station his defensemen side-by-side, instead of one behind the other. He figured correctly that the side-by-side positioning was better suited for shutting down the always-improving passing game. Before 1917 when Winsor made the switch, the thinking was that the first defenseman (known as the point) would meet the forward coming down the ice, and the second defender (known as the counterpoint) would be the safety valve. That system, however, would break down when a clever puck handler, such as Hobey Baker, simply skated around both defenders. U.S. Hockey Hall of Fame member John Garrison was on this squad. A year later, he would score an unassisted overtime goal to beat Canada 2–1 and give America its first World Championship.

Garmisch, Germany (1936): The increase in worldwide interest in hockey was evident when 15 teams arrived to compete in Garmisch. The United States won the bronze medal, despite the fact it gave up only one goal in the final round. The Americans tied Great Britain 0–0, downed the Czechoslovakians 2–0, and then lost to the Canadians 1–0 in a game that featured 60 minutes of overtime. Among those on the American roster were team captain John Garrison and Gerry Cosby who, as goalie, gave up just one goal in five games.

St. Moritz, Switzerland (1948): See main chapter text.

Oslo, Norway (1952): Having resolved its political differences through a compromise, the USA sent a strong team to Norway and won the silver medal. The Americans finally earned a tie with the Canadians. But a 4–2 loss to the strong Swedish team kept the Americans away from the gold medal. Among the players on the American roster was Len Ceglarski, who went on to have a successful coaching career at Clarkson and Boston College. At Boston College, Ceglarski would continue Snooks Kelley's tradition of recruiting only American players.

Also on the American roster was goaltender Dick Desmond, who had played on the strong Dartmouth team, plus Allan Van of St. Paul,

Minnesota, who played on five U.S. national teams. The leading scorer on the U.S. team was Ken Yackel (six goals and three assists for nine points).

Cortina, Italy (1956): The Americans, coached by feisty John Mariucci, won the silver medal. They defeated the archrival Canadians 4–1, but the Soviets arrived to begin their long dominance of international hockey. Two years earlier at the World Championship, the Soviets had the best collection of pure skaters the world had ever seen. They had stunned the Canadians with a 7–2 win in the championship game. The Americans, who hadn't sent a team to that championship, had seen the Soviets at the 1955 World Championship, where the Soviets posted a 3–0 win. At Cortina, the Russian power play was too much for the Americans, and they fell 4–0. The Americans' silver-medal success was aided significantly by the goaltending of Willard Ikola, another player from the Eveleth goaltending factory. Ikola became one of the most successful Minnesota high school coaches, posting a 616–149–38 record and winning eight state titles at Edina High School. Also on the team were John Mayasich, Dick Meredith, and Bill Cleary, who would also play for the 1960 team, plus Wendell Anderson, who would go on to be governor of Minnesota. Among the top players on the 1960 squad was John Matchefts of Eveleth, who was a superb college player at Michigan. He went on to coach at Colorado College and the Air Force Academy.

Squaw Valley (1960): See Chapter 8

Innsbruck, Austria (1964): The most interesting name on this Ed Jeremiah–coached team is Herb Brooks, who had persevered to land a spot on the 1964 U.S. roster after being cut from the 1960 squad. Brooks' brother David was also on the roster. Bill and Roger Christian returned from the 1960 gold-medal team, along with Paul Johnson. But the Clearys didn't play, and there was no John Mayasich, McCartan, or Tommy Williams. The Americans couldn't rediscover the magic from Squaw Valley and finished 2–5 in the tournament with victories coming against Germany and Switzerland.

Grenoble, France (1968): The game that will always haunt U.S. player Larry Pleau was a 3–2 loss to Canada. "[Canadian captain] Marshall Johnston scored two goals from the point and you could read the label on the puck as it headed past you," Pleau said. "That was a key loss for us." Coached by Murray Williamson, the Americans went 2–4–1 with a team that included future NHL players Pleau, Lou Nanne, Doug Volmar, and Bob Paradise, among others. Pleau and Nanne both had two goals and four assists for six points in seven games.

Sapporo, Japan (1972): See Chapter 9.

Innsbruck, Austria (1976): This Olympics came at a time when the WHA was heavily invested in American players, and many of the desirable players had gone to the WHA. Plus, Ron Wilson decided to return to Providence College. He was a dominant performer, particularly on the wider international ice rinks. It was a devastating loss for the squad. The Bob Johnson–coached Americans finished fifth. Buzz Schneider—who went on to be a key player on the 1980 U.S. squad—played on this team.

Lake Placid (1980): See Chapter 11

Sarajevo, Yugoslavia (1984): How do you follow the Miracle on Ice in Lake Placid? It was an impossible task for coach Lou Vairo, but that team ended up producing top-flight NHL players, such as Pat LaFontaine, Ed Olczyk, and Chris Chelios, among others. "David A. Jensen was a great player," Vairo said. "If he didn't get the injuries he had in Hartford, he would have had a fantastic NHL career. He was right there with LaFontaine and Olczyk as an extremely high-level player."

The Americans were young, and then LaFontaine became sick before the tournament started. Chelios played the entire tournament with a broken bone in his foot. America's success at

Dave Peterson coached the 1992 U.S. Olympic team in Albertville, France. (USA Hockey)

Lake Placid had also prompted the NHL to be more aggressive in scouting in the U.S. Suddenly, players such as Phil Housley, Tom Barrasso, Bobby Carpenter, and Brian Lawton were turning pro out of high school. The Americans posted a 2-2-2 record and finished seventh. "This team was treated disrespectfully," Vairo said. "I can tell you that this was a great hockey team, and they beat great hockey teams all year long. These kids were sensational."

What has been forgotten is that Vairo had to take a U.S. team to Japan in 1983 to win the B Pool. If the Americans didn't finish in the top two teams in the tournament, the United States would not have been eligible for the 1984 Olympic Games. Current Atlanta Thrashers president Don Waddell and Toronto Maple Leafs coach Ron Wilson both played defense on the team that went to Japan. "They saved me," Vairo said, laughing. Jim Craig, the 1980 Lake Placid hero, was in the net. Lawton played on that squad. "We played Norway in the final game and beat them 12–2 or 14–2, then we played them in the Olympics a few months later. Same Norwegian team, same goalie, and we tied 3–3. How do you figure hockey?"

Calgary, Alberta, Canada (1988): At a press conference during the Calgary Games, then–USA Hockey International Director Art Berglund compared the American squad to the Las Vegas, Nevada, Runnin' Rebels basketball team from that era. It was an apt description because these Americans were fast and talented, and they could push the puck up the ice. Future NHL players Brian Leetch, Tony Granato, Kevin Stevens, and Scott Young were on the team. Dave Peterson was the coach. Only the Russians scored more goals than the Americans in the preliminary round, but the USA failed to advance to the medal round because they gave up more than five goals per game. Players who were on that team probably feel like they were better than their seventh-place finish. They lost 7–5 to an impressive Soviet team that won the gold medal. "Leetchie hit the post in the third period when it was 6–5," said Jim Johannson, a player on that squad.

Albertville, France (1992): Thanks to the sterling play of goaltender Ray LeBlanc, the Dave Peterson–coached Americans had a shot at the bronze medal only to lose it on a 6–1 decision to Czechoslovakia. LeBlanc, of Fitchburg, Massachusetts, was a 27-year-old career minor leaguer who captured the hearts of Americans by posting a 5–2–1 record with a 2.00 goals-against average and two shutouts in the tournament. "More people in America know LeBlanc today than Brian Leetch," Berglund said during the Olympics, noting that LeBlanc had become a star on one of the world's greatest athletic stages. Keith Tkachuk, a future NHL 500-goal scorer played on that squad, along with future NHL players Young, Bret Hedican, Shawn McEachern, and Marty McInnis, among others. But LeBlanc was the story. "He was a good pro goalie at that time who had never gotten a chance," said Johannson, playing on his second Olympic team. "He was Mr. Dependable in the minor leagues." The Chicago Blackhawks promoted him to the NHL later that season and gave him a start. He gave up one goal, won the start, and never played another game in the NHL.

Lillehammer, Norway (1994): The Americans had the ex-Maine tandem of Garth Snow and Mike Dunham in the net, but were not a factor in the tournament, winning only one of their six games. That team included many future NHL players, including Brian Rolston, Todd Marchant, and Craig Johnson, among others. Future NHL coach Peter Laviolette played in his

second Olympic Games. He had also played for the 1988 team. The Americans were hurt by three ties with Slovakia, France, and Canada. The tie with Canada suggests the Americans might have underachieved, because Canada went on to win the silver medal.

Nagano, Japan (1998): This Olympics marked the first time the NHL allowed its players to participate, and it could not have gone much worse for the Americans. Using primarily the same stars who helped the Americans win the 1996 World Cup, the Ron Wilson–coached Americans stumbled to a 1–2 record, losing to Canada and Sweden in Group play, and then lost to the Dominik Hasek–led Czech Republic in the quarterfinals. The Czechs only used 12 NHL players and ended up winning the gold medal. To make their situation worse, 10 hours after the U.S. team was eliminated, unidentified American players caused $1,000 worth of damage to two rooms in the Olympic Village.

Salt Lake City (2002): See Chapter 21.

Torino, Italy (2006): This was viewed as a transitional year for the American program because the top players from 1996 World Cup team were beyond their prime years and the rising American stars hadn't yet reached their maturity. The result: an eighth-place finish for the Peter Laviolette–coached team. The Americans lost 4–3 to Finland in the quarterfinals. It's important to note that these Olympic Games came after the 2004–05 NHL season was lost after a lockout of players. "We lost a year of development for our younger players, and that hurt us in a transition year," said Atlanta Thrashers general manger Don Waddell, who was the general manager of the 2006 U.S. Olympic Men's Ice Hockey Team.

Vancouver, Canada (2010): See Chapter 22. ∎

Defenseman Jack Kirrane, one of the best U.S. shot blockers in the 1960 Olympic Tournament, stops another attempt against the Russians. (USA Hockey)

THE 1960 OLYMPICS
America's First Miracle Team

The frosty chill that Bill and Bob Cleary felt as they entered a Denver ice arena on a February morning in 1960 wasn't coming from the frozen rink. It was coming from the cold shoulders being directed toward them by their new U.S. Olympic teammates.

Not long before the team was to leave for Squaw Valley, the U.S. players learned that coach Jack Riley was cutting Herb Brooks and Bob Dupuis to make room for the Cleary brothers. The U.S. players had agreed to give the newcomers the silent treatment. "It was pretty controversial," said Roger Christian, one of the top scorers on the 1960 squad. "Everyone agreed not to talk to them."

"Hardly anyone would speak to us, and we barely got the puck in warmup," Bill Cleary recalled.

The truth is that the U.S. team's performance at the 1960 Olympic Games was as remarkable, if not more so, than the 1980 U.S. team's effort at Lake Placid. First, the Americans had never beaten the Soviets. Second, the Canadians were even better than the Soviets. Third, the U.S. team had not

looked sharp during the 18-game pre-Olympic tour. And finally, dissension over the late addition of the Clearys seemed to be tearing apart the team.

After a players' meeting was held in Denver prior to the Clearys' arrival, a message delivered to Riley said that the players weren't going to compete if the Clearys were brought in.

"I told [team manager] Jim Claypool, 'To hell with them,'" Riley said. "We'll bring our wives. We've got a nice place in Squaw Valley. We'll have a nice time."

Adding a player late wasn't a novel idea; American and Canadian teams had successfully done so in the past. In 1933 the late addition of Harvard standout John Garrison helped the United States capture the World Championship in Prague, and Riley had watched the Canadians bring in two players just before the 1948 Olympics to help them finish first.

The Clearys had let Riley know, through a message to Riley's brother, that they wanted to play. Everyone knew the Clearys hadn't tried out for the team because they were operating an insurance

The Cleary brothers, Bob and Bill, and the Christian brothers, Roger and Bill, were the top offensive players on the 1960 U.S. Olympic Team. There was a competitive rivalry between the two brother combinations because the Christians were from Minnesota and the Clearys were from Massachusetts. In that era, the East vs. West rivalry was prevalent in college and amateur hockey. (USA Hockey)

business and couldn't afford to leave their business for two months. But the Clearys could leave for two weeks, which would give them time to play in the tournament.

"I've read that I kissed their butts to get them," Riley said. "That's not what happened. They came to me."

A couple weeks before the tournament began, Riley spoke with hockey guru Walter Brown. "Walter," Riley said, "do you want to go into the Olympics with a chance to win or no chance to win?"

"I want a chance to win."

"Then I have to bring in the Clearys."

"Do it," Brown had said.

After the tournament, players said they weren't bothered by the addition of John Mayasich or Bill Cleary, whose arrival had been expected from the beginning. Everyone knew Mayasich and Cleary had been the top scorers on the 1956 team in Cortina. The players were more miffed because

they knew the Cleary brothers had come as a package deal. Bill Cleary wouldn't come without Bob. At that time, the players didn't believe Bob Cleary deserved to be on the team. That sentiment changed when they watched Bob Cleary play.

Before their first game, Bill Cleary addressed the tension with a brief, pointed speech: "I didn't come 3,000 miles to lose. We don't have to hug and kiss. I just want you to pass me the puck."

The Christian brothers were among the first to talk to the Clearys. McCartan would also tell his teammates, "We've worked too hard to let this get in the way." Jack Kirrane, a no-nonsense player, said he planned to play in these Olympics, "even if [he was] the only guy on the ice."

Players backed off their threat not to compete, but neither Riley nor anyone else on the team could be sure how well this team would gel once the Olympic tournament began. "No one gave us a chance," Bill Cleary said. "I think *Sports Illustrated* picked us last."

Deep down, the American players believed they were capable of winning the tournament. They could look down their bench and see an impressive collection of talent. John Mayasich, a University of Minnesota grad, and Bill Cleary, a Harvard man, were two of the best players ever in college hockey. Billy and Roger Christian were feisty and experienced international players who knew how to create offensive chances. Paul Johnson was a dynamic skater, a breakaway threat every time the puck hit his stick. This was an experienced team. Dick Rodenheiser, Dick Meredith, Weldy Olson, Mayasich, and Cleary had all played for the 1956 U.S. Olympic Team, which had won the silver medal.

Then there was Jack McCartan, on loan from the U.S. Army to play goal for coach Jack Riley's Olympic squad. Those on the U.S. team who didn't know McCartan knew of him. In addition to playing goal for the University of Minnesota's hockey team, McCartan had been an All-American third baseman. His career batting average at Minnesota was .349. In 1956 he batted .436 with four doubles, six home runs, and 17 RBIs in 13 games.

His career 2.95 goals-against average and .908 save percentage still puts him at the top of the school's goaltending leaders. "We all knew he had a great glove hand," Mayasich said.

The 26-year-old Mayasich was a veteran of several international tournaments. During the week, he was an advertising executive for a television station, but on weekends he played for the Green Bay Bobcats in the United States Hockey League.

He had been a high-scoring center in college hockey, netting 144 goals in 111 career games at Minnesota. In his senior season, he had 41 goals and 39 assists in 30 games. Opponents simply had

no way to shut him down. His moves were too crafty, his shots too hard. He credits former Chicago Blackhawks player Doc Romnes, his coach for just one year at Minnesota, with refining the puck-handling skills that would serve him well for decades.

Playing center on a line with Bill Cleary and John Matchefts at the 1956 Games in Cortina, Mayasich led the Americans in scoring with six goals and four assists. He had a hat trick in the USA's 4–1 win against Canada.

But the Bobcats liked to use Mayasich on defense because then he could dominate both ends of the ice. Riley, head coach at West Point, also liked Mayasich as a defenseman and let everyone know from the beginning that Mayasich was going to be added to the team right before the Olympics began. Mayasich didn't meet the team until the day before the games began in Squaw Valley.

Yet another product of Eveleth's hockey factory, Mayasich had his own unique calling card—a wicked slap shot that would have been the envy of any NHL player except Bobby Hull. "He was way ahead of his time on that slap shot," Cleary said.

Mayasich began experimenting with it during college when Eveleth goaltender Willard Ikola, then playing at the University of Michigan, told him how he had seen another player attempt it. With his skills, Mayasich was able to master the concept based solely on Ikola's description.

His slap shot was particularly befuddling to international competitors because it was completely foreign to players outside of North America. Mayasich remembered when he was playing for the Bobcats in an exhibition game against a Japanese national team, he uncorked a slap shot from center ice that beat the surprised goalkeeper. The goaltender appeared to have pulled a muscle trying to stop the shot. He fell in front of the goal and was rolling around on the ice in a fit of hysteria. But when his teammates and the Bobcats moved closer, they saw his hysteria was a fit of laughter, not pain. He had never seen anything like Mayasich's rocket launcher. The rest of the Japanese team joined the goalie in his bemused laughter. "It was comical to see them all laughing so hard," Mayasich said.

After the game, Japanese players examined the knob of tape Mayasich had at the top of his stick, thinking that had something to do with the velocity and timing of the shot.

With Mayasich supplying support, the Americans' high-powered offense gelled quickly, in spite of the rift caused by the Cleary brothers' arrival. The team was brimming with confidence after it won its first four games in pool play against Czechoslovakia, Australia, Sweden, and Germany. The four defensemen—Mayasich, Kirrane, Bob Owen, and Rodney Paavola—were playing well, McCartan was sharp, and the offense was clicking.

But the Americans knew they were still the underdog against the vaunted Canadians, whose roster included Harry Sinden, later a coach and general manager in the NHL, and Bobby Rousseau, who would go on to score 245 NHL goals and win four Stanley Cups as a member of the Montreal Canadiens. (Hockey historian Joe Pelletier has reported that the Canadian team originally wanted future Toronto Maple Leafs great Dave Keon but settled on Rousseau when Keon's St. Mike's Junior Team wouldn't allow him to play.)

The backup Canadian goalie was Cesare Maniago, who would end up in the NHL later that season. The Canadians were coached by Bobby Bauer, a member of the Bruins' famous Kraut Line with Woody Dumart and Milt Schmidt.

Against Canada, Bob Cleary jammed a rebound past goaltender Don Head on the power play to give the USA a 1–0 lead, and former Minnesota standout Paul Johnson intercepted a pass and streaked up the ice to beat Head with a lengthy shot.

In an interview for the Michigan State website 50 years later, Johnson's linemate, alternate captain Weldy Olson, estimated that Johnson fired the puck from 80 feet out to give the United States the two-goal lead. "[Johnson] went over the center red line and let it go," Olson said. "When we skated over to the bench, and I asked him why he shot so soon, he said, 'Oh, I had him beat.'"

Johnson was considered to have as much pure offensive talent as any player to come out of Minnesota in that era. "All the way through high school, he was the scourge," McCartan said. "He could control the game, do anything he wanted."

Canadian winger James Connelly finally tallied with 5:22 left in the game, but McCartan's strong goaltending preserved the 2–1 U.S. victory.

"It was shocking to us," said Sinden, now president of the Boston Bruins. "We were probably favored by seven goals against them."

To beat Canada, goaltender Jack McCartan made 38 saves, including 20 in the second period. One wire service report of the game said McCartan seemed to be operating "with radar to smother shots."

"McCartan played well in goal, much like Jim Craig did for the 1980 team," Sinden said.

Team Canada was really the Kitchener-Waterloo Dutchmen, Canada's best amateur team. Coming into Squaw Valley, their goal had been to avenge Canada's bronze-medal finish at the 1956 Games in Cortina, where they had also lost to the Americans. After being waylaid again by the 1960 U.S. squad, they were bitter. They believed they hadn't played well and blamed McCartan for their undoing.

"Beating the Canadians in hockey," Bill Cleary told the Associated Press immediately after the game, "would be like Canada beating us in baseball."

Riley was gracious in victory, telling reporters, "If we played the Canadians 10 games, they'd win nine of them."

He may not have believed that, and the American players certainly didn't. Although the Americans had passed an important test, the Soviets were still favored in their matchup with the USA two days later. "Though we had beaten the Canadians," McCartan said, "no one would bet his house on beating the Russians. We had never beaten them, and their power play used to do us in all the time."

It was clear the Soviets planned to dominate the sport. The Americans, who had been playing hockey in some form since the 1890s, had always finished behind the Soviets, who had only been competing internationally since 1955. The Soviets had beaten the Americans 4–0 at the 1956 Olympic Games in Cortina, Italy.

Yet there was cause for optimism: the Soviets had been tied 2–2 by the Swedes, the same Swedes the Americans had whipped 6–3. Roger Christian had netted three goals in that one-sided game, and McCartan had made 36 saves. Ex-Harvard winger Robert McVey, the Clearys' linemate, had also scored for the Americans, who led 4–0 after the first period.

The 1960 game against the Russians drew an overflow crowd to the open-air Blyth Arena at Squaw Valley. The team's trainer, the late Ben Bertini, had to clear the bench to get his players room to sit. Among those thrown out, according to Bill Cleary, was then–California governor Pat

Brown. "Everyone wanted to carry our skates just to get in," Cleary said.

The Soviets led 2–1 before Bill Christian, assisted by brother Roger, tied the game with a goal at 11:01 of the second period. Russian goaltender Nikolai Puchkov had mistakenly given Bill Christian about two feet of room on the short side, and Christian had ripped a shot about eight inches off the ice. "It was an easy goal," Christian would say later.

For the next 24 minutes, the Americans and Soviets fought for every inch of ice, neither side conceding anything.

Perhaps more than anyone else, the Christian brothers wanted this victory against the Soviets. Two years earlier, they had been on the first U.S. team to play inside the Soviet Union during the Cold War. In the four days they spent in Moscow, they were constantly reminded about the Soviets' successful launch of Sputnik into outer space in the fall of 1957. Their Soviet hosts had made Sputnik centerpieces to place on the tables where the Americans ate.

More than 15,000 Soviet fans had showed up in 1958 to watch the U.S. team lose twice to Soviet teams. The Christians remembered that the hotel, the food, and the conditions were bad. "We hated every minute of it," Bill Christian said.

Now it was 1960, and the games were on American ice. The Christian brothers knew they could pay back the Soviets in grand fashion. With 5:01 left in the contest, Bill Christian, the U.S. team's smallest player at 5'9" and 145 pounds, scored again, set up again by brother Roger and Tommy Williams, his other linemate.

"Tommy had knocked the puck out of the corner, and Roger took a shot," Bill remembered. "Puchkov went down. I was getting shoved around in front of the net. The puck came out, and I put it back in, just under Puchkov's head."

A boisterous crowd screamed with delight while the Americans fought off the Soviets in the closing minutes. The puck was in the Americans' end for many of the final minutes, and McCartan was brilliant preserving his country's first hockey win over the Soviets. "Every faceoff seemed to last an eternity," Bill Cleary remembered.

After the game, the teary-eyed Soviet coach, Anatoli Tarasov, entered the American dressing room and kissed Riley on the cheek, and Russian interpreter Roman Kesserlov gave Bill Cleary a bottle of vodka he had to pay off a bet they had made. The vodka still sits unopened in Cleary's Massachusetts home as a memento of the triumph.

Almost 20 years later, Bill Cleary entertained Coach Tarasov at his home overlooking the Charles River in the Boston area. Tarasov joked that he "ended up in Siberia" because of Cleary and his colleagues.

Aside from Tarasov, the Russians didn't accept the loss in 1960 very well. A bitter Nikolai Romanov, the Soviet minister of sport, told the assembled media: "Perhaps we would have won on a neutral rink, but naturally it is the right of the spectators to cheer their team as much as they can, and we just had to bear that handicap."

The Americans had no time to celebrate because they were scheduled to be on the ice at 8:00 the next morning to face the Czechs for the gold medal. Organizers expected the Canada–Soviet Union game to be for the gold, so the USA-Czech game was scheduled for early Sunday.

The Americans had defeated the Czechs 7–5 in pool play, but they were made uneasy because they had been forced to come from behind to do it. There was no denying they were facing a well-schooled team, quite capable of rendering their victories over Canada and the Soviet Union relatively meaningless.

As if to add some drama to the script, the Americans fell behind 4–3 after two periods. After watching this, Soviet team captain Nikolai Sologubov decided to make a visit to the Americans' dressing room, thereby creating a legend of Olympic competition. He couldn't speak English, and his message was lost until he began using charade-like hand gestures.

"When he put his hand over his mouth, we realized he was trying to convince us to take oxygen," Bill Cleary said. Sologubov believed the oxygen would reenergize the Americans at the high altitude of Squaw Valley, which was a mile above sea level.

When the Americans scored six goals in the third period to upend the Czechs, the media proclaimed Sologubov a true sportsman and saluted his noble gesture as one of the keys to the victory. But years later, most of the American players weren't so sure how much it really helped the team. Only eight players took the oxygen. "All I know is Roger Christian didn't take oxygen, and he scored three goals in the third period," McCartan said, laughing.

Some question whether Sologubov's gesture was genuinely noble or just an attempt to ensure that the archrival Czechs would not finish ahead of the Soviets. If the U.S. won, the Soviets would finish ahead of Czechoslovakia with the bronze or silver medal. On the other hand, Solly, as Sologubov was called by the U.S. players, was considered to be friendly toward the Americans.

"I played it up, because I knew it was a good story," Riley recalled. "But it wasn't a big thing in the dressing room."

Bill Cleary, who had played against the Soviets on several occasions, tended to be more idealistic about Sologubov's intentions. "We had played against them so often, I began to see them as

Fielding a team that sent just two players to the NHL, the USA defeated Canada, Russia, and Czechoslovakia in consecutive rounds to take the gold medal in Squaw Valley, California. (USA Hockey)

friends," Cleary said. "When they sat around and talked, they didn't talk about communism. Like us, they talked about hockey and women."

All the oxygen on Mother Earth wouldn't have helped the Americans if McCartan hadn't been as brilliant as he was during the tournament. He surrendered just 17 goals in seven games and was clearly the best goaltender in the tournament. Ironically, McCartan had been cut from the roster three months earlier at the open tryouts. In November he had tried out in Minneapolis and

believed he had played well enough to make the team. When he went down to look at the "cut list" that had been posted by Riley, he whistled to himself over some of the names on the list.

"I thought, *They are cutting some pretty good guys*, and then it hit me," McCartan said. "These were the guys they were keeping, and my name wasn't on the list."

McCartan was devastated. Walter Bush, then general manager of the St. Paul Steers senior team, called and stretched the truth to a U.S. Army general that McCartan was needed as an emergency backup. He really just wanted McCartan for his team, which turned out to be fortunate, because McCartan was in game shape when Riley called him a month later.

"That was my plan all along," Riley insisted in a 1996 interview. "He was in the Army and I knew I could get him back. He was mad at me, and he played great. Hell, they were all mad at me."

Members of the 1960 team say McCartan was the most valuable player of the tournament, although he prefers to modestly say the Americans' success was a case of every player performing to the best of his ability.

Many players did play key roles in the triumph. Kirrane, a stay-at-home defenseman, had been the perfect complement for Mayasich. "He was black and blue from blocking shots," Bill Cleary said. And the American players had been wrong about Bob Cleary, who was among the team's top scorers. The controversy was forgotten, although the team photo with Bob Cleary's head pasted over Herb Brooks' body is a permanent reminder of the upheaval that was present heading into Squaw Valley. The Christian brothers were the first of the players to talk with the Clearys. "After it was all over, I remember us all standing in the shower and the Clearys thanking us for talking to them," Roger said.

In 2009 a documentary by directors Tommy Haines and Andrew Sherburne aptly titled the 1960 team's exploits as the *Forgotten Miracle*.

The 1960 U.S. team didn't receive as much attention as the 1980 team for a variety of reasons, the lack of television coverage being chief among them. The TV industry was in its infancy in 1960; Squaw Valley was the first televised Olympic Games, and it wasn't blanket coverage like today's Olympics receive. This was still a black-and-white television era, and the Olympics weren't a made-for-TV event like they are today. The romance of the Olympics wasn't captured as well as it was even 20 years later in Lake Placid.

"People didn't even know where Squaw Valley was," said former USA Hockey official Art Berglund. "This was a great accomplishment, but it might have been better if it had happened in Oslo or Cortina, Italy, because people knew where those cities were."

Although the Olympics were a world event, they simply were not as all-consuming as today's Olympics. The world was a smaller place. "It was just a different time," Olson said. "Hockey was still relatively new to many areas. We didn't have the same coverage that they do now with the pros, but even in '80, there was just more publicity for it then there was [in the '60s]. We were happy if we got mentioned in the paper! And of course there was no Internet and no computers or anything else."

There were no invitations to the White House for this team, nor any notoriety that lasted beyond a week. With the NHL boasting only six teams, opportunities for U.S.-born players weren't there. The triumph at Squaw Valley might have received more attention had most of the players immediately signed pro contracts like they did in 1980.

McCartan and the late Tommy Williams were the only players to go to the NHL. Within a week's time, McCartan made 33 saves to help the last-place New York Rangers defeat the Detroit Red Wings 3–1 in his NHL debut. That night it appeared he might be headed for NHL stardom. But McCartan played four games with the Rangers that season and eight more the next season before settling into a lengthy minor league career. Williams would be considered a successful American pro hockey pioneer. Although Williams' life would never be quite as sweet as it was the day they won the gold medal, he would become the first American to score 20 goals in a season in 1963.

The U.S. players who won the gold in 1960 seemed unbothered by the fact that they didn't receive a massive amount of attention, such as what the 1980 team later received. They seemed to wear their anonymity proudly.

"We were proud to be the first," Olson said. "Our goaltender Jack McCartan said it best when they asked him about everything else that has happened since. He said, 'We live with one thing—quiet pride.' It's a great line, because that's what we had, and that's how we approached it."

Former Michigan State standout Olson went back to the U.S. Air Force.

Bill Cleary, who went on to become hockey coach and athletic director at Harvard, had made the decision not to pursue a pro career even before those games. Proud that he was paid only $15 a month to play with the U.S. team, he laments the Olympics are now dominated by highly paid athletes. "I wouldn't trade my chance to march in the Olympic parade of athletes for 100 Stanley Cup Championships," he said. "When it was over, we all went back to our lives. That's the way we wanted it."

As captain, Kirrane would be the one to greet Brundage at the medal ceremony. "Wasn't that ironic, given how the bastard treated us in 1948?" Riley said. "He said we were pros in 1948. Why weren't we pros in 1960?"

Cleary said he understood the Olympic dream best when he watched Kirrane receive his medal during the traditional medal-presenting ceremony. Kirrane's decision to join the 1960 Olympic team hadn't been as easy as it was in 1948 when he made the Olympic team as a 19-year-old with no responsibilities and no family. Married with three children, Kirrane had to take a leave of absence from his job as a firefighter to join the team. Later in his firefighting career, the seniority time he lost to chase his Olympic dream cost him a promotion. On December 7, 2010, his hometown of Brookline, Massachusetts, commemorated his hockey career by dedicating the outdoor facility at Larz Anderson Park as the Jack Kirrane Skating Rink. More than 500 people showed up to honor Kirrane, including 1980 U.S. Olympic captain Mike Eruzione, 1960 coach Jack Riley, and Bill Cleary.

"This is one of the toughest guys you will ever meet," Cleary said. "But when he went up to the podium to get his medal [in 1960], his knees were shaking and his hands were a pool of water. Seeing him like that is something I will never forget."

Back in Minnesota, Brooks, the last player cut from the 1960 team, watched the gold-medal game on television. He was hurt when he had been cut, even though he suspected it was going to happen. He told his roommate, Tommy Williams, that he thought he was in trouble, even though he had been scoring on the pre-Olympic tour. Williams, Brooks, and Bill Christian were the youngest players. "Christian and Williams were better than me," he said later.

When Brooks was cut, he had called home, and his father had told him, "Keep your mouth shut, thank everyone there, and come home." Two weeks later, he and his father were watching the television as his former teammates were en route to the gold medal.

When it became clear that the USA would win, Brooks' father turned to him and said, "It looks like the coach made the right decision." ■

Tim Sheehy (15) congratulates goaltender Mike "Lefty" Curran after Curran made 51 saves in a 5–1 win against Czechoslovakia at the 1972 Games in Sapporo. Curran's effort in that game probably rivaled any ever recorded by an American goalie, including Jim Craig's effort against the Soviets in 1980. (USA Hockey)

WHEN SILVER LOOKS LIKE GOLD
The 1972 Olympics

When the American hockey players stood on the medal podium at the 1972 Olympics, the color of the medal wasn't as important as the pride they had acquired in earning it.

"It was the only time in my life that second was good enough," USA's Mike "Lefty" Curran recalls.

The 1972 team's accomplishment in Sapporo, Japan, was considered remarkable at the time because the United States National Team had finished last at the 1971 World Championship. The Americans needed a 5–3 win against Switzerland in a pre-tournament game just to qualify for pool play. The 1972 team never seemed to get the recognition it probably deserved. "We were sandwiched between the boys in '60 and the boys in '80," Curran said years later.

America had the youngest team it had ever brought to the Olympic Games. It included teenagers like Mark Howe and Robbie Ftorek, plus a 20-year-old named Henry Boucha, who had been a Minnesota high school legend. It was a team with heart and character, exemplified by players like Stu Irving, who was in the U.S. military on a combat assignment when he was asked to play for the U.S. Olympic Team, and Ron Naslund, who was a quiet leader. The squad also had scorers, such as Tim Sheehy, Kevin Ahearn, and Keith "Huffer" Christiansen.

These players all badly wanted a spot on that team, and there was no waffling about whether it was best for their potential pro careers. Backup goaltender Pete Sears, another Vietnam veteran, quit his job to play for the team.

The gold medalists in 1972 were the Soviets, many of whom played in the famous 1972 Summit Series against NHL All-Stars. Those NHL All-Stars would need a late goal by Paul Henderson to win that eight-game series 4–3–1.

The 1972 Americans lost 7–2 to the Soviets. "It was the best game we played against the Soviets in seven or eight years," coach Murray Williamson said.

Curran's 51-save performance in a 5–1 win against Czechoslovakia was on par with efforts turned in by goaltenders Jack McCartan and Jim Craig in the gold-medal campaigns of 1960 and 1980.

Even though Curran had been a member of the U.S. National Team in 1969, 1970, and 1971, it wasn't a given that he would end up as the No. 1 netminder on Williamson's team. "He was difficult to handle," Williamson said. "We feuded. He was a colorful guy."

Prior to Curran's arrival, *Sports Illustrated* writer Mark Mulvoy had traveled with the team and then left without writing a word. "He just couldn't find much to write about it," Williamson said. "We didn't have any Dennis Rodmans or Charles Barkleys."

Curran's arrival added some sparkle to the team. Curiously, one of the goalies that lost out to Curran in the Olympic cuts was Dave Reece, who would gain ignominy four years later in goal for the Boston Bruins when Darryl Sittler set an NHL record of 10 points in a game. He scored six goals against Reece that night. He was a feisty competitor who would come charging out of a goal during a practice session if he thought teammates were shooting too close to his head.

Williamson had too much coaching savvy not to realize that Curran's talent, stubbornness, and experience would all be beneficial for a team that had too many younger players. "Players loved him," Williamson said. "Mostly they loved him because he stood up to me."

Players also realized quickly that Curran knew more about international hockey than anyone else on the roster. Ftorek, an intense competitor even at 19, remembered being perplexed by seeing his netminder starting to roam out of his net as soon as the team hit the island of Japan. Curran seemed to have altered his playing style during the flight overseas.

"Lefty, what are you doing?" Ftorek asked him.

"Robbie, these people don't shoot over here, so I cheat," Curran replied. "You just have to trust me."

Ftorek quickly did learn to trust Curran, as did the rest of his teammates. "After the second game I realized he knew what he was doing," Ftorek said. "The European teams didn't shoot. They would make the pass right across the crease, and he was always there to stymie them."

Coach Williamson also knew plenty about international hockey. He had coached the United States team at the 1968 Olympics and three other U.S. National Teams. In 1971 he was allowed to watch a Soviet training camp and grew fascinated with the Soviets' dry-land training ritual. The 1972 Olympians were rather surprised that their practice routine often included jogging, piggyback races, basketball, tennis, and strength-building exercises.

"The coach's tactic was that we were never going to lose a game because of conditioning," said Tom Mellor, a 1972 defenseman who went on to play briefly with the Detroit Red Wings.

On the final day of the competition, the Americans needed some help to earn a medal. They got it when Finland defeated Sweden and Russia crushed the Czechs. The silver medal would go to the Americans, much to the surprise of most of their opponents, who hadn't seen the USA win a medal since 1960.

The 1972 team's lifetime of anonymity probably began when NBC ended its coverage a few minutes before the Americans reached the podium for their medal ceremony. This was an era when networks were paying reasonable amounts for rights to televise the Olympics and didn't feel obliged to provide sunup-to-sundown coverage, as they do today. "That was the biggest disappointment in my entire career," said defenseman Dick McGlynn, now a Boston attorney.

Years later, NBC host Curt Gowdy told the *Boston Globe* that he had been stunned that the Americans had won the silver medal. "That was the real surprise of the 1972 Olympic Games," Gowdy said.

But he wasn't surprised that the 1972 team's accomplishments were often overlooked in the roll call of U.S. Olympic heroes. "There's an old saying: Finish second and no one remembers who you are," Gowdy said. "That's what America has come to. We hold up our fingers and say, 'We're No. 1.' That's all we're interested in, in college basketball, college football. That's the desired outcome, gold or No. 1."

But the U.S. players did come back from Japan satisfied with their efforts. They had all performed better than anyone had expected.

Mark Howe, the son of former NHL great Gordie Howe, was the youngest player in U.S. Olympic hockey history. He was a year younger than Jack Kirrane, who was 17 when he played for the 1948 team. Howe didn't have a point in the tournament, but Williamson said Howe held his own against the older, more experienced international competition.

Howe's presence created a stir; even the Soviet press recognized his legendary name. After the Soviet-USA game, Howe was surrounded by reporters from Izvestia, Pravda, and Tass. They couldn't seem to get enough information about Howe and his relationship with his dad.

"What does your father teach you?" the Russians asked Howe.

"He teaches me to do what the coaches tell me to do," Howe said. "But sometimes he doesn't like what the coaches tell me, and he tells me to do something else."

The Soviets loved that answer. As a 16-year-old, Howe had a perspective about the Olympics that older performers probably couldn't appreciate. Accustomed to an allowance of $10 per week, he was flabbergasted when team officials gave him $800 living expenses. Empowered by his wealth, he purchased two large suitcases to hold all of his loot.

The innocence of youth was one of the key ingredients of that 1972 team. Williamson told reporters at the Olympics that players such as Boucha, Howe, and Ftorek were too young to accept the fact that they would probably lose at the Olympics.

Boucha and Ftorek were among the leading scorers on the team. Both players would sign NHL contracts after the Olympics, and Howe would be in the World Hockey Association.

"Ftorek was one of the hardest-working son of a guns I've ever seen," said teammate Larry Pleau, now a consultant with the St. Louis Blues. "He wouldn't give you an inch, or a foot, without fighting you for it."

Boucha, a Native American from Warroad, Minnesota, impressed his teammates, just as he had impressed his opponents in Minnesota. Former NHL player Doug Palazzari, now the executive director of the U.S. Hockey Hall of Fame Museum in Eveleth, Minnesota, remembered a Minnesota high school tournament game when Boucha never left the ice. "When he needed a rest, he went back on defense," Palazzari said.

When Minnesotans talk about the best high school players of all time, Boucha's name comes up as often as Phil Housley, Neal Broten, or John Mayasich.

"Hank has great hands and real subtle speed," Ftorek said. "It didn't look like he was going fast, but he was really moving."

Any NHL scout or official from Sweden, Finland, or Czechoslovakia who watched the 1972 Olympic tournament and the performances of Boucha, Ftorek, and Howe could undoubtedly see the Americans were coming, and coming hard. But they wouldn't arrive for another eight years. ∎

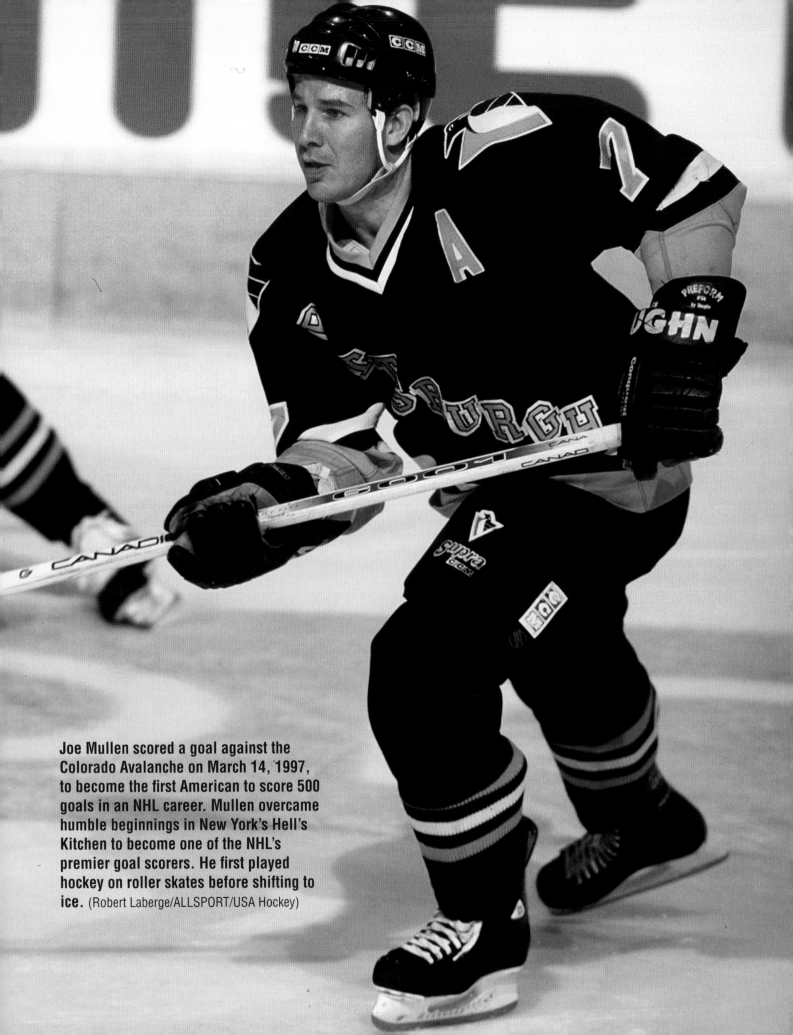

Joe Mullen scored a goal against the Colorado Avalanche on March 14, 1997, to become the first American to score 500 goals in an NHL career. Mullen overcame humble beginnings in New York's Hell's Kitchen to become one of the NHL's premier goal scorers. He first played hockey on roller skates before shifting to ice. (Robert Laberge/ALLSPORT/USA Hockey)

THE U.S. INVASION
Germs vs. White Corpuscles

As the National Hockey League doubled in size in 1967, the American player population in the league also doubled. It swelled from one U.S. player to two when Doug Roberts was called up by the Detroit Red Wings.

Roberts' arrival to join former 1960 U.S. Olympian Tommy Williams in the ranks of regular NHL players was considered such a monumental event that *Sports Illustrated* published a lengthy piece on it in its January 22, 1968, issue. Using his best sarcasm, *SI* writer Gary Ronberg called it "preposterous" that Roberts should be playing on a line with Gordie Howe because "as everyone knows, Americans are incapable of playing pro hockey, a game that is Canadian property."

At the time the article was published, there were 214 Canadians wearing NHL sweaters to go with the two Americans. Ronberg sounded like he was playing it straight when he wrote: "Of the scattering of Americans in minor league hockey, none could stickhandle well enough to claim any new

jobs created last year by the NHL's expansion [from 6 to 12 teams]."

Whether that was true or not wasn't as important as the fact that NHL general managers believed it was true. They did all of their player shopping in Canada because they believed Canada had the best merchandise. As a general rule, that was true. But there is evidence to support the idea that prejudice against American players did exist for many years, particularly in the 1940s, 1950s, and 1960s.

When Eveleth, Minnesota, native Aldo Palazzari made the Boston Bruins in 1943, he said players made him feel "like a germ that had just entered the body and all the white corpuscles were ganging up on me."

"One of my own teammates told me, 'Go home and play baseball,'" Palazzari remembered.

New York Rangers general manager Lester Patrick signed St. Paul, Minnesota, native Bob Dill before the 1943–44 season. At age 23, Dill registered six goals and 10 assists in 28 games. Dill was also handy with his fists and didn't mind challenging the NHL's toughest players.

Dill was the Deion Sanders–style athlete of the 1940s. He could thrive in two different sports. In addition to playing in the NHL, he thrived in baseball. He almost made it as a hard-hitting major league outfielder, advancing as high as the AAA minor league teams in Minneapolis and Indianapolis.

In his second NHL season, Dill scored nine goals and added five assists in 48 games. But when the regulars came home from World War II, Patrick ordered Dill to the minors. The Boston Bruins had interest in Dill, but Patrick wouldn't release Dill from his contract because he wanted him as a draw for the St. Paul farm team.

"[My dad] believed he could have played another five or six years in the NHL," Bob Dill Jr. said. "He was always ticked at Patrick about that."

Considering that Frank Brimsek and Mike Karakas held two of the six goaltending spots in the 1930s and the impact that Doc Romnes, Cully Dahlstrom, and John Mariucci made in Chicago, it would have seemed logical that the American share of roster spots would have continued to grow.

Right wing Fido Purpur of Grand Forks, North Dakota, was only 5'6", but he played 144 NHL games in the 1930s and 1940s with the St. Louis Eagles and Chicago Blackhawks, and seven playoff games for the Detroit Red Wings. In his best season, he netted 13 goals and added 16 assists for the Blackhawks in 1942–43. He played in the Stanley Cup Finals for the 1944–45 Detroit Red Wings, who were knocked out by Toronto.

Given how much hockey was being played in Minnesota, Michigan, and Massachusetts in that era, it is difficult to explain why more Americans didn't find a home in the NHL. Why didn't U.S. Hockey Hall of Fame member Ken Yackel from St. Paul, Minnesota, get a true shot to play in the NHL? The 1952 U.S. Olympian won the International Hockey League scoring championship with 40 goals and 74 assists for the Minneapolis Millers in 1960–61. He had 50 goals for the Millers the next season and generated another 100-point season in 1962–63. Yet despite his scoring prowess, the 195-pound right wing only had six NHL games on his résumé for the Boston Bruins in 1958–59.

Although the late Tommy Williams, nicknamed "Bomber," enjoyed a long NHL career, he too faced some discrimination as an American in the NHL. In the 1965–66 season, Boston Bruins general manager Hap Emms told Williams he wanted to send him to the minors for two weeks to improve his conditioning, even though Williams was second on the team in scoring.

"What gives?" Williams asked.

"Tommy," Emms said, "it's not your fault, but Americans can't play the game."

Williams exploded in anger and told Emms he could take the job and shove it. After listening to Williams' tirade, Emms said he would give Williams another game before he sent him down. It's unknown whether Emms really believed what he said, but Williams was so incensed he went out the next game and scored two goals and added two assists against the Canadiens in the Montreal Forum. Emms never did send Williams to the minors.

A review of the hockey stories of that era would suggest that Americans began to accept the idea that playing in America made a player less prepared to play in the NHL than a Canadian player.

"I really don't think I would have been hurt as much if I had grown up playing under Canadian rules," Williams said.

Asked about the lack of Americans in the NHL, Roberts replied, "It's a combination of things. First,

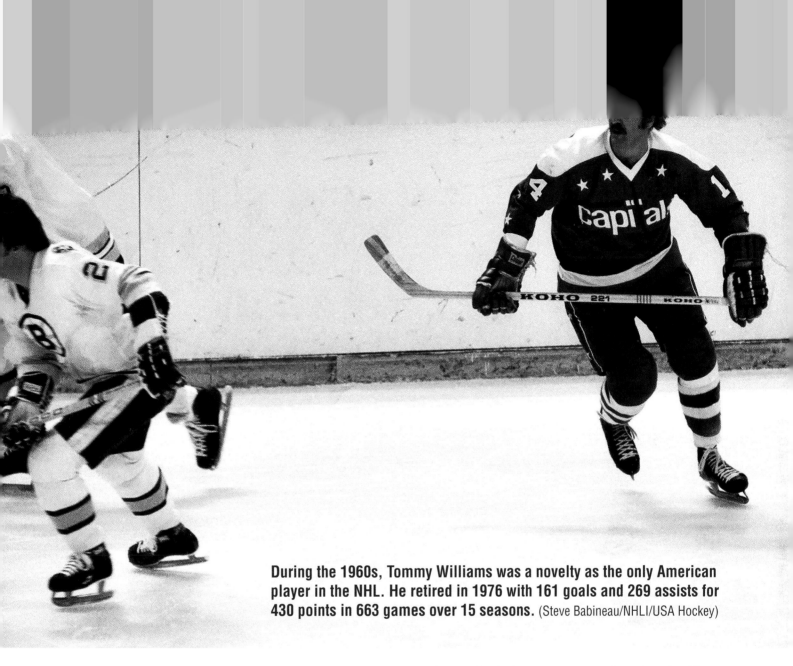

During the 1960s, Tommy Williams was a novelty as the only American player in the NHL. He retired in 1976 with 161 goals and 269 assists for 430 points in 663 games over 15 seasons. (Steve Babineau/NHLI/USA Hockey)

there's the difference in the rules: forechecking isn't allowed in American colleges and in the Olympics. But for me a tougher problem was simply skating."

The *SI* article opined that Canadian players were taught more frequently to keep their heads up and used this story to highlight this point: "In my very first NHL game," Roberts said, "we were playing the Rangers in Detroit and naturally I was nervous. I was awed. Alex [Delvecchio] passed the puck to me and I remember looking down and thinking, 'Gee, Delvecchio just passed the puck to me.' Then...the lights went out. I thought I had been hit by the team bus. It turned out to be Jim Neilson."

Some argue that the majority of American players simply weren't talented enough to play in the NHL, on the world's best six teams, in that era. There were only about 120 NHL jobs available until the 1967 expansion, and competition was fierce. Hockey was to Canada what baseball was to America. Canadian children grew up believing they had a birthright to those jobs.

Other factors inhibited American play, as well: the NHL didn't scout in the United States, it didn't pay particularly well, and the league didn't have the luster or popularity that it enjoys today. Children in Wayne, Michigan; Edina, Minnesota; or Worchester, Massachusetts, didn't grow up wanting to play in the NHL as they do now.

Some hockey aficionados insist John Mayasich, who played on the 1956 and 1960 Olympic Teams, was quite capable of playing in the NHL, but the league never discovered him. "He would have broken the bank if he was playing today," Bill

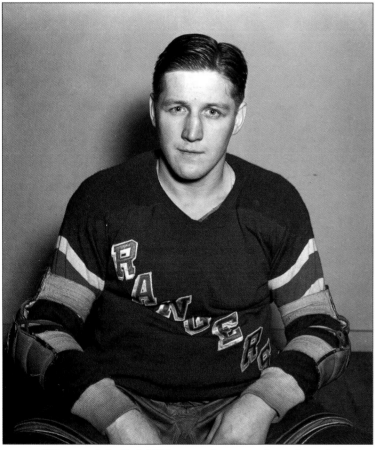

Minnesota's Bob Dill was a two-sport pro long before Bo Jackson was playing major league baseball and pro football in the same calendar year. In the 1940s, when Dill finished his hockey season, he grabbed his ball glove and headed for baseball spring training. Dill played two seasons in the NHL for the New York Rangers, but only advanced as high as AAA in baseball. (Imperial Oil – Turofsky/Hockey Hall of Fame)

Cleary said. "He would be making millions in the NHL." Had the NHL discovered Mayasich, it would have needed to make a significant offer to land him. Mayasich had a good job in the television industry and earned extra money playing senior hockey for the Green Bay Bobcats. He probably wouldn't have given up that long-term security for the short-term gratification of playing in the NHL.

The NHL didn't "wow" players with cash in the 1950s, 1960s, or early 1970s as it does today. In the 1950s, soon-to-be Olympic hero Bill Cleary was offered a contract to play for Montreal but turned it down to go into the insurance business.

Earlier, the Boston Bruins had an interest in Cleary after his college career. General manager Lynn Patrick offered him about $1,000 to sign and $5,000 to play. Cleary told Patrick he wanted $15,000 as a signing bonus and $10,000 as an annual salary. Patrick came back with an offer of $12,500 to sign, but Cleary heard they were cheating him and decided he wanted no part of pro hockey. Patrick made a final plea, talking about how important it would be to have an American player.

"You have a magic name in this area," Patrick said. "What you're saying," Cleary replied, "is that I'll be the monkey in the zoo that everyone is coming to see."

Cleary went into the insurance business instead and made more money than he probably would have in the NHL. American college players, with a degree in hand, usually could earn more outside of hockey. Hall of Famer Moose Goheen said no to the Boston Bruins in 1929 because he didn't want to give up his job with the power company. Bob Gaudreau, who played for the 1968 U.S. Olympic Team, was one of the top college defensemen of all time, but it made more economic sense for him to use his MBA from Columbia than to seek his fortune in the NHL.

Minnesota graduate Lou Nanne didn't join the NHL for a long time because the Chicago Blackhawks wouldn't pay enough to match what he could earn using his degree from the University of Minnesota. When Nanne graduated in 1963, Blackhawks general manager Tommy Ivan offered him a contract that paid him a $2,000 signing bonus plus an annual salary of $6,000. Nanne agreed to that figure, even though he was making a little more than that in chemical sales. Later, when Nanne asked for the contract previously agreed upon before he showed up at training camp, Ivan balked. "Not even Bobby Hull got a contract before training camp," Ivan said.

"Bobby Hull doesn't have a college degree, a wife, and a child," said Nanne, who decided to keep the security of his job.

For the next four seasons, the Hawks tried to land Nanne, but the pay gap kept getting wider. In 1967 they were offering $18,500, and he was already making $25,000 in marketing. Not until the Minnesota North Stars got his rights and Walter Bush began negotiating with Nanne, did a deal get done. It was completed over Frescas at the Dunes Hotel in Las Vegas. "We each wrote our figures down on napkins. It took 10 minutes," Bush remembered.

Larry Pleau, with his New England accent, was as American as firecrackers and sparklers on the Fourth of July. He was a 16-year-old sophomore at Lynn English High School in Massachusetts in 1963 when the Montreal Canadiens' Ralph Backstrom discovered him at the Doc O'Connor summer hockey camp. The Canadiens sent Scotty Bowman to woo Pleau. Ralph Backstrom told the director of player personnel, Sam Pollock, that the Rangers were also aware of Pleau.

According to Ron Caron, then a Canadiens' scout, Pollock's response was, "Take $5 and send him to the movies, because [Rangers general manager] Emile Francis will get there ahead of Bowman."

The Canadiens wanted Pleau to play junior hockey in Canada and to agree to be placed on their protected list. There was no NHL entry draft in those days. "I didn't even know what junior hockey was," Pleau remembered.

Bowman's pitch worked, and 16-year-old Pleau played for the Notre Dame-De-Grace Maple Leafs and then joined the Montreal Junior Canadiens for three seasons, playing alongside Serge Savard, Jacques Lemaire, Rogie Vachon, and Carol Vadnais. Another American, Craig Patrick—grandson of Lester Patrick—also played on that squad. Pleau was captain of the Junior Canadiens in his final season.

After the 1967 expansion, the NHL still didn't seem to need more American players. But the WHA-NHL wars in the 1970s created an explosion of job openings for Americans, particularly college players whose hockey résumés had previously failed to impress NHL teams. The WHA created headlines by signing away NHL stars such as Bobby Hull, Bernie Parent, John McKenzie, and Derek Sanderson, but they also began filling many of their roster spots with Americans. The New England Whalers won the first Avco Cup with a team coached by former Boston University coach Jack Kelley and a roster that boasted Americans such as Tim Sheehy, Larry Pleau, and Kevin Ahearn.

In a span of six years, from 1967 to 1972, the number of major league teams, if the WHA could be called that, increased from 6 to 28. The NHL had 16 teams and the WHA had 12. By 1974 the NHL had 18 teams and the WHA had 14. Major

Defenseman and University of Minnesota graduate Lou Nanne played his entire 11-year NHL career with the Minnesota North Stars. He was a recipient of the Lester Patrick Trophy in 1988–89, awarded for outstanding service to hockey in the United States. (Portnoy/Hockey Hall of Fame)

league hockey then offered 660 jobs, instead of the 120 that were available just seven years before.

"This wasn't evolution, this was revolution," said Whalers owner Howard Baldwin.

WHA teams in the United States, particularly New England and Minnesota, signed players who had some name recognition in those areas. The Minnesota Fighting Saints, for example, signed 1972 U.S. Olympic hero Mike Curran of

International Falls, Minnesota, and 1960 U.S. Olympian Jack McCartan of St. Paul. The Houston Aeros signed Gordie Howe and his two American-born sons, Mark and Marty.

Mark was 18 when he signed. Although later in his career he would be an All-Star NHL defenseman, Mark started his pro career as a left wing. He notched 38 goals in his first season to outscore his 45-year-old father and linemate, who finished with 31.

Mark Howe believed the 1972 U.S. Olympians played a significant role in helping the NHL conclude that there was hockey talent south of the Canadian border. "Up until that point," Mark Howe said, "I don't think anyone in hockey respected the ability of the American player."

The Detroit Red Wings signed U.S. Olympian Robbie Ftorek in 1972 but let him flee to the WHA, where he became a star player with the Phoenix Roadrunners and Cincinnati Stingers. Ftorek scored 31 goals in his first WHA season and then followed with season productions of 41, 46, 59, and 39 goals to establish himself as an elite pro player.

"He was the Bobby Clarke of the WHA," Pleau said.

Only 5'9" and 170 pounds, Ftorek was always forced to prove he could survive and thrive in a world where opponents were usually a head taller and 20 to 40 pounds heavier.

"His size was never a detriment because he was such a smart player," said Jacques Demers, who coached him in Cincinnati and Quebec. "He may have been the most intelligent player I ever coached."

Ftorek's pride was his guide when it came to dealing with the toughness of pro hockey. Demers remembers Ftorek suffered a nasty cut during the WHA All-Star Game and needed 65 stitches to close the wound.

The Cincinnati Stingers' next game was against the Birmingham Bulls, who boasted one of the roughest collections of tough guys pro hockey had ever seen. Demers knew the Bulls would attack Ftorek's wound like tigers after injured prey.

"Robbie knew they were going to kick the crap out of us, but he insisted on playing," Demers said.

Other 1972 U.S. Olympians to join the NHL included Henry Boucha, who took advantage of a bidding war between the Red Wings and Minnesota Fighting Saints to get a nice contract from Detroit. Craig Sarner, Jim McElmury, and Tom Mellor also played in the NHL, and Mike Curran, Keith Christiansen, Dick McGlynn, Wally Olds, Frank Sanders, and Kevin Ahearn ended up in the WHA.

"The assumption was that Americans couldn't play until they proved they could. It was like every GM was from Missouri, and they were saying, 'Show me,'" said Brian Burke, an Edina, Minnesota, native who played college and minor league hockey in the 1970s. He went on to become an agent, NHL general manager, and the NHL director of hockey operations.

The prevailing NHL attitude during the 1950s, 1960s, and 1970s was similar to the attitude professional boxing judges had about title bouts: to unseat the champion, one had to be unquestionably better, not just marginally better, and ties or close decisions always went to the incumbent. Canadians owned the vast majority of managerial positions in the NHL, and they were going to dethrone a Canadian player only if the American player was significantly better.

No one fought against that thinking more aggressively than agent Art Kaminsky, who was among the first American-based agents. With a client base made up primarily of college players, Kaminsky was like a salesman who had to jam his foot in the door to get teams to listen.

American Firsts

Here is a list of the first true U.S. players or teams to accomplish the following:

Play an NHL Game: George "Gerry" Geran (Holyoke, Massachusetts)—Montreal Wanderers, December 19, 1917. Won 10–9 over Toronto Arenas.

To Reach the Stanley Cup Final: Hugh "Muzz" Murray (Sault Sainte Marie, Michigan)—Played for the Seattle team in the 1918–19 Stanley Cup Final that was cancelled because of the Spanish flu epidemic.

To Win the Stanley Cup As an NHL Player: Clarence "Taffy" Abel (Sault Sainte Marie, Michigan)—1927–28 with the New York Rangers.

Score an NHL Goal: George "Gerry" Geran during the 1925–26 season. The NHL would count Ed Carpenter (Hartford, Michigan)—Quebec Bulldogs, January 1, 1920. Ottawa 3 at Quebec 2, but he was raised in Canada and considered himself Canadian.

Play for a U.S.-Based NHL Team: George "Gerry" Geran (Holyoke, Massachussets)—Boston Bruins, November 26, 1925. Lost 2–1 to Pittsburgh Pirates.

Play As an NHL Goaltender and Record a Goalie Win: Alphonse Lacroix (Newton, Massachussets)—December 1, 1925, with Montreal Canadiens. Won 3–2 over Boston Bruins.

Record an NHL Goalie Shutout: Mike Karakas (Eveleth, Minnesota)—November 14, 1935, with Chicago Blackhawks. Scoreless tie with Detroit Red Wings.

Be Drafted by an NHL Team: Curt Bennett (Cranston, Rhode Island*)—Drafted 16th overall by the St. Louis Blues in 1968.

Be Drafted No. 1 Overall: Brian Lawton (Cumberland, Rhode Island)—Drafted first overall by Minnesota North Stars in 1983.

Be the First Goaltender Drafted No. 1 Overall: Rick DiPietro (Winthrop, Massachussets)—Drafted first overall by the New York Islanders in 2000.

Win the Vezina Trophy As the NHL's Top Goaltender: Frank Brimsek (Eveleth, Minnesota)—Won with the Boston Bruins in 1938–39.

Win the Norris Trophy As the NHL's Top Defenseman: Washington Capitals' Rod Langway (Taipei, Taiwan**/ Randolph, Massachusetts)—Won in 1982–83 with the Washington Capitals.

Win the Lady Byng as the NHL's Most Gentlemanly Player: Elwyn "Doc" Romnes (White Bear Lake, Minnesota)—Won in 1935–36 with the Chicago Blackhawks.

Win the Conn Smythe Trophy as the NHL Playoff MVP: Brian Leetch (Cheshire, Connecticut)—Won with the New York Rangers in 1994.

Register 100 or More Points in a Season: Neal Broten (Roseau, Minnesota)—Scored 29 goals and 76 assists for 105 points for the Minnesota North Stars in 1985–86.

Score 20 or More Goals in a Season: Tommy "Bomber" Williams (Duluth, Minnesota)—Scored 23 goals for the Boston Bruins in 1962–63.

Score 30 or More Goals in a Season: Curt Bennett (Cranston, Rhode Island)—Scored 31 goals for the Atlanta Flames in 1974–75.

Score 50 or More Goals in a Season: Bobby Carpenter (Peabody, Massachussets)—Scored 53 goals for the Washington Capitals in 1984–85.

To Captain an NHL Team to a Stanley Cup Championship: Derian Hatcher (Sterling Heights, Michigan)—1999 with the Dallas Stars.

To Score 200 Career Goals: Reed Larson (Minneapolis, Minnesota)—Scored his 200th NHL goal while playing for the Boston Bruins in 1986–87, not long before Joe Mullen scored his 200th.

To Score 500 Career Goals: Joe Mullen (New York City)—Scored his 500th goal on March 14, 1997, against Colorado's Patrick Roy.

First NHL Game Played in the U.S.: December 1, 1924—Montreal Maroons 1 at Boston Bruins 2.

First NHL Game Played between Two U.S. Teams: November 26, 1925—Pittsburgh Pirates 2 at Boston Bruins 1.

First Team to Host an NHL Winter Classic: Buffalo Sabres—January 1, 2008, lose 2–1 to the Pittsburgh Penguins in a shootout in Ralph Wilson Stadium.

First Team to Host an NHL All-Star Game: Chicago Blackhawks—November 3, 1948, in Chicago Stadium. The NHL All-Stars defeated the Toronto Maple Leafs 3–1.

* Was born in Saskatchewan but moved to Rhode Island when he was three months old.
** Langway's father was in the military, stationed in China when Langway was born.

"It wasn't as much anti-American as it was pro-Canadian," Kaminsky said. "The GMs were all Canadian, the coaches were all Canadian, and the scouts were all Canadian. They just didn't believe there were better players than Canadian players."

Ironically, the Montreal Canadiens, one of the symbols of Canadian hockey pride, were among the first to see the value in signing Americans. Ron Caron, then the Canadiens' assistant general manager, liked American college defensemen because they were big, strong, and smart.

"The Americans had good goaltenders and defensemen," Caron said. "There was a concern they couldn't play on your first or second line, because they had no creativity with the puck. They were like robots. They could play defense, but they really couldn't score."

In 1972 the Canadiens chose Notre Dame player Bill Nyrop with the 66th pick in the draft. In 1977 they took New Hampshire defenseman Rod Langway with the 36th. In 1983 Langway would eventually become the first American to win the Norris Trophy as the league's top defenseman.

Langway was a superb athlete who played linebacker for two years at New Hampshire. At one point, the Dallas Cowboys were interested in him, and Kaminsky has hypothesized that Langway would have been an NFL draft pick had he stuck with football.

"He had great stamina, and he was a great competitor," said David Poile, who was general manager in Washington when he acquired Langway from Montreal. "It was like, 'Wow, how do we get this guy?'"

Nyrop was also a two-sport athlete who played spring football at Notre Dame and earned a spot as Joe Theismann's backup before deciding to concentrate on hockey.

Nyrop helped the Canadiens win three Stanley Cup Championships and then retired at age 26. He came back and played one season with Minnesota in 1981. Nyrop died in 1996 of lung cancer.

Montreal's interest in American players drew the attention of other teams. The Canadiens had a lineup full of Hall of Famers in the 1970s, and they clearly knew something about finding talent.

Yet, the NHL still was moving cautiously toward Americans. The best example of the trepidation about Americans could be seen in the journey of Joe Mullen, who scored 110 goals in 111 games for Boston College from 1975 to 1979 and was still sent to Salt Lake City when he turned pro with the St. Louis Blues. He played three seasons there, scoring 120 goals in 182 games before he was promoted. It was like the scouts didn't believe what they saw when they scouted American players.

"I hate to admit this," said Poile, "but I think the NHL management staffs and scouting staffs... we were slow on the draw to recognize the quality of the American. Just like we were on the Europeans."

In 1968 the St. Louis Blues made Curt Bennett the first American player chosen in the NHL draft, selecting the Brown University player with the 16th pick. He was actually born in Canada but moved to Rhode Island when he was three months old. His father, Canadian Harvey Bennett Sr., and two brothers also played in the NHL. Harvey Sr. had been in net for the Boston Bruins the night that Montreal's Maurice "Rocket" Richard scored his 50th goal in 1944–45.

In 1974–75, Bennett, a colorful character who majored in Russian Studies in college, scored 31 goals for the Atlanta Flames to become the first true American to score 30 or more goals.

The Minnesota North Stars were starting to draft Americans regularly by the late 1970s. Also in the 1978–79 season, Minnesota North Stars coach Glenn Sonmor decided to make NHL history by starting six Americans. Pete LoPresti was in goal, with Billy Butters, Gary Sargent, Tom Younghans, Mike Polich, and Jack Carlson.

Sonmor told the players just to stay on the ice long enough for photographers to capture the moment on film. "Dump the puck in, and come to the bench for the change," Sonmor said.

Problem was, the Chicago Blackhawks won the faceoff and carried the puck into the North Stars' zone. It seemed as if the Hawks were on a power play.

"It took us forever to get the puck out," LoPresti said.

Sonmor said afterward: "We will never do that again."

Kaminsky recalled that he had difficulty convincing general managers to come out and watch hotshot Minnesota freshman Mike Ramsey before that summer's draft. "I believe Scotty Bowman was the only general manager who came to the U.S. Olympic trials."

Bowman's Buffalo Sabres drafted Ramsey 11th overall in 1979, and he went on to play 18 seasons in the NHL.

Old habits didn't die easy, even though American players were beginning to make inroads after the Miracle on Ice. Kaminsky represented 16 players on the 1980 U.S. Olympic Team and was frustrated trying to get some NHL agreements in place before the Games.

"In most cases the offers were so bad, so awful, we didn't even bother," Kaminsky said.

One case involved University of Wisconsin center Mark Johnson, who had been college hockey's best player for two seasons. Before the 1980 Olympic Games, Penguins general manager Baz Bastien offered Johnson a $10,000 signing bonus, plus a three-way contract. He would get one salary if he made the NHL, a lower salary for the American Hockey League, and an even lower salary if he played in the International Hockey League.

After he led the Olympic tournament in scoring and put a gold medal in his trophy collection, Johnson was given a $75,000 signing bonus and a one-way contract. Ramsey, Jim Craig, Dave Christian, and Rob McClanahan all landed similar deals.

The gold medal opened the doors wider for American players and seemed to give renewed credibility to United States hockey. Ken Morrow, Mike Ramsey, and Dave Christian quickly became NHL standouts, and Mark Pavelich, Neal Broten, and Mark Johnson weren't far behind. Christian signed with the Winnipeg Jets immediately after the Games and scored eight goals and 10 assists in the final 15 games of the 1979–80 season. He had 28 goals in his first full season with the Jets.

During the next two years, team registration at the Amateur Hockey Association of the United States was up about 7 percent, and that was probably the maximum that could have been achieved, given the number of available rinks. It took time for rink construction to catch up to the hockey enthusiasm that swept the country. After 1980 NHL teams also approached the draft in a distinctly different way. Bobby Carpenter, a Massachusetts prep star, was selected third overall by the Washington Capitals in 1981 after unprecedented publicity surrounding his performance at St. John's Prep High School.

Sports Illustrated featured Carpenter on one of its covers as "the Can't-Miss Kid," and that alone was evidence of the inroads hockey was making in the United States.

In 1980 no U.S. high school player had been drafted in the first two rounds, and in 1981, four high school players, plus Chicago native Chris Chelios—who was about to head to the University of Wisconsin for his freshman season—went in the first two rounds.

Bowman helped the American cause by drafting Minnesota high school sensation Phil Housley No. 6 overall in 1982 and Boston-area goaltending standout Tom Barrasso No. 5 overall in 1983.

A Buffalo scout named Rudy Migay spotted Housley playing as a junior in high school, but Bowman didn't see him until after his senior season was over and he joined a local junior team.

"There was only one other scout there, a part-time scout for Philadelphia, when I saw him," Bowman said. "The first time he touched the puck he went through the whole team."

Bowman recalls that Housley looked so young at training camp that no one would have guessed he would score 19 goals and post 47 assists in his rookie season.

"The first day at training camp, he got on the team bus with his high school girlfriend," Bowman said, laughing. "We thought it was the bus driver's daughter, and then we found out it was Housley's girlfriend."

Bowman said he considers Barrasso "the more amazing story," because as a teenager he won both the Calder Trophy as NHL Rookie of the Year and the Vezina as the league's best goalie.

"He was unbelievable, especially given that he was only six months removed from high school hockey," said Gerry Helper, who was the Sabres' public relations director.

Bowman said, "The real reason we drafted Barrasso was that he was so good handling the puck...he was like Marty Brodeur."

Barrasso's quantum leap from a high school league to NHL stardom was the talk of the hockey world. "Although it surprised many around the league, I don't think it surprised Tom," Helper said, laughing. "It was the confidence he had in himself that allowed him to do what he did."

This bold drafting strategy was not out of character for Bowman who, in 1981, drafted highly skilled Czech star Jiri Dudacek with his No. 17 pick. Dudacek never came over to North America, but the move established Bowman's willingness to look outside the boundaries of Canada for talent. "He liked being unconventional," Helper said.

Carpenter, meanwhile, scored 32 goals in the 1981–82 season after jumping directly from high school.

"He was not a fighter, but he was really competitive," said former New York Rangers defenseman Tom Laidlaw. "I remember I would try to run him, but he would get his stick up. He never backed down."

The NHL still seems to prefer players who play Canadian Junior over college, although guys like Chris Chelios, Brian Leetch, Rod Langway, Bryan Smolinski, and others have made it clear that there are many different paths that lead to the final destination.

Some older American players look back at the 1950s, 1960s, and 1970s and wonder whether they would have made the NHL had they owned a different passport. But McCartan, whose NHL career lasted 12 games, isn't among them.

"I was up against Glenn Hall, Jacques Plante, and Gump Worsley," McCartan said. "The bottom line was I wasn't good enough. I wasn't one of the best six goaltenders in the world." ∎

Dave Silk celebrates after scoring Team USA's first goal in the team's first game of the 1980 Olympics as Buzz Schneider looks on. The U.S. tied Sweden 2–2. (USA Hockey)

THE 1980 OLYMPICS
Miracle at Lake Placid

Over the past 100 years, America witnessed Babe Ruth swat his 60th home run, Jesse Owens infuriate Adolf Hitler with a sterling Olympic track performance, Roger Bannister break the four-minute mile, Wilt Chamberlain score his 100th point in a single NBA game, Bob Beamon leap beyond 29 feet in the long jump, and Michael Jordan close out his Chicago Bulls career with a sweet, high-arc jump shot to win an NBA championship.

But when the Associated Press and *Sports Illustrated* selected their greatest sports moment of the 20th century, none of those momentous feats measured up to the greatest moment in American hockey history. In today's sports world, hockey remains an undercard event. But it is impossible to argue against the truth that the Americans' triumph over the Soviets in hockey at the 1980 Olympics is the most memorable event in sports history.

"It's the most transcending moment in the history of sports in our country," said Dave Ogrean, executive director of USA Hockey. "For people who were born between 1945 and 1955, they know where they were when John Kennedy was shot, [when] man walked on the moon, and when the USA beat the Soviet Union in Lake Placid."

Mike Eruzione's game-winning goal triggered a national celebration of epic proportion. People wept, strangers hugged each other, and people around the country uncorked stirring renditions of the songs "God Bless America" and "The Star-Spangled Banner."

More than 32.4 million people watched the tape-delay broadcast of the game, and for the first time in America's history, everyone in the country was talking about hockey. The euphoria about the win outlasted the night.

Ogrean, then a young public relations director for USA Hockey, boarded a plane to head home, thinking how nice it would be to catch up on the sleep he lost in the gold-medal revelry. The flight attendant's eyes widened as she noticed his Team USA hockey parka. But Ogrean cut her off with a quick shake of the head. He had just closed his eyes when the flight attendant announced over the public address system: "Ladies and gentlemen, in

6C, we have a member of the U.S. gold-medal hockey team." The plane filled with applause and hoots of delight.

"I really didn't want to take the time to explain to everyone that I wasn't a player, and besides, they wanted me to be a player," Ogrean said. "They wanted to come by and be a part of what had occurred at Lake Placid."

Thinking quickly, Ogrean figured he could pass for backup goaltender Steve Janaszak, who had been the only U.S. team member not to register a minute of playing time in Lake Placid at the Olympics. Figuring no one would know Janaszak, Ogrean signed many cocktail napkins that were passed his way.

Years later, he ran into Janaszak at a luncheon and confessed to the impersonation. He told Janaszak he signed 15 autographs using his name. "That means there are probably 16 napkins out there with my autograph," Janaszak joked.

No one could get enough information about the American boys who had toppled the Soviet professionals. *Sports Illustrated* published no words with their cover photo of the American players celebrating, because no words were needed. Undoubtedly, there were Americans who couldn't name their congressman but knew Eruzione was the hero at Lake Placid.

"Right after we won, I got bags of mail," Eruzione said. "It was like in the movie *Miracle on 34th Street* when they bring in all that mail to Santa. That's what I used to get."

The U.S. team, made up of college players and longshot pro aspirants like Eruzione and Buzz Schneider, defeated a Russian program that had dominated the Olympics since 1964. The U.S. team beat a Russian team that had seven players from the 1976 Olympic Team and one player who had played in three other Olympiads.

Somehow over time, the U.S. team has been miscast as a group of overachievers, even though the core group of players—Mark Johnson, Neal Broten, Mark Pavelich, Ken Morrow, Dave Christian, and Mike Ramsey—also made significant marks in the NHL. "Maybe we overachieved," Ramsey said. "But we were a damn good hockey team."

The USA had speed, defense, scorers, conditioning, goaltending, and coaching—a complete team, something the Soviets didn't realize until it was too late.

"Kenny Morrow told me a while ago that even his [Stanley Cup champion] New York Islanders teams didn't have the speed that we had," Eruzione said.

Eruzione said Eric Strobel probably had the team's best skating stride. "He took one stride and he was gone," Eruzione offered. "But what amazed me about Neal, Davy Christian, and Mark Johnson was how fast they were laterally. When I got the puck and headed across the ice, I was nowhere near as fast as I was going straight. Those guys seemed to pick up speed going laterally."

The Soviets had expected to win the tournament with the same ease with which they had dispatched all comers at the 1976 Olympics in Innsbruck, Austria. Further buoying their confidence was the 10–3 licking they had applied to the Americans in an exhibition at Madison Square Garden just one week before the world arrived at Lake Placid. To the younger Americans, the Soviets must have seemed like hockey gods. Boris Mikhailov, goaltender Vladislav Tretiak, Alexander Maltsev, Vladimir Petrov, Vasili Vasiliev, and Valeri Kharlamov were all members of the Soviet team that had played against the NHL All-Stars in the 1972 Summit Series. The NHL players were confident they would dominate the Soviets in all eight games. Instead, they needed a goal by Paul Henderson with 34 seconds left in regulation of the final game to win the tournament with a 4–3–1 record.

The Americans trailed in six of their seven Olympic wins, including the victory which ensured their gold medal, a 4–2 win over Finland. In the opening game of the tournament, defenseman Bill Baker scored with 27 seconds left to give the USA a 2–2 tie with Sweden. Would the Miracle of Lake Placid have occurred if Baker had not scored? Probably not. The tie was important because the Americans had a gloomy history with Sweden. They hadn't beaten the Swedes since 1960. Baker's goal lifted the team's morale like the thrust of a rocket booster.

The Americans then dominated the Czechoslovakians, winning 7–3 with six different goal scorers. That outcome surprised many, particularly the Czechs, who had entered the tournament with aspirations of at least a silver medal. The Czech team had the Stastny brothers—Peter, Marian, and Anton—who would later defect for a chance to play in the NHL with the Quebec Nordiques.

Then Norway was taken, followed by Romania and West Germany. Coach Herb Brooks had been worried about the Germans, because they had beaten the USA 4–1 in 1976 at Innsbruck, undermining coach Bob Johnson's hope of a bronze medal. They didn't have the talent to compete with the Americans. They weren't fancy, like the Swedes, Czechs, Finns, and Soviets. But they were dangerous because they played hockey as if it was trench warfare. They were tough and determined, not like the German players who the Americans whipped in the 1960s.

The competitive spirit the Germans unveiled at Innsbruck in 1976 also made the trip to Lake Placid.

The Germans claimed a 2–0 lead against the Americans after one period, scoring both goals with shots from beyond the blue line. The first shot was one chance in a thousand, a 70-footer by Horst-Peter Kretschmer that caught Jim Craig off-guard. The second goal was a 50-foot shot from the point by Udo Kiessling. Craig was screened on the play.

Enraged by their ineffectiveness, the Americans stepped up their game in the second period, but they weren't able to tie the game until Neal Broten scored with 1:29 remaining in that period. Rob McClanahan and Phil Verchota scored in the third period to complete the 4–2 win.

Although the Americans won, the game didn't help them in the standings. Ironically, at that point in the tournament, the Americans were trying to avoid facing the Soviets. The U.S. was tied with Sweden for first place in the Blue Pool, and the loser of the tiebreaker system would play the Soviets first in the medal round. The Americans wanted to win the Blue Pool to assure they would play the Finns first and then play the Soviets for the gold medal. Therefore, the U.S. hoped the Czechs would defeat the Swedes in the final Blue Pool game, assuring the United States would win the Blue Pool and face the Finns first. However, the Swedes beat the Czechs, so the United States hoped to beat Germany by seven goals so they would have a better goal differential against the Swedes and win the first tiebreaker and the Blue Pool. But the United States only beat the Germans by a two-goal margin. They would have to play the Soviets first. Destiny awaited.

Coach Herb Brooks wondered whether he had successfully exorcised the players' memories of the humiliating defeat they had suffered in Madison Square Garden at the hands of the Soviets. "Our guys were applauding the Soviets when they were introduced," he recalled.

One of Brooks' objectives before the Olympics was to "break down the Soviets to mortals." He told his players that the great Boris Mikhailov looked like Stan Laurel of the comedy team Laurel and Hardy. He hoped his players would stop looking at Mikhailov as if he was hockey's Zeus.

"You can beat Stan Laurel, can't you?" Brooks would ask.

As expected, the Soviets began an immediate offensive blitzkrieg, but the Americans were staying with them. Craig was looking as sharp as he ever had. The team was gaining confidence as the first period progressed, even if they were getting outshot badly. "When you are an underdog, all you are looking to do is keep the game close, so you will have a chance to win it in the end," Mark Johnson would say later.

Eruzione's goal was preserved in the minds of Americans as "The Goal" of American hockey history, but Johnson was the Americans' top scorer in the game against the Soviets and in the tournament. Because of his tremendous skill, teammates called him "Magic" Johnson, comparing him to the NBA superstar. Johnson was as slick with the puck as any player in the tournament.

He was 22 years old, yet he probably had as much hockey savvy as some of the veteran Soviets. Though he hadn't played as much as they had, Johnson possessed a sense about the game that other Americans did not. As the son of the legendary American coach Bob Johnson, he had soaked up every bit of insight that was available in every hockey school his father had run and when his father had coached the national team in 1975.

Johnson was a senior at Madison Memorial High School in 1976 when his father, needing a player at the last minute, decided to add his wunderkind son to the Team USA roster for the pre-Olympic tour. Mark held his own on the team, but Bob Johnson felt there would be too much pressure on his son if he took him to the Olympics. Everyone might believe he was there just because his father was the coach.

Although Johnson was probably the best player in college hockey, he had some concerns about making the 1980 Olympic team because Brooks and his dad were bitter rivals. When Brooks was at Minnesota and Johnson was at Wisconsin, they never had anything good to say about each other. "They got along like Germany and France," said agent Art Kaminsky, who considered himself friends with both men.

Mark Johnson said he was never comfortable that he would be on the team until the pre-Olympic tour in Oslo, Norway, when Brooks told him he was counting on him to be a leader as well as a player. Did he really believe Brooks might cut him because of his feud with his father? "Hey," Johnson said, "stranger things have happened in hockey."

But Brooks' desire to win at the Olympics meant more to him than prolonging any feud. He even patched up his considerable differences with Kaminsky, an important step because Kaminsky was going to represent most of the players Brooks wanted for his team. Kaminsky said that prior to their peace accord, Brooks considered him "vermin." Kaminsky jokingly responded, "And I thought he was a maniac."

After Brooks and Kaminsky had each vented their frustrations with the other, they decided to work together, knowing that a successful run at the Olympic Games would be best for all concerned.

On the ice, Mark Johnson lived up to his reputation. He had several big goals, including two against the Soviets. He wasn't intimidated by the Soviets. Every Sunday, he had played in what his father called "the Russian Game." His father had

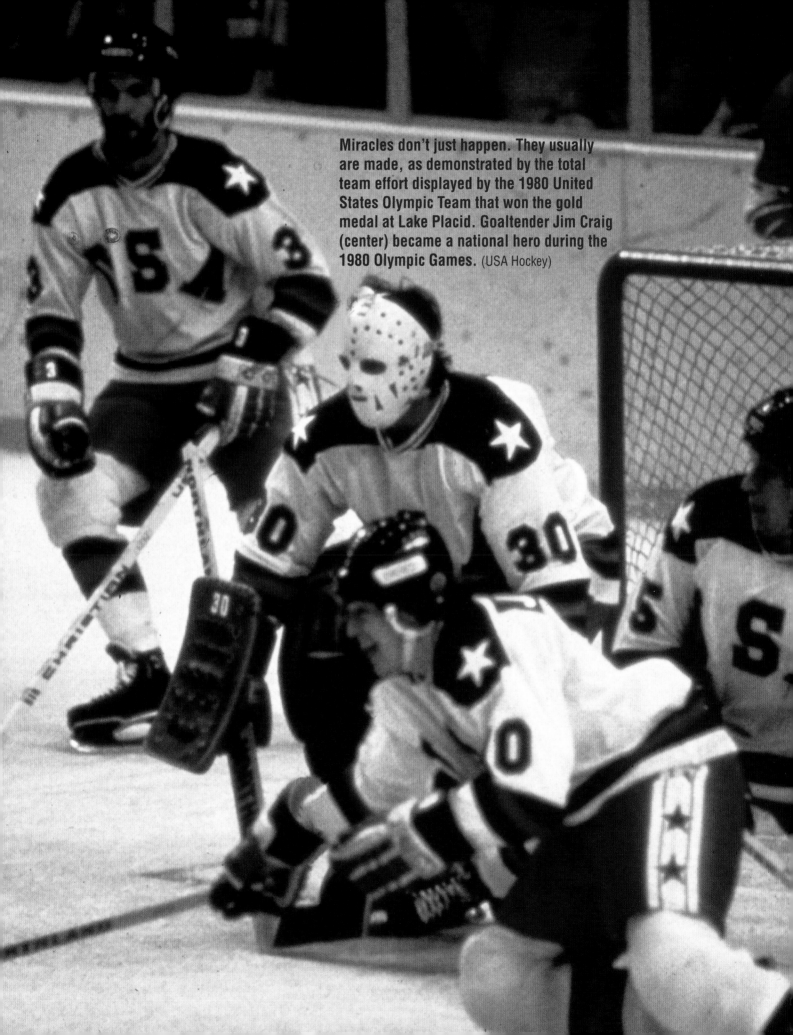

Miracles don't just happen. They usually are made, as demonstrated by the total team effort displayed by the 1980 United States Olympic Team that won the gold medal at Lake Placid. Goaltender Jim Craig (center) became a national hero during the 1980 Olympic Games. (USA Hockey)

Russian jerseys made with all of the top Russian names sewn on the back. Mark Johnson had played against Mikhailov many times, although the player wearing the jersey never had quite the same talent as the namesake.

With his team trailing 2–1 near the end of the first period, Johnson split two defenders to drive hard to the net after Christian cranked a long shot. Tretiak didn't surrender many rebounds, but this puck bounced off his pads as if it had a spring attached. It went directly to Johnson, who drilled it past him with one second left to tie the score at 2–2. The goal gave the USA a major lift going into the second period. After Johnson's goal, Soviet coach Viktor Tikhonov stunned one and all by removing Tretiak and replacing him with Vladimir Myshkin.

The Americans assumed Tretiak would be back, but he wasn't. This was a significant boost for the Americans. "We were in awe of Tretiak," Eruzione said.

Not many coaches would have had the courage to remove a Russian hockey legend from goal after only one period in the world's most important international hockey tournament, but Tikhonov was no ordinary coach. He was a dictator, as hated as he was successful.

Years later, when Johnson found himself playing on the same New Jersey Devils team with Slava Fetisov and Alexei Kasatonov, two other members of the 1980 Soviet team, he asked Fetisov why Tikhonov had pulled Tretiak.

Fetisov just shook his head and said two words with his thick Russian accent: "Coach crazy."

Vladimir Myshkin was hardly a second-rate replacement, as he had shut out NHL All-Stars 6–0 the year before. But clearly, Tretiak's presence had a negative psychological effect on the Americans, an air of invincibility, even if they had scored two goals against him.

The Soviets claimed a 3–2 lead early in the second period when Alexander Maltsev scored. But going into the third period, the Americans finally believed they could beat the Soviets. Johnson scored the tying goal on a power play at 8:39 of the third period.

Brooks was short-shifting his players to keep them fresh. Less than two minutes after Johnson's goal, Eruzione jumped off the bench with a burst of energy. He ended up in the slot, where Pavelich found him with a pass. Eruzione fired a 25-foot wrist shot that zipped past Myshkin, who was screened by Soviet defenseman Vasili Pervukhin. All of America rejoiced.

For the game's final 10 minutes, with the Americans clinging to a one-goal lead, the U.S. players finally understood why Brooks had always said, "Legs feed the wolf." He had worked them mercilessly in practice with the idea that USA would be the most well-conditioned team at the Olympics. In those final 10 minutes, their work paid off. They skated stride for stride with the Soviets and were not intimidated by the Russian players. They were invigorated by the challenge of beating them. But none of the Americans thought the game was theirs until the final second had ticked off the clock. The celebration that followed the game felt surreal to the players involved. Jim Craig was buried by the crush of his teammates, and sticks and gloves were scattered everywhere. Euphoria reigned, and for the next few hours, players were besieged by well-wishers. Fans lined the short distance between the arena and the media center, forcing the team bus to inch its way toward the press conference. As fans banged on the bus, one player—most seem to think it was Neal Broten—started singing "God Bless America." Other players quickly joined in.

Separating Myth from Reality about the Miracle On Ice

Myth: The USA beat the Soviets in the gold-medal game.
Truth: After beating the Soviets 4–3, the Americans still had to beat the Finns to win the gold. The Americans won that game 4–2.

Myth: Mike Eruzione was the USA's leading scorer.
Truth: He was the team's captain, but five players outscored him in Lake Placid.

Myth: The USA won all of its games in 1980.
Truth: The Americans tied Sweden 2–2 in the opening game.

Myth: The USA game against the Soviets was carried live on ABC in prime time.
Truth: The game was played at 5:00 PM and was broadcast on tape delay. The Soviets turned down a request to move the game to 8:00 PM.

Myth: The Americans overachieved against a superior Soviet team.
Truth: While the Americans clearly pulled off an epic upset, the Americans had a strong team, particularly with Neal Broten, Mark Johnson, and Mark Pavelich at center, and Mike Ramsey, Dave Christian, Ken Morrow, and Jack O'Callahan on defense. The Americans also had a hot goalie in Jim Craig.

Myth: Thousands upon thousands were in the arena to watch the game live.
Truth: The arena only had 7,700 seats.

Myth: Coach Herb Brooks got every player he wanted.
Truth: He wanted Joey Mullen, but Mullen turned pro with St. Louis. Many believe former Northern Michigan player Don Waddell, now president of the Atlanta Thrashers, would have made the team if he had not broken his leg early in the process.

Myth: Eruzione beat Russian great Vladislav Tretiak on his winning goal.
Truth: Vladimir Myshkin had been brought in as Tretiak's replacement in the second period.

U.S. team physician George Nagobads, a native of Latvia, talked with Soviet players after the Olympics. Most of them didn't seem mortally wounded by the loss, although Vasili Vasiliev was perplexed that the U.S. had managed to defeat his strong team.

"What did you give your players to eat or drink so in the third period they can skate like that?" Vasiliev asked. "Last period is always ours. In second period, when we were ahead 3–2, we celebrate."

Nagobads, who speaks some Russian, replied, "It's called the fountain of youth."

U.S. players were overcome with emotion after defeating the Soviets at Lake Placid in the 1980 Olympics. Americans had equally patriotic reactions around the country. The *New York Times* reported that people on the streets of Manhattan were hugging each other while spectators stood and spontaneously sang "The Star Spangled Banner." (USA Hockey)

In terms of strategy, the most important move that Brooks made was the decision to move Christian from forward to defense.

"The key was that when Davy got the puck he could skate it out of the zone," Eruzione said. "He could skate forever...he reminded me of watching John Havlicek with the Boston Celtics. They were both guys that could fly around without breaking a sweat."

Years after the event, it's easier to see that the Soviets badly underestimated the Americans' talent. After soundly beating the United States in Madison Square Garden, the Soviets never entertained the possibility that the Americans would give them a better game in their next meeting.

Also, the Soviets never thought that Craig was capable of playing as well as Tretiak did in his prime. Craig gave the United States the same quality goaltending Jack McCartan had supplied the gold-medal 1960 team. Brooks expected no less from Craig, who was his goaltending choice from the beginning.

Craig was a complicated man whose habit of saying the wrong thing at the wrong time made him a lightning rod for controversy. He came across as arrogant, even though those who knew him said he really wasn't like that. Overall, most teammates did like Craig, and all of them respected his ability. Craig oozed confidence like no goaltender they had ever seen.

Boston University coach Jack Parker recruited Craig out of Massasoit Junior College, actually grabbing him away from Jack Kelley, his former coach, who wanted Craig for his Colby team. Parker was honest with Craig, telling him from the beginning that he had offered a scholarship to Mark Holden of Weymouth, Massachusetts. Parker also had Brian Durocher penciled in as one goaltender. If Holden accepted, Craig wouldn't get a scholarship, as Parker didn't have three scholarships for goaltenders.

"I understand," Craig told Parker. "But I've seen Durocher and I've seen Holden, and I'm going to be your goalie."

Holden didn't go to Boston University. Two years later, in 1978, Craig was 16–0–0 with a 3.72 goals-against average and Durocher, grand nephew of baseball legend Leo Durocher, was 14–2–3, as they split duties during Boston University's national championship season in 1978.

"He's the best college goaltender I've seen with the exception of Ken Dryden," Parker said. "[Two-time Olympic coach] Dave Peterson used to tell me that Craig was absolutely perfect technically."

Parker remembered that when he watched Craig practice, it would seem as if "the net had disappeared behind him." Craig's best asset was his confidence. He hated to get beaten by a shooter. "When you are good, and you know you are good, it's the greatest feeling in the world," Parker said. "And Jimmy Craig had that feeling."

Brooks seemed to understand how to push Craig's buttons better than anyone. Just before the Olympics, Brooks told Craig he might have made a mistake by playing him too much. He left the impression that he didn't believe Craig was playing all that well.

"You are playing tired, and your curveball is hanging," Brooks said to him.

Those words might have devastated some players, but not Craig. He seemed to transform anger into energy. During the Olympics, he never looked tired.

Brooks was not like any hockey coach these players had experienced before. He was hockey's version of George Patton. In style, he was a combination dictator-philosopher whose instructions forced his players to think as well as act. Every day was an adventure in psychology for the guys wearing the red, white, and blue. "He got inside our heads," Ramsey said.

In a *People* magazine story, written by Jim Callo immediately after the 1980 Olympic Games, Craig said of Brooks: "I've played for him for six months and I still don't understand him. He drives me crazy."

Backup goaltender Steve Janaszak recalled a nose-to-nose confrontation when Brooks convinced left-winger Rob McClanahan to continue playing in the tournament opener against Sweden despite a severe charley horse. Brooks questioned McClanahan's manhood in a curse-filled tirade and called him a "cake eater." McClanahan responded with cursing of his own. The scene was ugly.

The enraged McClanahan went out and played as well as he could with his muscle knotted. "That locker-room scene is still vivid in my mind," Janaszak said more than a decade later.

Brooks' attack on McClanahan probably had little to do with McClanahan and more to do with the fact that the Americans weren't playing well in their first Olympic test. Brooks tried to unify his team against him, a technique he used on many occasions, and sent a message to his players that the team was going to overcome all obstacles. Players kept a notebook of what they called "Brooksisms." One of them was, "This team isn't talented enough to win on talent alone."

Mike Eruzione (waving flag) and his American teammates climbed on the medal stand to wave to fans after winning the gold medal at Lake Placid in 1980. Defenseman Ken Morrow (with beard, far right) would immediately sign with the New York Islanders and win a Stanley Cup. (USA Hockey)

"I'd cut my own brother to make a better hockey club," Brooks would say.

Before the game against the Soviets, Brooks took out a note card and read a prepared text: "You were born to be a player. You were meant to be here." His players believed him.

Brooks said the 1980 Olympic team members embodied qualities he admired most. "The players had big egos, but they didn't have ego problems. That's why all-star teams traditionally seem to self-destruct. We didn't."

The players' mental toughness was demonstrated when they came back from behind to beat Finland 4–2 to capture the gold medal two days after stunning the Soviets. It's been forgotten by many that if the United States had fallen to Finland, it would not have earned a medal at all, gold or otherwise.

But the American players understood the challenge. Champagne was sent to the American dressing room following the win over the Soviets, and not a single American player touched it.

"If we don't win tomorrow," Craig told the media gathering after the Soviet game, "people will forget us."

What made the U.S. team so special was that every player was a hero in his own way. Defenseman Jack O'Callahan's knee was so badly injured in the last exhibition game against the Soviets that he should have headed for surgery and not Lake Placid.

And there was the Conehead line of Mark Pavelich, John Harrington, and Buzz Schneider, named after the *Saturday Night Live* alien characters. All three players were from Minnesota's Iron Range, and none of them played a style that could be easily copied.

Eruzione recalled their strange play. "They were the only line that stayed intact because no one could play with them," Eruzione said. "I played with them once, and I had no idea what I was doing or where I was going."

Brooks liked to use the Conehead unit when he needed some creativity or a home run swing. When the play looked innocent, that's when the Coneheads were most dangerous.

Craig Patrick said years later that the well-traveled Schneider was probably the unsung hero of the 1980 squad. At 25, he was the oldest player on the team and the only returnee from the 1976 Olympic squad. Playing on his fifth national team, his leadership was probably as important as Eruzione's.

Schneider was among the leading scorers in the tournament. He had almost stopped playing hockey when he failed in a tryout with the Pittsburgh Penguins. Before then, Schneider had played briefly in Springfield, Oklahoma City, Birmingham, Hampton, Milwaukee, and Europe.

"I was the only player in the Penguins camp without a contract," Schneider said. "They only needed me as a practice body."

Superior skill is not why America loved those players as much as they did. Players have said global politics wasn't an issue to them when they were playing against the Soviets in 1980, but it was an issue to those who watched.

The United States' gold medal at the 1960 Olympics may have been just as dramatic, just as emotional, and maybe even as unlikely as the 1980 gold medal. But the 1980 victory was surrounded by political circumstances that weren't present 20 years before. The world had changed dramatically in the two decades between the gold medals. John F. Kennedy and Nikita Khrushchev had played a high-stakes game of chicken during the Cuban Missile Crisis. The arms race had become a dangerous sprint toward mutual destruction. Russia had become synonymous with evil. Therefore, the U.S. victory in 1980 held much symbolism for the American public.

The Soviets had helped create their negative image. After the 1960 debacle at Squaw Valley, they had begun sequestering their athletes, keeping them out of the public, thereby constructing a wall of mistrust. To Americans, Soviet athletes had lost their humanity. To those who watched international competition on television, Soviet athletes were state-run machines. Americans didn't know, or want to know, that Soviet athletes were flesh-and-bone human beings who struggled, complained, and fought the system as much as American athletes. The Soviets' dominance in hockey had humbled everyone, including the mighty Canadians, who didn't compete internationally in the 1970s

because they viewed the Soviets as professionals. Soviet players were Darth Vader on skates, unemotional soldiers from the evil empire.

Images of athletic Frankensteins created in laboratory experiments were conjured up because Americans couldn't believe that any country could produce better, more dedicated athletes than the United States. Steroids? Blood packing? Performance-enhancing drugs? Americans believed anything was possible with the Soviets.

Remember, the American public was a disillusioned group in 1980. By those Olympic Games, Iran's Ayatollah Khomeini had already kept 52 American hostages imprisoned for more than 100 days. The Soviets had invaded Afghanistan. At home, America faced domestic inflation, unemployment, and economic uncertainty. The United States didn't seem to be as mighty on the global scene as it once was. USA's win at Lake Placid seemed to reignite the country's pride about who the Americans were and what they were about.

Through a tough-love approach, Brooks had transformed American boys into heroes. In Brooks, many Americans saw the parent they wanted to be.

When the gold medal had been won, Brooks, in stoic fashion, immediately left the ice because he said the moment belonged to the players. Eruzione said he doesn't remember Brooks ever telling the players after a game that they had played well or had done a good job. That wasn't his way.

In the *People* story, he probably came the closest to saying how he truly felt about his players. Said Brooks: "Fathers and mothers love their children as I love this hockey team." ■

A product of USA Hockey's National Team Development Program, Patrick Kane was the No. 1 pick in the 2007 NHL draft and a Stanley Cup champion with the Chicago Blackhawks in 2010. (Bruce Bennett Studios/ Getty Images/USA Hockey)

USA HOCKEY
Expanding the Game Across America

When Tom Lockhart began running the American Hockey Association of the United States (AHAUS) out of his New York apartment in 1937, all of the registrations and paperwork fit comfortably into a standard shoebox. Today, with USA Hockey now boasting almost 500,000 registered players and approaching 100,000 registered coaches and officials, a much larger shoebox is required.

Unquestionably, the most important aspect of hockey's growth over the past 75 years has been its ability to expand beyond its traditional geography. The yesteryear American "hockey belt" of Massachusetts, Michigan, and Minnesota has been replaced by a newer model that has strong pockets of hockey growth all around the country. Today, there are registered hockey players in all 50 states, and California has become a major source for college and pro talent. "We now have as many players from the state of New York playing in the NHL as we have Russian players," said past USA Hockey president Walter Bush.

The expansion of hockey's footprint across America has resulted from several factors:

USA's gold-medal men's hockey performance at Lake Placid in 1980 inspired a talented generation of new players and brought attention to a sport that previously had seemed only a regional endeavor.

Wayne Gretzky's arrival in Los Angeles in 1988 made hockey a West Coast happening and helped draw attention to ice hockey and inline hockey. That supplied an even bigger boost for hockey than Bobby Orr's arrival, which also had an impact.

The NHL's increased popularity and expansion into Sun Belt cities—such as Tampa, Miami, Atlanta, Dallas, Phoenix, and Anaheim—plus nontraditional winter-sports cities, such as Raleigh, North Carolina, and Nashville, helped spawn youth programs in each of those cities. For example, since Florida, Tampa Bay, Atlanta, Carolina, and

Nashville debuted in the NHL, USA Hockey's registrations in its Southeastern District has shown a 492.5 percent increase, from 6,718 players in 1991–92 to 39,807 in 2009–10. Since the NHL's arrival in Phoenix, Dallas, and Colorado, USA Hockey's Rocky Mountain District has risen 276 percent, from 9,809 players in 1992–93 to 36,882 players in 2009–10. Also today, more than 20 million fans fill up NHL arenas every season.

The American women's gold-medal triumph at the 1998 Nagano Olympics and Cammi Granato's presence as the face of the sport have inspired young females to play the game.

The rapid growth of women's college hockey opened up scholarship opportunities for many female athletes.

Minor league hockey continues to have a significant impact. In 2009–10, the American Hockey League's attendance was almost 6 million, and the East Coast Hockey League drew more than 3 million. The Central Hockey League had attendance approaching 2 million.

Growth of the United States Hockey League and North American Hockey League have given the country a noteworthy junior hockey presence.

But also along the way there were people in the background trying to push the game forward while others were content to keep hockey a niche sport.

The first U.S. hockey development camp was actually the brainchild of Colonel F. Don Miller, head of the United States Olympic Committee, who came to AHAUS executive director Hal Trumble with the idea. The USOC was offering money to all sports for the purposes of developing talent. It was Trumble's idea to hold the first camp in Squaw Valley, the site of the 1960 Olympic Games, and to invite players from the Pacific Region. One of the players at that camp was a 16-year-old named Chris Chelios, who was playing in San Diego.

Lou Vairo had just started working for AHAUS in 1978, and he remembers lugging the skate sharpener on the plane with him. "I remember I was going to California for a week, and I had $8 in my pocket," Vairo said.

The coaches for the USOC hockey development camp were Bob Johnson, Grant Stanbrook, Lefty Smith, Vairo, Art Berglund, and Dave Peterson. The players at the camp came in all shapes and sizes and had varying degrees of skill. But the days spent at that camp opened up the eyes of all in attendance about the opportunities that could be unlocked for players if these camps were a regular occurrence.

"I always felt that if I had been born in Minnesota, I would have played in the NHL, and I still feel that way today," Vairo said. "But I wasn't. I was born in Brooklyn. We didn't have a single rink, and yet we still felt we could be hockey players and play for the New York Rangers. That's the way kids think. But the odds were so difficult."

Vairo had always wanted to improve the odds for players who were born outside of Massachusetts, Michigan, and Minnesota. After his Squaw Valley experience in 1978, he knew how. He began lobbying Trumble to fund an 80-player national development camp. He pushed Trumble to the point of annoyance. As Vairo recalls, Trumble told him, "We don't have the budget. Don't bring it up again."

The issue gnawed at Vairo to the point of anger. The next day after Trumble had ordered Vairo to speak no more of national camps, he marched into Trumble's office and said, "Hal, listen, I would have gone to the National Hockey League if I had grown up in Minneapolis like you. I think it's bullshit that we don't have a national camp, and I think you are a prick." Vairo expected to be fired. Trumble only said, "Aw, maybe I want to be a prick on purpose."

The next day, Trumble called Vairo into his office and said, "Go ahead, have your national camp."

But the battle was just beginning for Vairo, because he believed the only way to grow the sport was to have hockey's version of affirmative action when choosing players for the national camps. He believed every area of the country needed to be represented at the camp, and other movers and shakers in AHAUS, many of whom were his close friends, believed the spots should go to the best American players regardless of what state they were from.

"They thought it was a ridiculous idea," Vairo recalled. "They said the 500th-best player in Minnesota is better than any kid from Florida, or Texas, or Alabama, or New Mexico. I said, 'You are probably right, but the 500th-best player from Minnesota is never going to play for our national team. But who knows...the best kid from Texas might end up making it someday.'"

Vairo believed that when players from nontraditional hockey areas showed up and held their own against premium players from Minnesota, Michigan, and Massachusetts in these camps, it could change their lives.

"It helped their confidence and made them want to work harder," Vairo said. "That's what happened. Look at Joe Mullen or Mike Komisarek or Chris Higgins coming out of New York. Whoever thought guys from Long Island would end up playing for the Montreal Canadiens?"

USA Hockey has come a long way since the early years when there was squabbling over who would control American hockey, including the U.S. Olympic teams. As part of a compromise

As executive director of the Amateur Hockey Association of the United States (AHAUS), Hal Trumble took a largely a part-time operation operating deep into the red and turned the association into a prosperous full-time, professionally staffed organization. Trumble was inducted into the U.S. Hockey Hall of Fame in 1985 and into the International Ice Hockey Federation Hall of Fame in 1999. (USA Hockey)

reached after two U.S. teams showed up for the 1948 Games, Brundage insisted that the 1952 U.S. Olympic Team be formed by an eight-man committee. Four members were named from the U.S. Olympic Committee: Daniel J. Ferris, Asa Bushnell, W.E. Moulton, and Eddie Jeremiah.

Representing AHAUS were Brown, Bob Ridder, Fred Edwards, and Leonard Fowle. The group decided Ridder should be general manager and

Eveleth's John "Connie" Pleban should be the coach.

Ridder's take-charge approach strengthened AHAUS's reputation in the hockey world. He organized a very successful, well-financed trip for the 1952 U.S. Olympic Team, including a string of exhibition games to pay for the USA's participation in Oslo, Norway. Ridder even had the Americans play an exhibition game against the Boston Bruins, which was certainly a novel idea at that time.

Some of the exhibition games were against college teams, which were far less concerned about the bottom line than they are today. This was before Nike deals, equipment contracts, and logo licensing. This was before colleges distinguished between revenue sports and nonrevenue sports.

"I remember we played Michigan, and we were supposed to share the gate," Ridder recalled. "But they said, 'Oh, hell, why don't you take the whole thing?'"

The 1952 team won the silver medal at Oslo, and Ridder and Pleban earned high praise for their efforts. "What I learned in 1952 was that nobody complains about success," Ridder said.

Ridder had become an important player in AHAUS. He was invited back to be general manager of the 1956 team, and he and John Mariucci led the team to the silver medal. The stability of Ridder's leadership, with Brown working in the background, helped the American program recover quickly from the embarrassment of the 1948 mess in St. Moritz. The Americans were now looked upon as a well-organized power on the international circuit.

AHAUS's youth hockey movement was also on the move, although not quite at the same pace. AHAUS president Lockhart, a former cyclist and track-and-field competitor, had organized the Eastern Amateur Hockey League in 1932 and had correctly realized that hockey wasn't going to grow nationally without a strong governing body. However, it took Ridder's Minnesota Hockey Association to spark the youth movement. By 1949 AHAUS was sponsoring national youth tournaments.

Minnesota's important role in the growth of national youth hockey is ironic because the state's program wasn't nearly as large as it had been prior to World War II. The late hockey historian Don Clark, a pioneer in the Minnesota program and a past president of the organization, said Minnesota was the nation's hockey hub in the mid- to late-1930s. For example, the 435 teams registered in the state for the 1935–36 season was a number that put Minnesota not far behind some of Canada's major metropolitan areas. But then the war took away coaches, fathers, organizers, players, and interest in the game.

By the 1950–51 season, Minnesota was up to 560 teams again, although only 101 chose to register with the Minnesota Hockey Association and AHAUS. It was still an uphill battle for Lockhart, Ridder, Clark, and others to convince team managers that the $2 cost for each team to join AHAUS was worthwhile. Slowly, teams began to see the benefit of national insurance, unified age groupings, and uniform rules, among the other benefits and services AHAUS offered. But it certainly didn't occur overnight. At one point in the early 1950s, only seven teams were registered in New York. Even by 1959, AHAUS had only 720 registered teams, and 26 percent were located in Minnesota. It took about 20 years to reach the then-attractive goal of 1,000 registered teams.

One of AHAUS's problems in that time was a lack of publicity—ironic because Brown and Lockhart both had reputations as promoters. Even some of AHAUS's members weren't sure exactly what the organization was doing or where it was headed.

In 1955 Walter Bush, a former Dartmouth player fresh out of law school, decided to drive from Minneapolis to Duluth to attend an AHAUS meeting at the Spalding Hotel. He attended only to determine why the AHAUS was claiming 2 percent of the gate receipts for his Minneapolis Culbertson's senior team. He didn't know the meeting would alter the course of his life. Ridder was impressed with Bush and told Brown that he believed Bush had some potential to be a mover and a shaker in the organization. In 1959 Bush, only 29 at the time, was named general manager of the USA National Team. That same year, he became a member of the AHAUS Board of Directors, a position he has held continuously since then. In 1964 AHAUS suffered a loss when Walter Brown died unexpectedly in Hyannis, Massachusetts. For more than 30 years, Brown had been an important figure in the USA's involvement in international hockey.

To be sure, Brown was a promoter and businessman, a man who once invested $1,000 in the Ice Follies and helped transform it into a national investment. (His minimal investment was worth $100,000 when he finally got around to selling his stock years later.) He helped bring Bob Cousy to the Boston Celtics and broke the color line in professional basketball by bringing in Duquesne's Chuck Cooper. Brown was a colorful character, full of laughter and savvy in the ways of the world. During the Depression, he turned down a gift of a Rolls-Royce because he didn't believe it was proper for folks to see him driving a Rolls at a time when many were unemployed. An extremely generous man, he always had a few dollars for every cause. "Walter Brown was a great but humble man, one characterized first and last by human kindness," said Asa Bushnell.

Brown's death left a huge hole in the AHAUS organization. Though Brown was officially vice president of AHAUS, he had also been an unofficial guru for the organization. Everyone turned to Brown to solve problems. "He had also financed a lot of teams when there were no funds available," Walter Bush said.

It was impossible to replace Brown, who was loved as much by the Europeans as he was by the Americans. "But after 1964, people started calling Ridder when they had a problem," Bush said.

In 1972 William Thayer Tutt succeeded retired Lockhart as AHAUS president and pushed the idea that the organization needed to be operated more like a business. Tutt, whose family owned the Broadmoor Hotel, had a strong international

William Thayer Tutt and Art Berglund chat with 1972 Olympic coach Murray Williamson at the Broadmoor World Arena in Colorado Springs in 1971. (USA Hockey)

Current USA Hockey Chairman of the Board Walter Bush poses with his predecessor, William Thayer Tutt. Tutt led AHAUS from 1972 to 1986, when Bush took over. (USA Hockey)

Tutt donated space in the Broadmoor Hotel for AHAUS offices, giving the few AHAUS employees a unique workplace. "Elegant offices, and we had access to the Broadmoor Hotel cafeteria. You could get a BLT, an ice tea, and a slice of blueberry pie, and it didn't cost you a buck," said Ogrean, who started as the organization's public relations director.

Under Tutt's command, AHAUS brought in Hal Trumble as executive director in 1972. Trumble was a prominent IIHF referee and an experienced administrator. He managed the 1972 U.S. Olympic Team before taking the job as AHAUS executive director. The Minnesota North Stars, with Bush as president and as one of the co-owners, provided office space for Trumble at the Met Center. But the following year, Trumble and Tutt moved AHAUS to Colorado Springs.

"Tutt was a larger-than-life figure," Ogrean said, likening him to the Shakespeare character Falstaff. "Thayer was a man of girth, appetite, and humor," Ogrean recalled. "He loved food and drink. He loved camaraderie. He loved international friends. He would sometimes burn the candle at both ends. That is perhaps a characteristic that has been passed on to others in our organization. He is a legendary figure in our sport."

Tutt was once president of the International Ice Hockey Federation and then was on the IIHF Council for a lengthy time. He was succeeded on the IIHF Council by Walter Bush, who was succeeded by Tony Rossi. "[Tutt] started a chain of international leadership that now dates back more than 40 years," Ogrean said. Trumble brought another layer of credibility to the job, because he was highly respected in Europe because of his refereeing experience. In 1968 he was the referee in both the bronze- and gold-medal games at the Grenoble, France, Olympic Games. "When he was

background, having spent 27 years as a member of the International Ice Hockey Federation Council. His international affiliation began in 1959 when he had successfully bid for the 1962 World Championship to come to his Broadmoor World Arena in Colorado Springs. The Americans won the bronze medal that year, although the absence of the Russians and Czechs for political reasons had weakened the field.

hired, it began the process, both literally and figuratively, of taking the organization out of the shoebox," said Ogrean.

Some of Trumble's startup programs—such as officiating education, coaching registration, and a registrar system—still exist today. Volunteer Ken Johannson, father of two-time Olympian Jim Johannson, was the architect of the coaching education program, and then Gary Fay was hired to professionalize it.

"Hal Trumble laid the foundation for the professional organization on which we have just continued to build," Ogrean said.

Trumble served as executive director from 1972 until 1986. Tutt also liked the idea of having his administrator working out of his hotel. Tutt's keen interest in international hockey helped fuel the organization's increasing involvement in international competition. Tutt had been the first to invite Soviet teams to this country in the 1960s. He also hired Art Berglund, a former Colorado College scoring leader who would play an integral part in the development of American hockey over the next 20 years. In 1977, when AHAUS sent its first official American team to the IIHF World Junior Championship, Berglund, then managing Tutt's Broadmoor World Arena, was named manager of that team.

"If there wasn't an Art Berglund, there wouldn't be USA Hockey, especially not at the level that it has gotten to," Jeremy Roenick said during his U.S. Hockey Hall of Fame induction. "[He] introduced me to a very different world."

Under Trumble's command, the U.S. was involved in international hockey for teenagers before the World Junior Championship officially existed.

American hockey players' involvement in the tournament for the best teenage players actually began three years before, when a Midwest Junior Hockey League All-Star Team represented the USA in Leningrad. One of the players on the USA squad was Paul Holmgren, who would go on to play and coach in the NHL. Members of that team were picked by coaches John Mariucci and Murray Williamson and sportswriters Charlie Hallman and John Gilbert. The second World Junior Tournament was officially held in Winnipeg in 1978, although four games were played at the Met Center in Bloomington, Minnesota. The American roster was again filled by players from the Midwest Junior Hockey League, which is now the United States Hockey League, started by Walter Bush and Murray Williamson.

Berglund, who helped start the concept of elite summer camps for the United States' top 15-, 16-, and 17-year-old players, has been general manager of 20 United States National Teams. He has also helped develop U.S. coaches. NHL and college coaches such as U.S. National and Olympic women's coach Ben Smith, Minnesota's Doug Woog, Yale's Tim Taylor, and Toronto's Ron Wilson and Northern Michigan's Walt Kyle got a boost in their careers when Berglund recommended them for United States National coaching positions.

Berglund received the Lester Patrick Award for his contributions to American hockey. Born in Fort Frances, Ontario, he is an American citizen, and no one is more emotional about American hockey than Berglund.

In 1986 Walter Bush succeeded Tutt as president of AHAUS. "If you had a vote to determine what nonplayer has had the most influence in American hockey in this century, Walter would probably win the thing," Ogrean said.

Bush has an air of aristocracy mixed with a gifted legal mind, a razor-sharp business acumen, and a collegial attitude. He's an idea guy and quite comfortable in social settings. In many respects, he is like his mentor, Walter Brown.

It's difficult not to like Bush, unless you stand in the way of something he is trying to accomplish. On the 19th hole, he's gallant, noble, and a first-rate storyteller. Behind closed doors, he is a warrior. For example, one of his causes was getting women's hockey into the Olympics. "Some have the impression that Walter is a bon vivant who likes to crack a lobster, crack a beer, and crack a golf ball more than 200 yards," Ogrean said. "He does like all of that.... He's an astute politician whose influence in hockey circles is enormous. It's almost impossible to describe how much he contributes to hockey in America."

"[Bush] is a man of boundless energy," said Ron DeGregorio, who succeeded Bush as USA Hockey president. "I don't like it when I have to be in Toronto and Detroit on consecutive days. He doesn't mind going to Russia for a two-hour meeting."

In 1986 Bush was in Mexico on vacation when he received word that Trumble was leaving AHAUS to join former NFL coach George Allen to set up a sports training academy in California.

When Bush got off the phone, he turned to his wife, Mary, and asked her, "If you could pick one person in the world to be executive director, who would it be?"

"Bob Johnson," she said without hesitation.

The timing couldn't have been much better, because Johnson was in the midst of a 10-game losing streak. But he still needed to be talked into the move, even though he had long before viewed the job as one he wanted later in his career. Johnson's arrival gave the organization increased visibility and perhaps changed the focus ever so slightly toward hockey matters, rather than organizational matters.

Johnson was a hockey guy, not an administrator. He was far more concerned about the quality of American goaltenders than about which insurance carrier the organization should choose. One of his first acts was to get the organization to change the name from Amateur Hockey Association of the United States (AHAUS) to USA Hockey, a move his staff applauded. "I know he was bothered once when he gave his business card to someone on an airplane and they thought AHAUS was a construction firm," Bush said.

It was a simple move, yet it was a step that suggested that the organization was ready for another growth spurt. "When you would call someone and [say] you were from the Amateur Hockey Association of the United States—by the time you got that all out, you forgot why you had even called," Berglund said.

Berglund also didn't like the word *amateur* in the title. In Berglund's opinion, Americans didn't view the word *amateur* with the same hallowed respect that Avery Brundage had for the word. To Brundage, the word meant players weren't paid to be athletes. "But to the public, *amateur* means 'not as good,'" Berglund said. "When you say someone is an amateur in this country, what you are saying is they don't know what they are doing."

Bob Johnson never lost his enthusiasm for promoting American hockey, but he didn't enjoy politics or paperwork. More important, he missed coaching. "He was born to be a coach," Bush said. "The only thing I asked him was that if he got a deal he couldn't turn down, to let me know. And he did."

When the Pittsburgh Penguins called, Johnson left in 1990. He was replaced by Baaron Pittenger, who had recently retired from the U.S. Olympic Committee, where he spent 14 years, the last as its executive director. Pittenger held the USA Hockey post until June 24, 1993, when Dave Ogrean took the job.

An ambitious, progressive administrator with all-star people skills, Ogrean marshaled in a more diversified game plan for the organization. The days of USA Hockey representing only young male ice hockey players were over. Females were starting to play the game with increasing frequency. He was executive director until 1999, left to join the United States Olympic Committee, and then came back to be executive director in 2005.

Ogrean's ability to build consensus has helped modernize USA Hockey. Under Ogrean's leadership, USA Hockey unveiled the American Development Model (ADM) during the 2009 season, a program designed to enhance the development and enjoyment for younger players. USA Hockey surpassed 100,000 registered players in the 8-and-Under category, and the new program is specifically aimed at creating a fun environment for that age group. Included in the model is a change to cross-ice games and age-specific training.

"We studied and stole the best ideas from other countries and other sports," Ogrean said. "But for us, it's a cultural change. But as we have been successful in educating more and more people about what the ADM stands for, we are having tremendous success in getting people to jump on the bus."

At the beginning of the 1990s, USA Hockey had a membership of about 200,000. When Trumble had moved the USA Hockey office from Minneapolis to Colorado Springs, all he needed was an office in the Broadmoor for him and a secretary. In 2011 USA Hockey had 90 employees.

USA Hockey has come a long way since the day Lockhart and his cronies came together in 1937, or even since Ridder and his Minnesota friends met in St. Paul in 1947. With 474,592 registered players in 2010–11, USA Hockey has far more players than anyone had envisioned so many years before. In 2011 USA Hockey was pushing toward 70,000 registered female players. DeGregorio succeeded Walter Bush as USA Hockey president in 2003, and he has also helped modernize USA Hockey's approach with online registration and a risk management plan. DeGregorio is known for his passion about the sport. He's 64 and still plays goaltender in men's leagues multiple times a week. "He's always got the hockey gear in the back of his car," Ogrean said.

He was also what Ogrean terms "the blocking back" on USA Hockey's 1996 decision to institute the National Team Development Program (NTDP) in Ann Arbor, Michigan. In theory, USA Hockey invites the country's best 16- and 17-year-old players to train and play together all season.

It was a controversial decision because it is an expensive undertaking for about 40 players. The idea was that better performances at international tournaments by U.S. teams and producing more elite players would help grow the overall game in the United States. Today that program is a staple of USA Hockey's programming. Assistant executive director Jim Johannson has been asked to speak to other countries about how the Americans operate that program.

First-round NHL draft picks routinely come out of the NTDP or have NTDP backgrounds. Rick DiPietro (2000), Erik Johnson (2006), and Patrick Kane (2007) are all American-born former NTDP players who were drafted No. 1 overall in NHL drafts. In 2010–11 there were more than 50 players in the NHL with NTDP backgrounds. Said Ogrean: "[DeGregorio] has always been fearless in pursuing change if he knew it was the right thing to do to make the sport and organization better." ∎

The outdoor hockey game matching Michigan State against Michigan at Michigan Stadium in Ann Arbor drew a world-record crowd of 104,073 in 2010. (Leon Halip/Getty Images/USA Hockey)

USA HOCKEY
COLLEGE HOCKEY
Dead Fish and Lively Insults

When the outdoor hockey game between Michigan State and Michigan drew a world-record crowd of 104,073 in Ann Arbor in 2010, it was a fitting symbol for a sport that has always prided itself on being both a competition and a happening.

College hockey is uniquely American. Boisterous fans; painted faces; raucous student sections; crude taunts; loud and lively pep bands; organized, manic mascots—those aren't hockey elements borrowed from Canada. There's a zaniness and tradition to college hockey that simply doesn't exist outside college arenas. Where else but in college hockey would New Hampshire fans celebrate their first goal of the game by hurling a dead fish onto the ice? Where else but in college hockey is there a history of some enterprising North Dakota students acknowledging the arrival of the visiting Minnesota Gophers team by throwing a dead gopher onto the ice? Where else but in college hockey is there a true story of the Minnesota mascot Goldy Gopher once body-slamming Bucky Badger to the ice during a pregame ceremony?

The chanting in Cornell's 4,267-seat Lynah Rink, opened in 1957, is organized to the point that there is a website dedicated to making sure everyone knows the words and protocol. Fan intensity in college hockey is historically over the top. Fans in most college arenas chant "Sieve! Sieve! Sieve!" when the opposition goalie surrenders a goal. At Rensselaer Polytechnic Institute (RPI), the Big Red Freakout has been an annual event for more than 30 years. Fans dress from head to toe in red and cheer as loudly as humanly possible. In 1987 red plastic horns were given to fans for the Freakout. The racket from those instruments reached such a high decibel level that the NCAA immediately banned plastic horns from future college hockey games. At Michigan, fans will start chanting, "Ugly parents! Ugly parents!" when opposition parents stand to cheer. Legendary Michigan coach Red Berenson recalls that fans once singled out an opposing player's mom for wearing a polyester suit. "They started chanting, "Kmart! Kmart! Kmart!' every time she stood," he said.

Insulting the opposition is a college hockey tradition that may date back to the early 20th century when Ivy League schools clashed. It has been around for as long as anyone can remember. More than 40 years ago, when Cornell started recruiting Canadians into its agriculture program, Harvard fans started greeting Cornell players with, "Welcome Canada's future farmers" or "Hey, Cornell, if you're here, who is milking the cows?"

College hockey is as competitive as it is festive. Nowhere in sports are bragging rights more cherished than in college hockey, and nothing illustrates its competitiveness better than Boston's Beanpot Tournament. Since 1952, teams from Harvard, Boston University, Boston College, and Northeastern University have met for an annual tournament to determine the city's college champion.

David Silk has a 1980 Olympic gold medal stashed away, but in a speech at a Beanpot Tournament luncheon, he once said he considers his memory of winning the 1978 Beanpot Championship for Boston University among his most cherished. "I'll never forget being handed the Beanpot and being able to show it to my family and friends and all those other people in the stands, maybe taunting the other team's band," Silk said.

What Silk enjoyed most about the Beanpot were the bragging rights that accompany a championship. He enjoyed running into his vanquished foes from Harvard, Northeastern, and Boston College at Red Sox games or on the Boston Common and being able to say, "Better luck next time."

"That's a feeling absent from international hockey or the NHL," Silk said. "It's tough to walk up to [Vladimir] Krutov, [Sergei] Makarov, and [Slava] Fetisov and say, 'Hey, sorry about that.'"

The outdoor game at Ann Arbor on December 11, 2010, was in keeping with the carnival-like atmosphere that has always defined college hockey. Michigan players didn't know whether it was more impressive playing in front of the 104,073 fans or seeing 71-year-old Berenson applaud when the attendance record was announced.

"I actually saw him smile and saw him clap, and that doesn't happen much," Michigan player Jon Merrill said.

Michigan Stadium has a capacity of 109,901, and the original Michigan crowd was announced at 113,411. But Guinness World Records adjudicator Mike Janela was on site to verify the crowd size for the Michigan victory. After a month of reviewing ticket scans and other evidence, the final attendance figure was verified to be more than 9,000 less than originally announced. However, it was still more than enough to shatter the previous world hockey attendance record of 77,803, set in the spring of 2010 when the Germans defeated Team USA 2–1 in a domed soccer stadium at the IIHF World Men's Championship in Gelsenkirchen.

The outdoor-game craze actually began in college hockey with the historic Michigan vs. Michigan State game at Spartan Stadium on October 6, 2001. That game, drawing a crowd of 74,544, ended in a 3–3 tie. Future NHL Vezina Trophy winner Ryan Miller was MSU's goalie in the contest. Atlanta Thrashers forward Jim Slater scored the tying goal with a minute to go in regulation. Norris Trophy–winning Chicago Blackhawks defenseman Duncan Keith also played for MSU.

"That event was a game-changing experience," said former Central Collegiate Hockey Association commissioner Tom Anastos. "We might not have the [NHL's] Winter Classic if they hadn't done what they did."

The idea was originally hatched by Michigan State assistant coach Dave McAuliffe.

"It was amazing what they did, considering that there was no one to call, to ask what to do back then," Anastos said. "There was no blueprint."

On February 11, 2006, Wisconsin defeated Ohio State 4–2 in a game played outdoors in the Frozen Tundra Hockey Classic at Lambeau Field, the Green Bay Packers' home field. More than 38,000 people watched Boston University defeat Boston College 3–2 in an outdoor game played at Fenway Park on January 8, 2010, a week after the Philadelphia Flyers and Boston Bruins played the Winter Classic there.

Rivalries have been important to college hockey almost from the moment the sport was introduced on United States campuses in 1896. Before then, college athletes were playing what they called "ice polo." The game's objective and strategy were similar to hockey as it is known today, except teams had only five players and used a ball instead of a puck. The ice-polo stick resembled the modern-day field-hockey stick.

In the summer of 1894, American and Canadian athletes at a tennis tournament at Niagara Falls began talking about what they did in the winter. They discovered they were both playing different versions of the same game and decided to meet the following winter to determine who had the better game.

In the April 1951 issue of the *Brown Alumni Monthly*, Alexander Meiklejohn offered a firsthand account of that Canadian–United States hockey summit of 1895, which was played in Montreal,

Lambeau Field in Green Bay, Wisconsin—home of the NFL's Packers—hosted the Frozen Tundra Hockey Classic on February 11, 2006. More than 40,000 fans saw the Wisconsin Badgers defeat the Ohio State Buckeyes 4–2. (David Stluka)

Ottawa, Kingston, and Toronto. According to Meiklejohn's account, large crowds showed up to watch the ice polo–hockey doubleheader in each city. The U.S. participants included Byron Watson, Bill Jones, and George Matteson of Brown; A.C. Foote and Malcolm Chase of Yale; F. H. Clarkson of Harvard; and Billy Larned of Columbia. C.M. Pope, a reporter for the Associated Press, also accompanied the United States team to the tournament.

The Canadians won all four hockey games—"easily" according to Meiklejohn's remembrances 56 years after the event. "Their game was much more highly developed than ours, as shown by their established league, with a regular schedule and big buildings [for] large crowds of spectators," Meiklejohn wrote.

Meiklejohn continued, "They had a couple of other advantages [in addition to their] greater skill. First, they used flat-bladed speed skates against our rockers. And second, our hitting stroke with one hand would not move the puck along the ice."

The Canadians had an easy time playing polo, although the Americans did manage to win two of the four ice-polo matches, while the other two games ended in a tie.

"It was pretty generally agreed among us, as a result of the trip, that the Canadian game was better than ours," Meiklejohn said.

The Americans brought back some Canadian skates and sticks, and before long, collegians abandoned ice polo in favor of ice hockey. In the west, Minnesotans had also picked up Canadian hockey from the Manitobans.

Reporter Pope's attendance at the games turned out to be a benefit. He returned to New York and raised money for building the St. Nicholas Ice Rink, which would become America's hockey center. The American Amateur Hockey Association was also formed in 1896.

The earliest known written documentation of a college hockey game is a newspaper account of a 2–2 tie between Yale and Johns Hopkins University. The February 3, 1896, edition of the *Baltimore Sun* states that a game, played at North Avenue Rink, drew "the largest crowd of the season," suggesting there had been other games earlier.

At the turn of the century, the *Spalding Guide to Hockey* said Baltimore was probably "the most enthusiastic ice hockey city in the country." The Baltimore Hockey League was formed in 1897 and included Johns Hopkins University.

Enthusiasm for the sport spilled over into a court battle to decide the 1896–97 championship. (So much for the notion that the litigious side of sports was a modern creation.) In the championship game for the Northampton Cup, the Maryland Athletic Club led 2–1 over the University of Maryland. With only a few minutes remaining in the game, the college players scored what they considered the tying goal. The shot appeared to be too high to many, including the Maryland Athletic Club players. Following a heated argument, referee G.B. Macrae of the New York Athletic Club ruled that it was a goal and signaled for overtime to begin. Taking advantage of their momentum, the college players scored again to win 3–2, or so they thought.

The Maryland Athletic Club protested the referee's decision to the league's governing body, which heard testimony from those attending the game. The ruling: the shot was high and the Maryland Athletic Club was the winner. The *Spalding Guide to Hockey* said the University of Maryland student body reacted "with great indignation" and sought legal vindication. The school retained three prominent Baltimore attorneys, who argued passionately before Justice Bailey. On October 16, 1897, seven months after the game was played, Justice Bailey ruled in favor of the University of Maryland. In his decision, he said the "umpire's decision on the question of goals should be final."

College hockey in Hobey Baker's day was well attended and actually well chronicled in newspapers. By the 1930s, college hockey started to enjoy immense popularity, particularly on the East Coast, where a Harvard-Yale game drew 14,000 fans to Boston Garden in March 1930. College hockey had also spread to the West Coast campuses of USC, UCLA, Loyola, and California. "Some of the best college hockey in the country was played out West," hockey historian Don Clark has said.

And where did those schools go to look for players? Eveleth, Minnesota, of course. There were Eveleth players on teams around the country.

But college hockey, as it is today, didn't take shape until after World War II. Hockey enthusiasm was high after the war. At Harvard's open tryout in 1946, about 180 students showed up, a mixture of the traditional students and veterans in their mid- to late-twenties who had come home from the war and wanted to pick up where they had left off.

Eddie Jeremiah's Dartmouth College teams from 1942 to 1946 were the first college hockey dynasty of the modern era. During one stretch, Dartmouth won 46 consecutive games, a college record. Throughout the 1940s, they were considered invincible by most of their rivals.

"Being on Jerry's team was like being with a smash Broadway musical," one of his former players, Jim Malone, said when Jeremiah retired in 1967. "It was a long run."

Dartmouth's dominance ended when the NCAA began crowning the national champions in Colorado Springs at the Broadmoor World Arena in 1948. The University of Michigan defeated Dartmouth in the first championship game in 1948.

Dartmouth's experiences cemented the idea that Western teams had an unfair advantage because many were using older Canadian players. Teams from the West won 18 of the first 20 national championships. Vic Heyliger's Michigan team won six more (1951, 1952, 1953, 1955, 1956, and 1964); Denver won five (1958, 1960, 1961, 1968, and 1969) and was a runner-up in 1963 and 1964.

Minnesota coach John Mariucci, who primarily used players straight out of the Minnesota high schools, was particularly incensed about playing against the older Canadians. Those older Canadians included Colorado College's Jack Smith, who was 36. Teammates called him the Silver Fox.

"Tony Frasca was 30 when he was coaching at Colorado College, and he had players older than he was," said USA Hockey's Art Berglund, who played at Colorado College. "Only the real good Americans got to play."

Given today's rigid NCAA eligibility guidelines, it's difficult to fathom that the University of Michigan's 1957 NCAA runner-up team actually used a player, Wally Maxwell, who had played two games for the Toronto Maple Leafs in the 1952–53 season.

"There were games when the only American on the ice was the referee," said Bob Ridder, whose ties to USA Hockey brought him to many games.

Teams from the East also didn't like playing the game in Colorado Springs every year, believing it was also a disadvantage to them. In 1958 NCAA officials decided to play the championship game in a different venue every year. Most believe it was Mariucci's lobbying that paved the way for that change.

At one point, Mariucci vowed to never play the University of Denver because of all the older Canadians Murray Armstrong was using on his roster. The night before, Colorado College's line of Ike Scott, Bob McCusker, and Red Hay had physically dominated the young Minnesota team. (Colorado College also had Cy Whiteside, who would eventually become one of the toughest competitors ever to play in the International Hockey League.)

Not many of Mariucci's players really wanted to take the ice against the Colorado College team. After losing the game 7–2, Mariucci launched into another sermon about how overage players shouldn't be allowed in the game. The University of Denver's coach, Murray Armstrong, hearing about Mariucci's comment from a reporter, said that Mariucci should be ignored because he "was just a paper salesman."

Mariucci was, in fact, a part-time coach who also worked for a paper company. But that didn't stop the anger from rising in Mariucci's face when he read Armstrong's comments.

"I will never play Denver again," he said to everyone within earshot.

Mariucci had enough influence to convince Michigan State, University of Michigan, Michigan Tech, and University of North Dakota to abandon the existing Western Intercollegiate Hockey Association in favor of an informal league in which mandatory scheduling wasn't required. Eventually, the University of Denver and Colorado College ended up in the league, but Mariucci still wouldn't play Denver for many years.

Fate would bring them both to the NCAA tournament in 1961. As the Gophers were exiting the plane, Mariucci handed Canadian-born but naturalized U.S. citizen Lou Nanne a sign to carry. It read: "We fry Canadian bacon."

Acknowledging he had one Canadian-born player on his team, Mariucci introduced his team at the NCAA banquet as "19 future presidents and one future prime minister."

With many of the top Canadians playing for Denver, Michigan, and other schools in the West, Western teams continued to dominate the NCAA tournament. "Then, Ned Harkness and Jack Kelley changed things," said Jack Parker, the current Boston University coach.

Harkness at Cornell and Kelley at Boston University began recruiting more Canadians and started to compete favorably with the teams in the West.

With Hockey Hall of Fame goalie Ken Dryden in net, Cornell won the NCAA title in 1967 by defeating Boston University. The Big Red team was a finalist in 1969 and won the title again in 1970. Kelley's Boston University teams won back-to-back titles in 1971 and 1972. No other Division I team was able to win back-to-back titles again until Don Lucia's Minnesota Gophers were able to accomplish that feat in 2002 and 2003.

One of the most memorable teams in college history was the 1969–70 Cornell squad that is the only Division I hockey team to record a perfect season.

When Dryden finally left Cornell in 1969, Boston University coach Jack Kelley offered what turned out to be a premature prayer of gratitude. "Thank God we got rid of Dryden," Kelley growled. "Now all we have to do is beat them."

A year later, coaches were still trying to figure out how to beat Cornell. The Harkness-coached school posted a 29–0 record, culminated by a 6–4 win against Clarkson in the NCAA championship in Lake Placid.

The year before, the Big Red had graduated four All-Americans, including Dryden. They were said to be rebuilding and weren't considered a prime contender for the national championship.

"But at one of our first meetings, I can remember [Coach] Harkness emphatically telling us that we were going to win the national championship," said Brian McCutcheon, the team's leading scorer that season, who later became Cornell's coach.

Coach Ned Harkness has called his 1969–70 Cornell team the "greatest college team ever."

Harkness' short summation of a special season may explain the lure of college hockey better than a thousand words ever could. "You win a lot of lunch money by asking people who the goaltender was on that team," McCutcheon said. "Most people would be willing to bet that Dryden was the goaltender."

But Dryden had graduated the year before and had signed with the Montreal Canadiens. (His last year at Cornell, they had lost the championship to Denver.) The following fall, Cornell's goaltending chores transferred from Dryden, who was 6'4" and 210 pounds, to Brian Cropper, who was 5'5" and 125 pounds.

Cornell had six one-goal wins during their season, including a 3–2 win against Clarkson in the Eastern College Athletic Conference Championship Game, in which John Hughes scored with 14 seconds left to notch victory No. 27.

"I don't remember us talking about the streak much," McCutcheon said. "But we went into every game expecting to win."

Since then, only the 1992–93 Maine Black Bears (42–1–2) have come close to matching Cornell's feat.

Boston University's Kevin Schaeffer celebrates with the trophy after the Terriers' 2–1 victory over Boston College to win the 2007 Beanpot tournament. (Elsa/Getty Images/USA Hockey)

Harvard athletic director Bill Cleary said some of his favorite coaching moments involved players who weren't stars. Cleary's favorite Beanpot story occurred in 1977 when he recruited a soccer-tennis player to replace one of his injured hockey warriors.

Lyman Bullard had played some junior varsity hockey, but was known as a tennis and soccer player. He had two very attractive qualities: he was an athlete, and he roomed with Harvard goalie Brian Petrovek, which meant that Coach Cleary knew where to find him.

"Bullard answered the phone when I called and assumed I had called to talk to Brian," Cleary said. "I remember he wished me luck in the Beanpot, and then I asked him, 'How would you like to wear the Harvard colors and play with us in the Beanpot?' He let out this tremendous whoop."

Bullard actually scored a goal and added two assists as Harvard won the tournament. "Those were the only two games he ever played," Cleary said. "He never expected to be called up. But he was an athlete, and he was ready. That's what college sports are all about."

Hockey East commissioner Joe Bertagna once said, "What is interesting [about college hockey] is what also holds us back."

Essentially, college hockey needed larger schools to help it gain visibility without ignoring that the charm of the sport often centers on some of the smaller schools. "A big part of who we are is Saturday Night in Potsdam, New York, [Saint Lawrence] or Saturday night in Sault Sainte Marie [Lake Superior State] or Houghton, Michigan, [Michigan Tech] or Troy, New York [RPI]," Bertagna said.

The Frozen Four's success in recent years has expanded college hockey's visibility. Since the NCAA began to put the event only in large arenas in 2002, the event's average crowd size has been above 18,000. The event averaged more than 19,000 when it was played in St. Louis in 2007. In 2010 the Frozen Four was played in an NFL stadium for the first time, in Detroit's Ford Field, and an NCAA hockey-record 37,592 fans showed up to watch Boston College defeat Wisconsin 5–0 in the title game. The semifinals had drawn 34,594 fans.

Meanwhile, college hockey's impact on the NHL continues to grow. About 40 years ago, Berenson was viewed like an alien because he was a helmet-wearing ex-college player. "I was considered an intellectual geek," Berenson recalled.

In the 2010–11 NHL season, just under 28 percent of its players had college backgrounds. "I think what this means is that college hockey has become a more realistic option for playing in the NHL," Los Angeles Kings defenseman Jack Johnson said.

Today, there are also 10 NHL executives with college hockey backgrounds: Toronto's Burke (Providence), New Jersey's Lou Lamoriello (coached at Providence), Atlanta's Don Waddell (Northern Michigan), Pittsburgh's Ray Shero (St. Lawrence), New York Islanders' Garth Snow (Maine), Nashville's David Poile (Northeastern), Washington's George McPhee (Bowling Green), Philadelphia's Paul Holmgren (Minnesota), Boston's Peter Chiarelli (Harvard), and Dallas' Joe Nieuwendyk (Cornell).

"To me the growth of college parallels the growth of hockey in the United States," said St. Louis Blues general manager Doug Armstrong. "In places like Texas, California, and Missouri, players are now growing up thinking about NCAA hockey. That's how they think. I think college hockey is only going to get bigger." ■

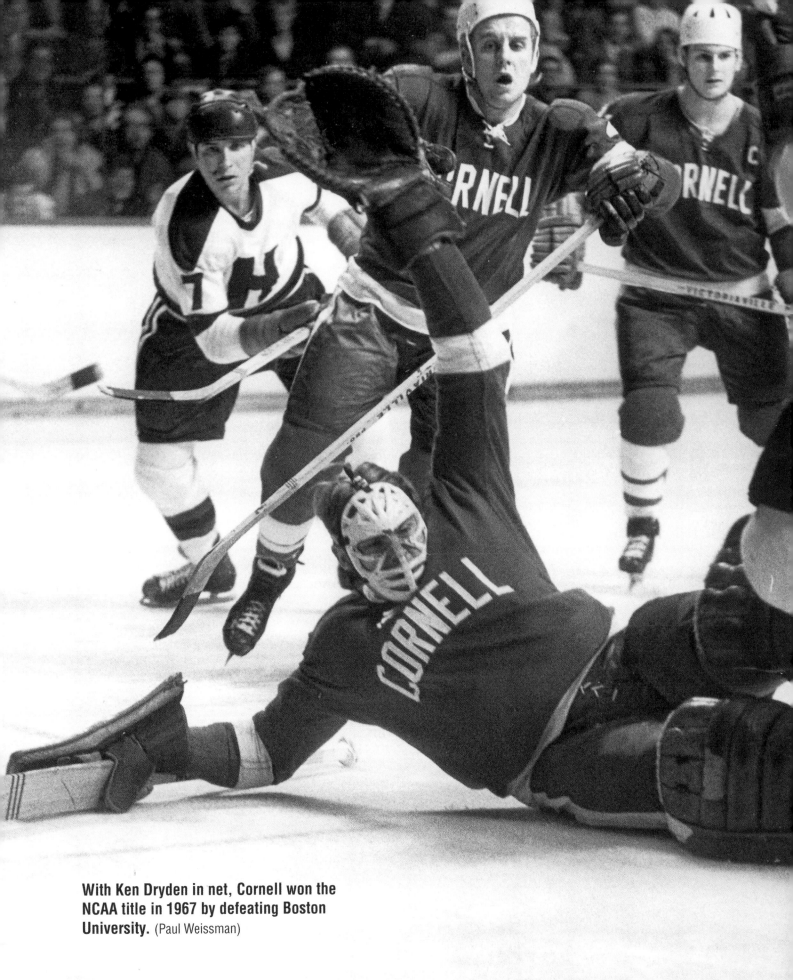

With Ken Dryden in net, Cornell won the NCAA title in 1967 by defeating Boston University. (Paul Weissman)

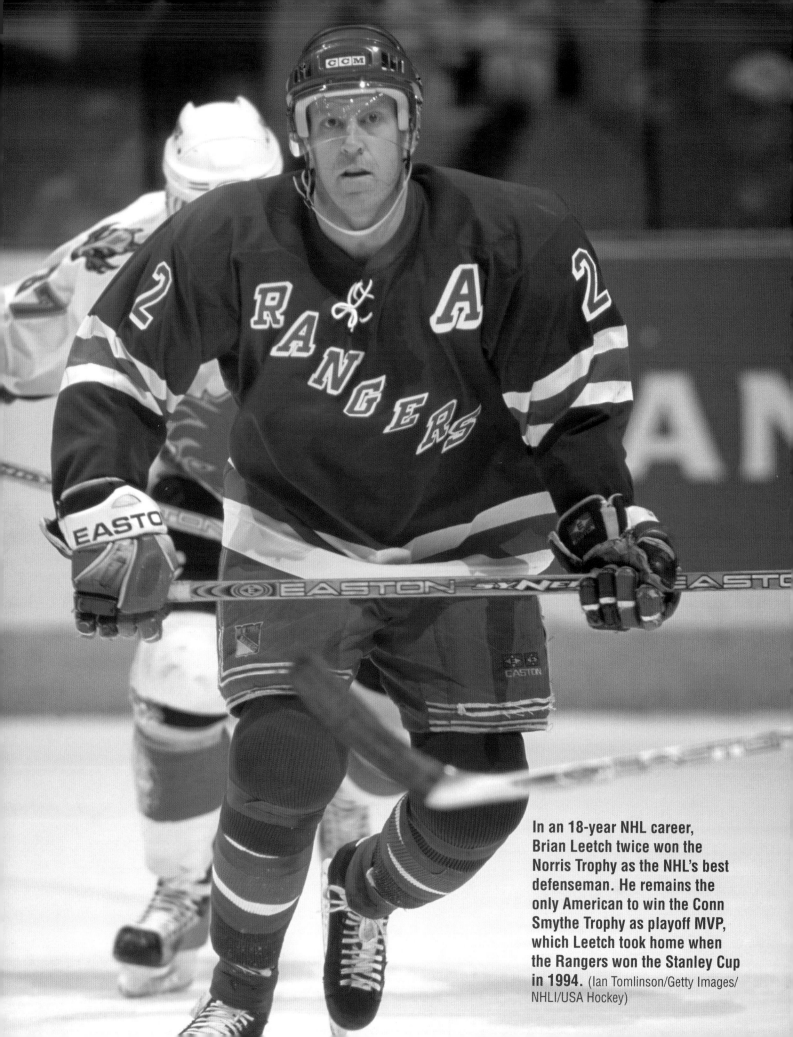

In an 18-year NHL career, Brian Leetch twice won the Norris Trophy as the NHL's best defenseman. He remains the only American to win the Conn Smythe Trophy as playoff MVP, which Leetch took home when the Rangers won the Stanley Cup in 1994. (Ian Tomlinson/Getty Images/ NHLI/USA Hockey)

THE GREATEST GENERATION
USA Hockey in the 1980s and Early '90s

Noted sports physiologist Jack Blatherwick's mission before the 1988 Olympic Games was to train the U.S. hockey players to handle the puck and create plays at elite-level speed.

What it meant in practical terms was that he was helping the Americans keep up with 19-year-old Brian Leetch.

"Leetchie could do everything at the highest speed," 1988 U.S. Olympian Jim Johannson recalled. "And we were all training to do that. We had to learn to play hockey at a higher pace, and Leetchie was already doing that."

Leetch broke his ankle on his first shift at the U.S. Olympic tryout camp in Greensboro, North Carolina, in 1987, and as he was being helped off the ice that day, everyone at the sports festival would have bet that Leetch was going to be on the U.S. Olympic squad seven months later.

"You are always going to remember the guy who wore white skates," Johannson said.

But Leetch didn't need those white skates to find the spotlight. He was among the most dynamic flag carriers during what could be called American hockey's greatest generation. If we use the NHL arrival of Pat LaFontaine and Chris Chelios in 1984 as the starting point of this generation and the arrival of Derian Hatcher, Bill Guerin, and Keith Tkachuk in 1991–92 as the end point, what we see is a large collection of stars who made a difference in international tournaments and on their respective NHL teams.

This group of premium players may have been USA's prize for winning the 1980 gold medal at Lake Placid. This generation of players was the secondary explosion of talent that was inspired by the Miracle at Lake Placid.

"It was hard to find any U.S. player from my era that hadn't had a real profound impact from that

Jeremy Roenick moves the puck while playing for the Blackhawks in 1995. Roenick scored 513 goals in 20 NHL seasons. (Glenn Cratty/Getty Images/USA Hockey)

Olympics," said U.S. Hockey Hall of Fame member Mike Richter, who joined the New York Rangers in 1989. "This was real to us because we had watched it on television."

Jeremy Roenick was a small, passionate 10-year-old player who felt empowered by watching the Americans excel in his sport. "Watching Mike Eruzione score probably the most important goal in U.S. history, I wanted to be an Olympian and a professional hockey player and to be Mike Eruzione," Roenick said. "I wanted to achieve greatness."

Although it is impossible to know how the landscape would have been different had Eruzione not beaten Vladimir Myshkin with his wrist shot, it is not unreasonable to think that USA Hockey might have lost some of these athletes to other sports had hockey not become the hottest game in town.

To appreciate how strong the American hockey group was in its heyday, consider that these eight forwards from that time period—Brett Hull (741), Mike Modano (561), Keith Tkachuk (538), Jeremy Roenick (513), Pat LaFontaine (468), Bill Guerin (429), Tony Amonte (416), and John LeClair (406)—combined for 4,072 NHL goals. That's an average of 509 goals per man.

"Not only were they great players, but they were the best at their positions in the NHL," USA Hockey consultant Art Berglund said. "We have a lot of great players now, but we don't have as many All-Stars as we had with this group."

And that forward list doesn't include Doug Weight, who had more than 1,000 points in 1,200-plus NHL games or Brian Rolston, Kevin Stevens, and Scott Young, who have combined for more than 1,000 goals. Massachusetts native Stevens, a 1988 Olympian, was a two-time 50-goal scorer. As of the 2010–11 season, Modano, Weight, and Rolston are still playing in the NHL.

American goalie Mike Richter entered the NHL in 1989 and ended his career with 301 regular-season wins, a World Junior Championship bronze medal, Stanley Cup championship, a World Cup championship, and an Olympic silver medal.

America's defense was All-Star caliber during this time period. In addition to Leetch and Chelios, the American-born defense that arrived in the NHL in that era included Kevin and Derian Hatcher and Gary Suter.

Chelios and Leetch combined for five Norris Trophies and four Stanley Cup championships. In 2010 the *Hockey News* listed the top 10 American-born players in NHL history, and Chelios and Leetch were No. 1 and No. 2. On the *Hockey News* list, 6 of the 10 players arrived in the NHL between 1984 and 1991. LaFontaine (No. 3), Modano (No. 4), Roenick (No. 8), and Richter (No. 10) were the others.

"We put USA Hockey on the map in terms of being a world power," Roenick offers. "Even though the 1980 team won the Olympics and the gold medal, I don't think they were considered a world power. I think people said, 'Holy shit, we just pulled off the greatest miracle of all time.' Now we have our generation...we are in the fight for first place every year. No more seventh- or eighth-place finishes."

The coming-out party for the group probably came at the 1991 Canada Cup when the Americans finished second to Canada. Brett Hull and Modano both had nine points in eight games. Roenick had a big tournament. The Americans lost 4–1 and 4–2 to Canada in the Finals. The team was coached by Tim Taylor because Bob Johnson had been diagnosed with cancer just before the tournament.

In previous Canada Cups, the Americans were at a clear talent disadvantage. In the first Canada Cup, the Americans had players such as Craig Patrick, Lou Nanne, Mike Polich, and Mike Milbury trying to compete against a Canadian team that had Guy Lafleur, Larry Robinson, Bobby Orr, Darryl Sittler, Phil Esposito, Gilbert Perreault, and Marcel Dionne, among others.

"In 1991 we were able to fill our holes with very elite players, and that was the first time we were able to do that," Tim Taylor said. "We were able to put together a real team."

There was undeniably a sense that the Americans had jumped off the porch and were ready to run with the big dogs.

"In that time period, Russia's skill intimidated you, and the Swedes could sometimes outskill you, and the Canadians could play harder than you,"

In 1998, John LeClair became the first American-born NHL player to record three consecutive 50-goal seasons. (Mitchell Layton/Getty Images/USA Hockey)

Johannson said. "Then all of a sudden...Americans have high-end skill guys who can run you over."

Richter recalls being on his first U.S. National Junior Team and being impressed with the talent level. "And then each year after that I would be more impressed," he said.

This generation had depth beyond its top-end stars, such as Tony Granato, the 1988 Olympian who had four 30-goal seasons in the NHL, or defensive forward Joel Otto. "I compare Otto to Bob Gainey," said 1972 U.S. Olympian Mike "Lefty"

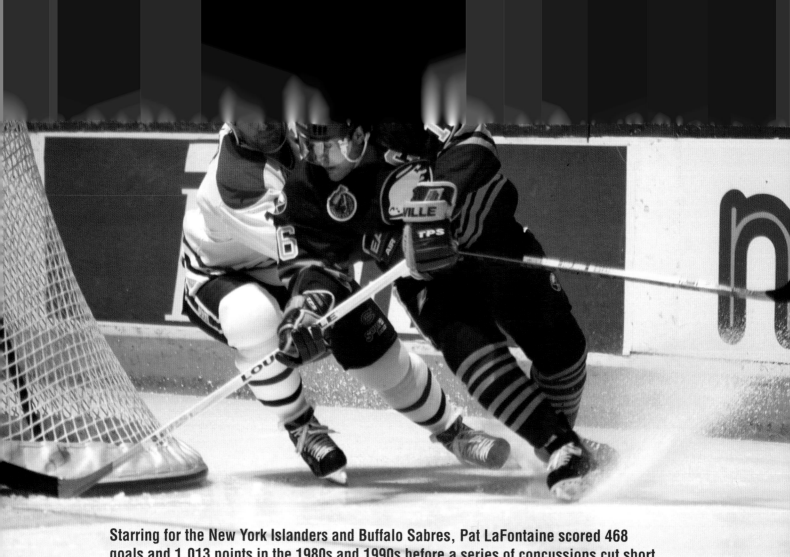

Starring for the New York Islanders and Buffalo Sabres, Pat LaFontaine scored 468 goals and 1,013 points in the 1980s and 1990s before a series of concussions cut short his career. (Denis Brodeur/NHLI via Getty Images/USA Hockey)

Curran. "Not to take anything away from Bob Gainey, but he had fewer points than Joel Otto did. But he hoisted the Cup five or six times. I always say he was fortunate to be born into royalty and Otto wasn't."

But it was the American superstars who defined this generation.

"In the first couple of skates at Providence [at World Cup training camp], guys were going up and down the ice at 100 mph," Modano recalled.

Young recalled that everyone in the dressing room was amazed by how fast all the players seemed and the way the puck was being tic-tac-toed around the ice.

Keep in mind that the top four American centers in this generation were LaFontaine, Modano, Roenick, and Weight. Modano, LaFontaine, and Roenick all scored 50 goals at least once in their careers, and LaFontaine, Modano, and Weight all netted at least 100 points once in their careers.

"We were competitive with each other," Modano said. "Who was the best American? But when we got together on our U.S. team, we left our egos behind."

Drafted originally by the Chicago Blackhawks, Roenick was a tornado on skates, whirling around the ice at high speed regardless of what was in his path. As a rookie, he had his front teeth knocked out on a cross-check by St. Louis Blues defenseman Glen Featherstone during a playoff game. Roenick never left the game and came back to score an important goal on the power play.

"All of us adapted that kind of Canadian mentality," Roenick said. "We got pushed around by the Canadians for years and years. Then we realized if we are going to beat them we have to adopt their mentality."

The Hatchers had contrasting styles. Kevin was the offensive threat, posting 12 consecutive seasons of scoring 10 or more goals, and Derian essentially helped define the role of the shutdown defenseman.

"We all felt that we had enough skill to hold up against the Canadians, but we needed the age that these guys brought us," Modano said. "They were very feisty, very tough."

Berglund views the arrival as an indication of the Americans starting to attract athletes who might have gone to football in other years. "If these guys had grown up in Texas, they might have been tight ends," Berglund said.

Attracting premium athletes into hockey has always been an issue for the U.S. program. One of the most intriguing prospects of the 1984 NHL draft was Tom Glavine, a crafty center, who was drafted by the Los Angeles Kings. He chose Major League Baseball, but it is fun to wonder what he could have done in hockey. He would have been a member of hockey's greatest generation.

In the spring of 1991, Weight (Lake Superior State) and Amonte (Boston College) literally signed minutes apart with the New York Rangers. "The Rangers had them on two different floors of the same hotel, and [Rangers general manager Neil Smith] was running up and down trying to

negotiate with them separately," said agent Steve Bartlett, who represented Weight.

Neither player had a lengthy stay in New York, but Weight ended up as one of the league's top play-making centers, and Amonte had eight seasons of scoring 30 or more goals.

"Weight, Amonte, and others helped bring credibility to the college game," Bartlett said. "There are still some who will argue the college game vs. major junior, but I think that debate is far less one-sided than it used to be thanks to [American players from that era]."

LaFontaine took off his USA jersey after the 1984 Olympics, put on a New York Islanders sweater, and promptly scored 13 goals in his first 15 NHL games.

"When you say LaFontaine's name, the first thing I think of is speed," said former NHL defenseman Tom Laidlaw.

Laidlaw recalls that LaFontaine changed the Rangers vs. Islanders rivalry because he seemed to be jet-propelled. "We were used to playing against great Islanders players," Laidlaw said. "But [Clark] Gillies, [Bobby] Nystrom, [Bryan] Trottier, and Mike Bossy didn't have the speed that he had. I was used to battling it out with those guys along the boards. Now all of a sudden LaFontaine is flying through the neutral zone, and if you were standing still he would fly by you."

Leetch may have had the greatest flair in the group, because it seemed like he was always a threat to take the puck end-to-end. He was not Bobby Orr, but he didn't seem to know that. In his fourth full NHL season, he became only the fifth defenseman, and the first American, to register 102 points.

"He knew when to go," Young said. "No one knew how to defend against him even in the pros... the way he'd come up the ice against you, he would

Chris Chelios of the Detroit Red Wings warms up prior to Game 1 of the 2009 Stanley Cup Finals.
(Jim McIsaac/Getty Images/USA Hockey)

always get by you. It was hard to angle him off."

Chelios is the alpha male of the American group from that era. He played in the NHL until he was 48, earning a reputation as one of the game's ultimate warriors. He trained as if he were preparing to join the U.S. Navy SEALs, spending his summers in Southern California, where noted hockey trainer T.R. Goodman guided his intense routines. In addition to an hour of weight-training with no breaks, the Chelios routine included a 40-mile bike ride along the Pacific Coast Highway and as much as 16 miles of paddle surfing in the Pacific.

"Paddling is underrated as an exercise," Chelios told *Sports Illustrated* in 2007, explaining how he used the ancient Hawaiian technique of standing on a 12-foot-long board while paddling with a seven-foot oar. "It's a real workout when you're dealing with waves or going against the wind. The paddle is like a hockey stick used for balance and steering. Paddling works everything: legs, stomach, shoulders, back."

During the season, Chelios was known to ride a stationary bike for 45 minutes while in the sauna. He called it his "aerobic wash."

"That's just crazy," his former Red Wings teammate Dan Cleary said. "I tried it, and it just burns your nostrils."

Detroit assistant general manager Jim Nill credited Chelios' work ethic for his durability and longevity. Late in Chelios' career, he suffered a serious knee injury that could have threatened his career if Chelios had let it.

"The team was on the road, and the arena was dark," Nill says. "I came in and heard something, and it was Chelios skating down the ice. It wasn't long after his surgery. He wasn't allowed to turn, so he'd lift himself on the boards to turn around...he was by himself. No one there to see it."

Fittingly, the movie *300* is among Chelios' favorites. It's the story of a small army of Spartans that held off an overwhelming force of Persians. Anyone who knows Chelios knows that he would fit in well with the Spartans. His real name is Christos Kostas Tselios.

Red Wings forward Kris Draper even stuck him with the nickname "Sparta." "His mom is from there so it has to be in his bloodline."

Chelios has long been viewed as the league's ultimate playoff warrior. In his early years he piled up penalty minutes, and not all from hooking and holding. From 1987 to 1994 he averaged about 203 penalty minutes, with a high of 282 for the Chicago Blackhawks in 1992–93.

"Oh, he was nasty," says Nill, who played against him. "He stands up to everyone and backs down to no one."

"He had a will about him," Cleary said. "If you picked a fight with him, you had better make sure he'd gone, because he wouldn't quit."

His reputation for being ruthless in pursuit of success dates to his collegiate playing days at Wisconsin. Johannson played at Wisconsin with Chelios for one season and recalls Chelios had his own code about what was acceptable behavior by an opponent. In a game against Minnesota, Johannson recalled Pat Micheletti, who would later play briefly for the Minnesota North Stars, scored a goal against Wisconsin that earned an experience with the wrath of Chelios.

"A guy missed the net wide, and the puck comes out the other side and [Micheletti] taps it in and does a huge dance," Johannson said. Chelios didn't like the dance. "He hadn't made a play. He just happened to be standing in the right spot," Johannson said. "Cheli thought he was showboating."

To the best of Johannson's recollection, Chelios skated past Micheletti and said, "This will be one of your last shifts." Two shifts later, Micheletti was hobbled by a foot injury.

"In fairness to Cheli, I don't think he wanted to hurt him severely," Johannson said. "He just wanted to make a statement."

Chelios retired as the second-oldest player in NHL history, only behind legendary Gordie Howe, who retired at age 52. "Gordie made me promise that I wouldn't break his record," Chelios said.

Chelios scored 185 goals, 763 assists, 948 points, and finished with 2,891 penalty minutes in 1,651 regular-season games. He also played in more postseason games than anyone in NHL history (266). He played in four Olympics (1984, 1998, 2002, and 2006) and also represented the U.S. in three Canada Cups (1984, 1987, and 1991), the World Cup of Hockey twice (1996 and 2004), and the World Junior Championship (1982).

In any discussion about who should be considered the greatest American player of all time, it's difficult to get past Chelios, who played 26 seasons in the NHL.

Roenick refers to Chelios as "Captain America" because he was the symbol of America's hockey perseverance.

"He is the godfather of American hockey," Roenick said, "and I think many of the guys feel that way about him."

Chelios was tough, fearless, passionate, and proud to be an American hockey player. In that regard, he may be the symbol of USA Hockey's greatest generation. ∎

Brett Hull was the leading scorer in the 1996 World Cup of Hockey, with seven goals and four assists in seven games. (USA Hockey/ Bruce Bennett Studios)

THE 1996 WORLD CUP
Slaying the Lion in the Lion's Den

When coach Ron Wilson entered the U.S. dressing room on the morning of the championship game of the 1996 World Cup, he was King Arthur in search of Sir Galahad.

To beat Canada in Montreal, with a championship at stake, Wilson needed someone to pull the sword from the stone. Tony Amonte wasn't the USA's best player or even one of its leaders, but in the first six games of the tournament, the Massachusetts native had proven himself a warrior.

Amonte had played as if he had turbo-charged skates and nitro in his veins. Whenever the USA needed a lift, Amonte had scored, created a scoring chance, or stapled an opponent against the boards with a well-timed check. Sometimes just the sight of Amonte jetting up the ice at Mach 2, with his long hair flowing and his USA jersey flapping behind him, was enough to rally his teammates.

Wilson was looking for someone who would pick up the flag and inspire the troops if it became necessary that night. He thought Amonte might be the one.

"Tony," Wilson said, "you are going to be America's Paul Henderson."

"Who the hell is Paul Henderson?" Amonte joked.

Most of the 28 million people in Canada—and Amonte—knew Henderson scored the game-winner to beat the Soviet Union in the famous 1972 Summit Series. In the United States, men and women over age 55 know where they were when John F. Kennedy was assassinated. In Canada, men and women over 50 know where they were when Henderson fired the puck past Vladislav Tretiak in Moscow.

But if Amonte was to be anointed as a hero in waiting, he preferred his model to be made in America. To U.S. hockey players of Amonte's

Rolston the Hero in 1996 World Championship

Everyone knows about Mike Eruzione's one-for-the-ages goal. Some know about Tony Amonte's game-winner at the 1996 World Cup. But few know that Brian Rolston delivered one of the most significant goals in American hockey history.

New Jersey Devils winger Rolston scored a short-handed goal at 4:46 of overtime to beat Russia 4–3 in the bronze-medal game at the 1996 World Championship. His tally ended a 34-year medal drought for the Americans at the World Championships. While trying to kill a penalty, Rolston found himself on a two-on-one break with Anaheim Ducks right wing Joe Sacco and fired a shot far-side past Russian goalie Mikhail Shtalenkov.

"Other countries always took the World Championships more seriously than the U.S.," Rolston said. "But that was a time when we were stepping up in the world of hockey. It was a big time win for U.S. hockey."

The Americans had to rally from a 3–0 deficit to win the contest. Rolston also had USA's first goal, and San Jose Sharks forward Chris Tancill and Buffalo Sabres center Derek Plante also scored.

Another key player for USA was goalie Parris Duffus, who made 32 saves, including three in overtime to preserve the win. He had a 2.54 goals-against average in the tournament. Duffus had a strong history in the World Championship, posting a career 2.20 goals-against average in 14 games. "You were wondering why this guy couldn't play in the NHL," Rolston remembered.

Duffus played just 29 minutes in the NHL with the Phoenix Coyotes in 1996–97.

generation, the list of fabled hockey heroes was restricted to the U.S. team that captured the gold medal at the 1980 Olympics in Lake Placid. When Amonte contemplated his destiny, he immediately thought of the man whose goal had vanquished the Soviets 16 years before. Most of the players on the U.S. team at the 1996 World Cup had been inspired by what happened at Lake Placid.

"Can I just be Mike Eruzione?" Amonte asked.

"Yeah," said Wilson. "You are both ugly, you are both Italian, and you are both from Boston University. You can be Eruzione and score the big goal for us tonight."

Neither man realized how prophetic their conversation would be.

Weeks before, when Team USA's World Cup training camp began in Providence, Rhode Island, the highly organized Lou Lamoriello brought in a white coach's board divided by a line down the middle. On one side, Lamoriello had written a long list of points he would raise with players at the opening meeting. The other side Lamoriello had left blank so that coach Ron Wilson could jot down an outline of his opening remarks.

"What are you going to say?" Lamoriello asked his coach.

"I have some points I want to make, but I really don't know what I will say until I get there," Wilson replied. "I'm usually better when I'm unrehearsed. I'm at my best when it comes from the heart."

"Can you at least give me an idea?" Lamoriello persisted. "Lou," Wilson said finally, "you are just going to have to trust me on this." Wilson knew his address to the team was important.

But Wilson was an engaging speaker, and not long into his opening talk, players began to believe this was a guy who they could follow. Wilson told them that the days of America coming to international tournaments with a goal of being respectable were over. This team would enter the tournament to win—anything less would be considered failure.

He challenged each player to ponder what he would be willing to do to win the World Cup. "If USA-Canada were tied 2–2 with two minutes to go in Game 3, what would you be willing to do?" Wilson asked. "We all know that Mark Messier will do anything it takes for Canada to win in that situation."

He looked at Brian Leetch, the captain of the USA's World Cup team, and asked rhetorically if Leetch would be willing to tangle with Messier, his New York Rangers teammate, if the game was on the line.

He looked at John LeClair and asked whether LeClair would go after Eric Lindros, his Philadelphia Flyers teammate, if the game was tied 2–2 in the final two minutes.

Wilson had another message as well, one he would repeat over the next few weeks: he compared hockey's history to a bus ride, with Canadians always in the driver's seat and Americans always asked to ride in the back of the bus.

"I started out in the luggage compartment," said Wilson, who was the only American college player on the Toronto Maple Leafs in the 1978–79 season. "Some of you are closer to the front now. But the Americans have never driven. Now it's time for us to drive the bus."

Wilson saw some nods. Before arriving in Providence, he and USA Hockey officials knew the team was talented enough to win. Now he was confident they were hungry enough to win. Canadians had long understood the importance of sacrificing personal agendas for the sake of

winning. Through the years, top Canadian players have accepted third- and fourth-line assignments without complaint. Colorado Avalanche star Joe Sakic had won the Hart Trophy as the NHL playoff's most valuable player in June, but when the World Cup started, he was probably going to be on the third line.

Wilson quickly won over the leaders of the team—Brian Leetch, Keith Tkachuk, and Joel Otto, among others. Bonding with Hull was very important to the American cause. Five years before at the Canada Cup, Hull hadn't mixed well with coach Tim Taylor, who had taken over after Bob Johnson was diagnosed with a brain tumor. Publicly, Wilson said he wasn't going to let history influence his program. Privately, Wilson wanted to make sure he and Hull were reading from the same page.

"I just told him great players have to play their best against the best competition," Wilson said. "I told him we needed him to be among our best players."

The meeting was important for Hull, who wasn't shy about saying he didn't appreciate his experience at the 1991 Canada Cup. Harmony and togetherness were important to the Americans, especially since the team had to face the Canadians in the first game. Even though the Americans could lose that game and still win the tournament, the first game was very important to their collective psyche. The Americans had never beaten Canada in a tournament where the best NHL players were competing. The first game, played in Philadelphia, would not necessarily give them a home-ice advantage, because Flyers captain Eric Lindros played for Canada. Philadelphia fans might have a difficult time rooting against big No. 88.

The importance of the first pool-play game against Canada was evident before it was 20 seconds old. Keith Tkachuk broke Claude Lemieux's nose in a fight. The physical play continued when Derian Hatcher decked Lindros behind the net. The symbolism was more important than the hit. It let the Canadians know that this tournament wasn't going to be like the Canada Cup of 1976 or 1991.

The Americans trailed 2–1 after one period, but Doug Weight's goal at 3:27 of the second period tied the score and restored the USA's confidence. Even if Lindros was the Flyers' most important captain since Bobby Clarke, Philadelphia fans were clearly pro-American. They cheered enthusiastically when Scott Young's goal at 10:48 put the USA ahead for good. Team USA won 5–3. It seemed appropriate that USA Hockey had finally removed one of its Canadian shackles in the city where the United States' independence was born.

Chelios had left a woman at the altar to attend the game. Actually, he left her at the receiving line. His sister, Eleni, was getting married in Chicago a few hours before Chelios was scheduled to face off against the Canadians in Philadelphia. But the fact that it wasn't Chris getting married didn't make it any easier for him to slip out. His sister and her new husband, Don, were understanding, but Chelios' father, Gus, wasn't very happy about his decision.

"My dad's still not talking to me," Chelios said after the game. "This one is going to take time to heal." Teammates told Chelios if family harmony wasn't restored after the World Cup, they would all petition his father to get him pardoned.

Next up was a Labor Day tilt with the Russians and a game against the Slovakians the next day. The Americans expected to beat the Russians, even though on paper the Russians had as many elite players. Behind a goal and two assists from Pat LaFontaine, the U.S. earned a 5–2 victory.

Just as had been anticipated, the USA's tough collection of physical wingers, including roomies Tkachuk and Guerin, were having a major impact. Players like LaFontaine and Hull had more freedom to move because guys like Tkachuk, Adam Deadmarsh, and Bill Guerin were holding up the opposition or making them pay a price along the boards.

The win over Russia meant the USA had the No. 1 seed, regardless of how they did against the Slovakians. Wilson rested key players, but they destroyed the Slovakians 9–3 anyway. That meant they would have a bye in the first round.

The team was humming. Team harmony was exceptional, and everyone was having fun. Players were razzing Tkachuk regularly about his bout with Lemieux. Posted on the wall of Team USA's dressing room was a New York Athletic Commission boxing scorecard for the Tkachuk-Lemieux tussle. Tkachuk had been credited with a 10–1 decision. The card also noted that all of Tkachuk's previous fights had been with "undersized amateur opponents" and that Tkachuk "had the potential to be a thug." Guys loved the humor—Lemieux wasn't one of the most popular men in hockey. Every move the coaching staff made was working. Placing Mike Modano on a line with Keith Tkachuk and Bill Guerin was like asking a sheep to party with two wolves. Modano is mellow, and Tkachuk and Guerin are maniacal. "Before the game, they look like they want to pound me to get me more intense," Modano said.

But the Tkachuk-Modano-Guerin trio, mismatched in terms of personality, proved to be an excellent blend on the ice, particularly against Slovakia. Tkachuk had three goals and an assist; Modano had two goals and an assist; and Bill Guerin had an assist, a slashing penalty, and a multitude of hits and dirty looks that intimidated

Mike Modano scored two goals and added four assists for the Americans at the 1996 World Cup of Hockey.
(USA Hockey)

the Slovaks. To opponents, playing against Guerin was like entering a radiation zone—prolonged exposure was ill-advised.

Tkachuk was a throwback to the 1950s, when the leading scorer on an NHL team was usually the toughest player as well. Gordie Howe, Maurice "Rocket" Richard, Milt Schmidt—all of them were captains who could score, hit, fight, and control the game in any number of different ways. Tkachuk was the 1990s version of those players, right down to his willingness to do whatever it took to be successful.

The way Modano handled the ribbing he took from Guerin and Tkachuk was indicative of how

close-knit the American team had become. Guerin and Tkachuk helped keep everyone loose. In Philadelphia, they put on a synchronized-swimming exhibition in the Jacuzzi.

Having earned the bye, the Americans wouldn't play again until six days later, when they faced the Russians in Ottawa. The Americans were ready for the Russians, but they weren't ready for Ottawa's fans.

One sign of how far USA Hockey's program had come was that Uncle Sam had surpassed Boris Mikhailov on Canada's list of leading hockey villains. Remember Mikhailov had outraged fans by laughing in Bobby Clarke's face after the Russians had whipped Canada's NHL All-Stars 20 years prior. In 1996 he coached the Russian team against the Americans in the game in Ottawa, and the Canadian fans cheered his players as if they were born in Moose Jaw, not Moscow.

When Team USA coach Ron Wilson entered the postgame press conference after the United States defeated Russia 5–2, he had a right to act as if he didn't know where he was.

"Let's make this quick," Wilson joked pointedly. "It's a long flight from Moscow to Philadelphia."

Don Cherry, color analyst for *Hockey Night in Canada*, told a reporter he was disappointed the Canadians had cheered for the Russians. "If we were bombed by Iraq," Cherry asked, "who would come to our defense? The Russians?"

Ottawa might as well have been Moscow to Brett Hull, who was booed unmercifully by the fans. The Canadians reacted to him as if he had become hockey's Benedict Arnold. Fans started chanting "Traitor! Traitor! Traitor!" after the Canadian-born Hull scored his second goal to give Team USA a 4–1 lead at 14:48 of the second period.

This fan reaction was at most bizarre and at the very least unexpected. After all, Hull had played for the USA in 1991 without abuse, and that was after he had won the Hart Trophy as the NHL's Most Valuable Player. Born in Belleville, Ontario, and raised in Winnipeg and Vancouver, Hull had the right to play for either Canada or the USA because his mother was a U.S. citizen. In 1986, when both the USA and Canada had scouted Hull for their national teams, only the USA had wanted him.

"When I was a sophomore in college, [Canada's] Dave King and [the USA's] Dave Peterson came to watch me play," Hull said. "Dave King said I was no good or whatever. He didn't come and see me afterward, but Peterson did."

Although Hull says he's no superpatriot, his only regret was that he had but two goals to give to his chosen country. The Ottawa fans' booing and taunting bothered him. "It wasn't like I high-sticked anyone," Hull said.

Team Canada, meanwhile, was struggling just to reach the final round. The Canadians needed a goal by Theo Fleury with 12.5 seconds left in second overtime to win a semifinal game against Sweden.

Watching that game from his hotel room, Wilson was definitely cheering for Canada. Everyone in USA Hockey believed it was important to face Canada in the final. If the Americans won the tournament without beating Canada in the best-of-three series, doubters would suggest their triumph was a matter of good fortune, not good playing.

But in Game 1 in Philadelphia, Canada showed it wouldn't easily abdicate its title as the hockey world's undisputed ruler. Steve Yzerman scored at 10:37 of overtime to give Canada a 4–3 win against Team USA.

"It's like a heavyweight fight," Wilson said. "They are the reigning champ. We didn't use our knockout punch. They got off the ropes and beat us."

Yzerman's game-winner was a fluttering shot from a bad angle that fell into the net after goaltender Mike Richter hit it with his glove. "I think the shot was going wide until Mike Richter hit it," Yzerman said.

Team USA had forced overtime after a goal by John LeClair with 6.3 seconds remaining in regulation. The goal was actually netted by Canadian defenseman Eric Desjardins, who accidentally knocked the puck through his own goaltender. Moments before, linesman Kevin Collins had waved Mark Messier out of the faceoff circle. With

Adam Graves in his place, the USA's Joel Otto won the draw, and the USA gained possession for a final drive to the net. LeClair was credited with the goal because he was battling in front of the net.

Then Yzerman scored in overtime. Adding insult to the loss was the fact that Collins had missed an offside call that should have stopped the play before Yzerman scored.

Fate seemed to have sided against the Americans. Although the Canadians were gracious in triumph, they had to be thinking, *Same old Americans. They can't find a savior when the game is on the line. Haven't we seen this before?*

For years the Canadians had attacked the Americans in waves, believing they would eventually shake the Americans' confidence. Now, out of respect for the Americans' aggressive forechecking and talent, they were sitting back, playing defense, and waiting for their chances. Instead of attacking like sharks as they usually did, the Canadians were lying in the weeds like equally dangerous snakes.

The loss brought a sense of reality back to the Americans, who had known no adversity until Yzerman's shot crossed the line. But it didn't undermine their confidence. The Americans expected Game 2 to be different, and it was.

If the old script had been followed, the Canadians would have closed out the Americans in the second game. Instead, the Americans defeated the Canadians 5–2.

Team USA produced its best effort against the Canadians since the United States shocked Canada en route to the 1960 Olympic gold medal. Canada's favorite ex-patriot, Hull, scored a key goal at 15:24 of the second period to put Team USA ahead 3–2. He got the breakaway when Adam Foote's shot hit Chelios and deflected directly to Hull, who scooted down the ice the way his father, Bobby, had done so many times at Chicago Stadium. Hull, who had played well defensively throughout the tournament, had been hanging out like a schoolyard cherry-picker when the puck found him. "I would like to say Hullie was cheating on that play," Wilson joked. "But I should say 'anticipating.'"

Canada played without its leader, Mark Messier, who was sidelined with the flu. Because of his previous history of playing with illness and injury, it was presumed Messier's symptoms were quite severe. With Messier bedridden, the Canadians were sluggish.

Team USA goaltender Mike Richter made 35 saves to shut down Canada's offense. Richter was sharpest in the third period when Canada outshot the United States 18–8. "He took [the Game 1] loss hard," Wilson said. "I think he felt he let the team down."

Chelios went after Lindros at every opportunity. He and Lindros swung sticks and traded jabs. Obscenities spewed from their lips. Taunts rose from their mouths. They were like two gladiators, only the forum was in Montreal, not Rome.

On a night when Canada was looking for Lindros to lead the charge, it was his American-born Philadelphia Flyers linemate, John LeClair, who was the important offensive player, with two goals in the game. "He doesn't need Eric to be a great hockey player," Wilson said.

"Both teams have one hand on the World Cup," Wilson said after the second game. "It will be a slugfest to see who can get the other one on it."

The third game was billed as Canada's most important since its 1972 showdown with the Soviet Union. Canada fell behind 3–1 in that series before rallying to win 4–3–1, capturing the title on Moscow's soil in perhaps the most dramatic series in hockey history.

Doug Weight celebrates with teammates after a goal during the 1996 World Cup of Hockey.
(Doug Pensinger/Getty Images/USA Hockey)

The day before the game, Messier said he would play in Game 3, as if anyone really doubted he would. The Canadian media tried to coax him into guaranteeing a victory as he had during the 1994 playoffs. With the Rangers trailing 3–2 in a best-of-seven series, he guaranteed the Rangers would defeat the New Jersey Devils. He then went out and scored a hat trick to make sure it happened. In New York sports lore, his guarantee will be forever lumped with Joe Namath's prediction that his New York Jets would beat the Baltimore Colts in the 1969 Super Bowl and the myth or reality of Babe Ruth calling his home run hit.

But Messier offered no such guarantee in 1996.

When the Americans took the ice for Game 3 in Montreal, they were greeted by a multitude of Canadian flags. The province was divided over the issue of Quebec independence, but it was unified in the belief that Team Canada needed its support.

"We have to beat the lion in the lion's den," Wilson said before the game. No miracle was required to win the World Cup of Hockey that day.

"In the past, we said we could beat Canada," said Doug Weight. "But when we were in our hotel room, all alone, did we really believe it? Maybe not, but this team believed it."

They believed it when the Canadians were peppering goaltender Mike Richter with shot after shot in the second period. They believed it when the USA's Keith Tkachuk, who may be the NHL's best power winger of all time, received a controversial game-misconduct for slashing Adam Foote. They believed it even when Foote scored with 7:10 left to give Canada a 2–1 lead. After Foote scored, Chicago Blackhawks winger Tony Amonte and Philadelphia Flyers winger John LeClair started chirping on the bench. "We're still going to win," LeClair said.

Less than four minutes after Foote scored, the Americans began to remove themselves from the canvas. Brett Hull redirected Derian Hatcher's shot from the point past goaltender Curtis Joseph for what looked like the tying goal. But the referee indicated the goal would be reviewed by the replay official. Was Hull's stick above his shoulders? If it was, the goal would be disallowed. Hull was so nervous that he kept chirping at the officials that he hadn't even touched the puck. But the replay would show he had, but his stick wasn't too high.

Emotions boiled over on the bench, and Wilson suddenly realized that his team was in the 2–2 tie that he had talked about the first day of training camp.

"This is what we talked about," he shouted at players. "It's 2–2. We know what to do, and the Canadians don't. They thought they would be up 5–1 at this point."

The LeClair-Smolinski-Amonte line was up next for the Americans. That trio had been the USA's best all-around line in the tournament. Bryan Smolinski had been an unsung hero, doing a job at both ends of the ice. LeClair was leading the tournament in goals. Amonte was the designated hero. When he left the bench, it seemed as if his skates were barely touching the ice. He skimmed the surface of the ice like he had been expelled from a torpedo tube. He honed in on a point in front of the net as if his conversation with Wilson had preordained what was about to occur. The puck was on his stick, and in a flash, he tucked it in under the crossbar with a shot that flew upward like it had been lofted with a seven-iron.

The American bench boiled over. But again, the play would be reviewed because the referee thought Amonte might have kicked it in. The replays confirmed the goal, and for the second time in a minute, the American bench got to celebrate a goal.

Wilson quickly rechanneled his players' emotions, reminding them that 2:35 remained in the game. In the final two minutes, Wilson chose to use Leetch and Derian Hatcher as his two primary defensemen. Given that Chelios was available, it showed the respect Wilson had for Hatcher. Much to the surprise of 28 million Canadians, Team Canada would not pull off any last-minute heroics to turn defeat into victory.

Symbolism was available for those who needed it. With 47 seconds left, Mark Messier and Wayne Gretzky, two icons of Canadian hockey, misfired on a goal that would have tied the game 3–3. Messier had made a perfect pass to Gretzky, who was all alone in the goalmouth. Gretzky had probably redirected that same Messier pass into the goal a hundred times, but this time he couldn't handle it, and the puck skipped away. A second later, Derian Hatcher swatted the puck 180 feet down the ice and into the empty Canadian net. Adam Deadmarsh added another empty-net goal to make the final score 5–2.

When time expired, sticks went skyward and gloves were tossed all over the ice. Keith Tkachuk was carrying an American flag when he came back on the ice. Tears, laughter, relief—the gamut of human emotions was available for inspection on the Molson Centre ice.

This wasn't Lake Placid. No political implications were present. There would be no trip to the White House, no interruption of normal programming to tell the world of this victory, no appearances on *Good Morning America*. But everyone in the hockey world understood the significance of this moment.

No one understood more than Ron Wilson. He had played for the USA in international tournaments when the Americans didn't believe they had a chance against the Canadians.

After the celebration had moved from the ice to the dressing room, Wilson knew that it would be impossible to have a moment alone with his players once the door had opened and relatives and press were allowed in. Amid the shouting and hoopla, he had a moment of quiet to tell his winter knights they deserved their victory. He left them with only one final thought. It was Independence Day, and the Americans were driving the bus. ∎

Neal Broten—here with the Minnesota North Stars in the 1980s—was 39 years old, retired, and had been off the ice for a year when he joined the USA team for the International Ice Hockey Federation Qualification Tournament in November 1998. Broten scored six points in three games as the U.S. won the tournament. (Steve Babineau/NHLI via Getty Images/USA Hockey)

1998 QUALIFYING TOURNAMENT
The Old Men of Klagenfurt

When USA Hockey officials hatched the idea to use retired players at a crucial international tournament in 1998, the plan initially read more like a Hollywood script than an effective strategy to build a national team.

"It was really like the movie *Space Cowboys*," USA Hockey's executive director Dave Ogrean said. "It was like we were asking Clint Eastwood and James Garner to go into space."

Instead of asking senior-citizen astronauts to rescue a decaying Russian satellite, which happened in the plot of *Space Cowboys*, USA Hockey officials Lou Vairo and Art Berglund were asking NHL retirees Neal and Aaron Broten, Mark Johnson, and Joe Mullen to blend with a patchwork roster of younger players and European League veterans to rescue the Americans from the embarrassment of falling into the *B* Pool at the World Championships.

What began as a crazy idea turned out to be one of the most fascinating, feel-good stories in American hockey history.

Mullen was 41 and hadn't played in 17 months when he agreed to play, and Neal Broten was about to turn 39 and had also been out of the NHL for more than a full season when they signed on. The decision of Aaron Broten and Johnson to play was even more remarkable, considering that neither had played pro hockey in more than six years. At the time, Johnson was 41 and Aaron Broten was 38.

The mission that they agreed to undertake was to travel to Klagenfurt, Austria, to compete in an International Ice Hockey Federation Qualification Tournament. The Americans had to finish in the top two places in that tournament or they would be banished to the *B* tournament, where there was no guarantee that they would escape in a timely fashion.

The Americans found themselves in this predicament because they had finished 12th at the World Championship in Switzerland six months before. The problem in Switzerland was simple: the Americans didn't come close to bringing their best players to the World Championship. That tournament had been played three months after the 1998 Olympics. The majority of USA's stars were either still in the NHL playoffs, weary from a long season that included the Olympics, or still peeved that they weren't selected to play for USA in the Olympics. The end result had been that the Americans struggled to score goals in Switzerland; lost to France, Italy, and Sweden; and tied Germany. USA had been outscored 19–9.

To make matters worse, the 1998 Qualification tournament was being held from November 5–8.

Lou Vairo (left) and Art Berglund (right) were behind the concept of using retired NHL players to compete in Klagenfurt in 1998. (USA Hockey)

Trying to find available pro hockey players in North America in November is like trying to find available tax experts in the week before April 15.

Ben Smith, fresh from helping USA's women win the gold medal at the 1998 Games, was selected to coach the team, and 1984 U.S. Olympic coach Lou Vairo, also a USA Hockey staffer, was picked to be his associate coach.

In that summer, when Berglund was beginning to think about USA's roster, it was a conversation between him and Lou Vairo that was the catalyst for using retired NHL players.

The names of Neal Broten, Mark Johnson, and Aaron Broten were among the first to be discussed and other names followed.

Berglund, Smith, and Vairo loved the idea to the point that Vairo and Berglund also wanted to invite Joe Mullen. Vairo didn't believe there was any risk because he had always felt that a 22-person roster was too large anyway.

"Even if they can't play," Vairo insisted, "their mere presence, leadership qualities, gold medals, Stanley Cup championships, NCAA championships will add something to the team. Plus, these guys had a USA Hockey stamp on their heart."

Smith dubbed the older players "The Over the Hill Gang."

"The funniest part was the program," Johnson recalled. "They listed our names, numbers, and current teams. It was Joey Mullen. Retired. Neal Broten. Retired. Aaron Broten. Retired...it was hilarious. If you were an opponent or a fan, you were wondering, *Who the heck are we playing against?*"

In the opening game against Kazakhstan, Johnson lined up for a faceoff against 18-year-old Nikolai Antropov, who had been the Toronto Maple Leafs' first-round draft pick five months before. Johnson was old enough to be his father.

At age 41, Joe Mullen hadn't played in 17 months when he joined the team in Klagenfurt. Mullen, who scored more than 500 goals in his NHL career, contributed three assists in the tournament. (Mike Powell/Getty Images/USA Hockey)

"I'm thinking, *What the heck have we got ourselves into?*" Johnson said, laughing.

Former NHL player and active German Leaguer Corey Millen, 34 at the time, was named the team's captain.

Paul Broten, Neal and Aaron's younger brother, was playing in the International Hockey League. He was 33 at the time. Former NHL players Mike Hartman, 31, and Bob Sweeney, 35, were playing in Germany, and they agreed to play. Defenseman Greg Brown, 30, a 1988 Olympian and former NHL player, was also on the squad. Former Hobey Baker winner and Boston College's all-time leading scorer David Emma was 29, and he came aboard.

He actually had been playing for the Klagenfurt team in the Austrian League.

The goalies were Derek Herlofsky, Chris Rogles, and Parris Duffus, all of whom were having strong careers in Europe.

Duffus' importance in American hockey history was established in the spring of 1996 when he was the starting goalie for the U.S. National Team that won the bronze medal at the World Championship. It was USA's first medal at that tournament in 34 years.

Some younger players were added: the Carolina Hurricanes loaned defenseman Mike Rucinski, 23, to the team. There was even a nonpro, University of North Dakota senior Jason Blake. His coach, Dean Blais, had offered to loan Blake to USA Hockey for the tournament.

"He threw a few names out there that were playing, and it gave me goose bumps," Blake said.

A Minnesota native, Blake had grown up watching Broten playing for the Minnesota North Stars. Everyone in the Minnesota hockey community knew the legend of the Broten brothers. "[Blake] was the baby of the group," Smith said. "You could tell he was kind of in awe of some of those guys."

Mark Johnson, shown here as a 22-year-old member of the 1980 Miracle on Ice Olympic team, came out of retirement to play for Team USA in Klagenfurt.
(Bruce Bennett Studios/Getty Images)

When the team was being put together, Berglund told Vairo about wanting to add a young undrafted defenseman who was playing in the Finnish League. "His name is Brian Rafalski," Berglund said, "and he should be playing in the National Hockey League."

None of the three opponents in the Qualification Tournament were kingpins of international hockey but neither were most of the teams that defeated USA at the World Championship the previous May. A veteran of international hockey, Vairo understood that all countries have skilled players and pride. Vairo flew to Switzerland to watch Kazakhstan play a couple days before the tournament. Coached by the former Soviet National Team player Boris Alexandrov, Kazakhstan defeated Switzerland, and Smith made sure his players understood the importance of the tournament.

But Smith didn't have to say too much, because half the players on the team had been leaders during their pro careers. "I remember coming out of the coach's room before the first game, and I saw Neal Broten standing up in front of the team, and I just turned around and walked away," Smith said. "They were going to know how to handle it."

With all of the experience Vairo had in international hockey, he had not been around a team quite like this one. He recalled John Lilley sitting at his stall in the dressing room and missing the wastebasket with an eight-foot launch of a wadded-up ball of tape. The tape clunked off the rim and hit the floor.

"I was about to tell John to go pick it up, but I didn't," Vairo said. "Mullen was just in his jock-strap and skates, and he went over, picked it up, and sat back down. I looked at John Lilley, and he was stunned. That was leadership. All Mully was saying was, the equipment men are not our slaves, make sure you throw it in the trash. We had the cleanest dressing room in the tournament."

As it turned out, the tournament that started with angst over what kind of team the U.S. could pull together ended with Berglund saying, "It was one of the greatest teams we ever put together."

The Americans won all three games by a combined score of 12–1. Estonia was dispatched by a 7–0 verdict. USA defeated Kazakhstan 3–0 and toppled the host country 2–0.

"Neal was the best player in the tournament," Vairo said.

Hartman had 1,388 penalty minutes in 397 NHL games in the 1990s. With 316 penalty minutes in one season with the Buffalo Sabres, he was definitely known for his fighting ability. But in Klagenfurt he was known for his good humor and his scoring.

"Hartman was probably the happiest guy because he got to play with Neal," Johnson said, laughing. "Neal set him up, and he looked like a 50-goal scorer."

He also produced two goals and four assists to tie Broten for the points lead. "We started to call him Gretzky," Vairo recalled.

Vairo also recalls the self-restraint Hartman showed when Kazakhstan players began to play vindictive hockey near the end of their loss to the Americans. Their sticks were up. U.S. player Ken Gernander even lost a tooth. Emotions were boiling over. Hartman wanted to defend his teammates, but Vairo and Smith reminded him and other players that under international rules they would have to sit out a game for fighting. He told Hartman the team couldn't afford to lose him.

To make sure no U.S. players or Smith would be suspended, Vairo took it upon himself to represent the Americans. "I went to the end of the bench and yelled at Alexandrov," Vairo said. "I told him to

get his team under control or I would come after him and everyone else. I was angry. You shouldn't come to play in a tournament and lose a tooth."

Mark Johnson pulled his groin early in the first game and really couldn't play after that. But he insisted on sitting on the bench in his uniform for the final two games. Aaron Broten played all three games but didn't register a point. Mullen had three assists, playing the same style he always played in the NHL.

"Joey looked like he was in a pinball machine, pucks bouncing off of him, *bing, bing, bing,*" Vairo said.

The finale against Austria is mostly remembered as a fun game because of the festive atmosphere and the fact that the Americans had already wrapped up the tournament. "It was probably a 6,000-seat arena with 7,000 fans in it," Smith said.

As always seems to be the case in international hockey, the home team was friskier in its own barn with the crowd urging it on.

"It was almost like a soccer-type atmosphere, maybe a little louder," Rucinski said. "There was a buzz in the arena."

Ramped-up crowd or not, the Austrians couldn't handle the Americans. Neal Broten was the star of the show, leading the tournament with three goals and three assists.

"I remember they would put the old guys on the power play, and they would dominate," Rucinski said.

Before the tournament, Vairo had fretted most about Neal, because the other three players were all coaching, and they were at least on the ice every day. Neal Broten hadn't been on the ice at all since he retired.

Vairo had arranged for Broten to skate at the University of Minnesota before the tournament. "What I never knew until after the tournament was that Neal never went," Vairo said. "But he was still our best player. You can't beat talent. Either you got it, or you don't. You could have gotten Babe Ruth out of a sound sleep at 3:00 AM, half drunk, with a big gut, and he could wake up and hit a line drive. Other guys could work out eight hours per day and swing and miss three pitches. That's just the way it is."

It wasn't as if Broten didn't feel the impact of his inactivity. Before the final game against Austria, the coaches asked Neal whether he wanted to center a line with his two brothers on the wing.

"That would be great," he said, "as long as we can be the fifth line."

Neal admitted he was exhausted. "He was sensational in those first two games to solidify, but I think both his groin and hip flexor were all barking at him," Smith said, laughing.

The three Brotens playing on a line together on a U.S. team was a remarkable story by itself. Not since Gord, Roger, and Bill Christian played on the same USA team at the 1958 World Championship had three brothers been on one American national squad. The Brotens are among the most storied families in American hockey history, like the Christians, Suters, Millers, Mullens, Roberts, and others. Together, the three Brotens had played 2,169 NHL games and combined for 36 NHL seasons.

The sight of three Brotens lined up side-by-side was highly emotional for their father, Newell, who had made the trip.

"He came down around the bench, and he was crying," Vairo remembered. "He said it was the best thing he had ever seen. He said, 'My boys have never played on the same team.'"

Vairo told Newell Broten that he should be a sperm donor. "Three shots and you had three boys

At the time a college student at North Dakota, Jason Blake was loaned to the United States team for the 1998 Qualification Tournament. Blake has gone on to score more than 200 NHL goals over 13 seasons. (Matthew Manor/HHOF-IIHF Images)

who played in the NHL and on the U.S. National Team," Vairo told Newell. "You should be selling that stuff around the States."

In the name of making the game even more enjoyable for players, Vairo and Smith put together a Boston College line of Emma, Sweeney, and Mullen. Smith recalls everyone trying to set up Mullen for a goal, but it didn't happen.

"There wasn't a player on the team that disappointed us," Vairo said. "Every one of them, as players and people, was just sensational."

Millen had two goals and one assist. "He did the heavy lifting because he was still in the prime of his career," Smith said. "The [retired players] appreciated that he was nearer to the top of his game than they were."

Sweeney chipped in a couple of goals in that tournament, and Rucinski had a goal and an assist.

When Rucinski was playing on that team, he said his emphasis was on playing well because he wanted to further his NHL career. But he said he appreciated the novelty of the event years later when he looked up the statistics and sent them to his brother to show him who he had played with at that tournament.

"When I was there, I probably let it go too fast," Rucinski said. "I should have stopped and said, 'Look at these guys.'"

In looking back, Rucinski said the highlight for him was playing with 1980 Olympians Johnson and Broten. "That 1980 team was everything to me," Rucinski said. "I would watch that and cry... those guys did that, and I got to play with them. Now that is cool."

Vairo recalls NHL teams scouting Rafalski at that tournament, and by the next season he was playing in the NHL with the New Jersey Devils.

"One of the highlights was after we clinched after the second game, Lou Vairo went right into the kitchen at the hotel and cooked us up an Italian meal," Johnson said, laughing.

The consensus memory of the tournament is that a good time was had by all, right through the trip to U.S. customs, when the veterans played a prank on an unsuspecting Blake.

As the hockey bags were hauled into the secure area for screening, Blake noticed that the trained dogs had stopped at his bag, prompting customs agents to ask who owned that particular bag.

"When I went over to the bag, they asked if I had anything out of the ordinary in the bag, and I said no," Blake recalled. "Then they opened my bag, and there were about 40 pieces of fruit in there. Of course I had never touched my equipment, but the guys had filled my bag with oranges, apples, and every fruit possible."

It was, of course, illegal to transport fruit from one country to another, which meant Blake had to provide a reasonable explanation for an act that he knew nothing about. "They all were laughing as I had to go in the back and explain," Blake said. "It was all in good fun. I got a kick out of it, although not at the time, because I thought I was going to get in trouble."

In 2010–11, Blake and Rafalski were still active in the NHL, and Smith said when he sees Blake, now with Anaheim, or Rafalski, now with Detroit, "flying across my screen on *ESPN Sportscenter*, I think about that team."

"It was probably one of the most satisfying and unique coaching experiences I ever had," Smith said.

When Smith is hanging around hockey people, he likes to throw around a couple trivia questions that are guaranteed to stump the panel. "I like to say, 'Does anyone know who Mark Johnson's last coach was? Was it in Hartford, or Pittsburgh, or New Jersey?'" Smith says, chuckling. "Or I say, 'Joe Mullen scored more than 500 goals in the NHL. Who was his last coach?'"

No one guesses correctly that it was Smith.

Vairo has always had one regret about that 1996 team. "The guy we forgot to ask to be on that team was Dave Christian," Vairo said. Christian was a retired member of the 1980 U.S. Olympic Team. Said Vairo: "He would have been a perfect fit for that team." ∎

Kelly Dyer, left, and Erin Whitten both starred in goal for the USA national team in the late 1980s and early 1990s. Dyer and Whitten also both played men's minor league hockey. (USA Hockey)

USA HOCKEY WOMEN'S HOCKEY
Playing Like a Girl

The Granato family in Downers Grove, Illinois, has always loved hockey—the way the Kennedys loved politics and the Earnhardts loved racing. On weekends and during Christmas vacation, brothers Tony, Don, and Rob Granato often made a joyful journey to Schroeder Park each morning to play hockey, so naturally, younger sister Cammi did the same. From breakfast to bedtime, she skated alongside her brothers in one of America's true equal-opportunity pickup games.

"I never realized I was the only girl until later," Cammi said. Those innocent, fun-filled games at the park were Cammi Granato's first steps of what would be a difficult climb to the summit of women's ice hockey. Once outside the boundaries of Schroeder Park, Granato soon discovered some players, and a surprising number of adults, didn't want to see a girl playing what they considered a boys' game. She was treated as an interloper, an outsider, a minority trying to gain entrance to an exclusive club. All the affirmative action and Title IX legislation in America couldn't protect Granato

when she went into the corners with a boy who didn't believe she belonged on the ice.

When her peewee team was informed that girls weren't welcome at a tournament in Kitchener, Ontario, team officials listed Cammi Granato as "Carl" Granato. "I wore a baseball cap pulled down," Granato recalled.

At the Peewee National Boys' Tournament, Granato scored a goal and was immediately decked by an opposing player. Her linemate, Jeff Jestadt, popped her assailant with such force that he's probably still feeling it. "I was lucky, because it was like I had 19 brothers out there looking out for me," Cammi said.

Once, before a game, her cousin Bob Granato switched jerseys with Cammi because the opposing team's players were threatening to single out her No. 21 for special abuse. Imagine their surprise when No. 21 turned out to be 6 feet tall, and not 5'6".

When Granato entered bantam hockey, where checking is allowed, she was subjected to a higher degree of danger. One opposing coach told Granato's

Cammi Granato became a star women's player at Providence College, scoring 89 goals during her junior and senior seasons, a school record. (Jeff Gross/Getty Images/USA Hockey)

coach that if Cammi played, "We will break her shoulders."

A similar situation was playing out in River Falls, Wisconsin, where Karyn Bye would have her name listed as K.L. Bye on tournament scoresheets to prevent players from taking the usual "extra runs" at her. But her years of playing tough hockey against the boys also paid off for her when she made the boys' high school team and then went on to become a star in women's international hockey. Bye was a novelty in high school. River Falls parents would often make the opposing team's parents guess which player was the girl. Given that Bye had short hair and everyone was

wearing a full face shield, it was very difficult for anyone to say for sure, especially since her talent level was on par with most of the boys on the team. Usually the opposing team's parents would say the girl was the player with the long hair, who happened to be a boy with a mustache.

Because of the lack of female leagues, many early pioneers in women's hockey were usually forced to test their skills against boys before finding elite-level women's competition. That was certainly true for goaltender Karen Koch, who may have been the first American woman to be paid to play hockey.

Koch was from Gibraltar, Michigan, and she signed to play for $40 per game for the Marquette Iron Rangers in the United States Hockey League in 1969–70. She was a 19-year-old freshman at Northern Michigan University when she made the Iron Rangers through an open tryout.

"She's got a lot of guts," said Iron Rangers left wing Robert Caster in an Associated Press story written about Koch (pronounced *Cook*) in 1969.

In an article in *Marquette Monthly* written by her former Iron Rangers coach Leonard "Oakie" Brumm, he admitted that he didn't even know Koch was female until team captain Barry Cook informed him 20 minutes into practice. Cook only knew because another Northern Michigan student had told him. Koch had purposely come into the practice with her mask on.

When Brumm pulled aside Koch to talk to her, she admitted that she had enrolled at Northern Michigan specifically to play for the Iron Rangers. She also confessed that no Detroit-area senior team would give her a chance. Brumm told Koch he would give her a "fair shot."

"In subsequent practices she showed remarkable ability," Brumm wrote. "Her only drawback was her size. Both of our goalies were big guys.

They stopped more pucks by accident than she did on purpose."

Normally Brumm preferred to keep 18 skaters and two goalies on his roster, but he decided to keep 17 skaters and three goalies in 1969–70 because he wanted to see what Koch could accomplish in games. His decision wasn't greeted warmly by veterans who didn't like having a woman on the team, even though, according to Brumm, most of them admitted that she was as skilled as the Iron Rangers' regular backup.

Undeniably, there was a marketing advantage for the Iron Rangers to keep Koch. Her arrival had spawned calls from several news outlets in both the United States and Canada.

The Iron Rangers' first game of the season was scheduled to be played in Sault Sainte Marie, Ontario, and rumors began to percolate that Koch would start there. The team asked Brumm to allow Koch to face the local mayor, a former player, in a one-on-one shootout contest before the game. The Iron Rangers went along with the promotion, and Koch knocked away the mayor's shot. She received a standing ovation.

In consideration of the big crowd, Brumm started Koch, and she stopped 10 of 12 shots in the first period. He replaced her with No. 1 goalie Brian Lunney, and the Iron Rangers won 5–3.

A crowd of 5,000 showed up in Green Bay, and Brumm felt obligated to start Koch again. She was in the 1–1 game in the first period when she was injured by veteran Paul Coppo's slap shot and had to leave the contest. Coppo had played for the U.S. National Team in the 1960s.

"She played as well as any previous backups when I used her," Brumm wrote in his *Marquette Monthly* article. "She wasn't solid enough to start and play regularly because the league was too good."

Koch didn't last the entire season, but not because of her ability. She refused to wear a mask in games, even though Brumm ordered her to wear one. He released her with 10 games left in the season. Koch left school and went to Canada with the hope of playing, only to have the Canadian Amateur Hockey Association bar her from playing on men's teams.

Team USA celebrates after its 6–0 win over China in the semifinals of the 1997 IIHF Women's World Championship. The United States won the silver medal in that tournament, falling to Canada in the finals. (Paul J. Sutton/USA Hockey)

The origin of women's hockey is less defined than its male counterpart. Canada had prominent women's teams even before World War I. It is believed that there were women's games played in Canada in 1892, even before the men's college game developed in the United States. The modesty of women's apparel at that time dictated that female athletes develop their own unique style. *A Brief History of Women's Hockey,* released by Canadian Hockey, states women would "protect pucks under their skirts" as they stickhandled down the ice, and goaltenders would spread their skirts across the goal line to stop the puck. Female goaltenders would sew lead linings into their hems to help them stop pucks. "Considering how high the skirts are worn now, that wouldn't be much help," said U.S. goaltending legend Kelly Dyer.

Women's hockey in America developed slower, although there were early women's teams. The first known U.S. women's team was the Seattle Vamps, playing as early as 1916. NHL legends Frank and Lester Patrick discussed the formation of a women's Pacific Coast Hockey Association, but it was never launched. Hall of Famer Bill Stewart, who guided the 1937–38 Chicago Blackhawks to the Stanley Cup championship, coached the 1924 Radcliffe women's team.

But the Depression, followed by World War II, stifled the growth of women's hockey in Canada and the United States. In terms of structure and recognition, women's hockey didn't regenerate in the United States until the 1970s when college teams began to appear. In the 1980s, USA Hockey began crowning champions in girls' peewee (11 and 12) and midget (15 and 16) age groups. At the same time, women's college hockey was beginning to gain a foothold. When the Eastern College Athletic Conference began holding playoffs to crown what was really the national champion, U.S. women's hockey was here to stay.

The nation's first continuous women's college program arrived at Brown in the mid-1960s, after Brown's men's coach Jim Fullerton, now a member of the U.S. Hockey Hall of Fame, had allowed Nancy Schieffelin to play in one of his practices to show his players how talented she was. The event created a buzz on campus, and soon a group of women was knocking on the door of the school's physical education director, Arlene Gorton. The group wanted to start a women's team.

About 20 women were on the first team, coached by Sarah Phillips, and Fullerton allowed the team to practice with the men's team for a short period to gain experience. According to the Pembroke Center at Brown, team members originally sold rule sheets at men's games to raise money to buy equipment. The team was playing by the 1965–66 season. Eventually the team became known as the Pembroke Pandas. Initially, the team had to play against Canadian teams because that was the only available competition. In 1971 Cornell started a team. In 1976 the first Ivy League women's tournament was held, and Cornell won.

One of the early women's pioneers was Colby College's Lee Johnson, a member of the Massachusetts Hall of Fame. She came to Colby when the program launched in 1975 and led the team in scoring for four seasons, even though she played defense. On February 26, 1979, she was listed among *Sports Illustrated*'s Faces in the Crowd because she had 23 goals in the first 14 games of the season.

Cindy Curley and Lauren Apollo were premium American players in the 1980s. "I remember seeing Cindy Curley playing for the Assabet Valley team [in Concord, Massachusetts] and saying I want to be like her," said 1998 U.S. Olympian Katie King. "To me, Cindy Curley and Lauren Apollo seemed they were six-foot-eight."

In 1987 the Americans played in an unofficial World Championship Tournament that was held in Toronto. The team wasn't sponsored by the Amateur Hockey Association of the United States. Instead, Assabet Valley coach Carlton Gray organized the trip, pledging $6,000 of his own money, according to a *New York Times* article. That news story reported that goaltender Jackie Haggerty quit her job as a crane operator to play in the tournament.

In the first official World Championship, Curley had 11 goals and 12 assists for 23 points in five games.

"I remember I was at my first U.S. development camp, and the national team was there practicing," King said. "I remember watching these players and thinking that they were so good. I remember thinking, *I want to be that good*. I was 14 or 15. It wasn't like I was 9 or 10. There were a lot of people that came before us that didn't get to play in the Olympics."

The Americans did play a lead role in championing women's hockey on the international front. Former USA Hockey Chairman of the Board Walter Bush was the mover and shaker in making women's hockey an Olympic sport in 1998. USA Hockey committee member Bob Allen had also lobbied aggressively for the sport.

"It was very difficult to get women's hockey in the Olympics," Bush said. "I wrote a letter to the IOC and suggested they put women's hockey into the Olympics. I got a letter back, about four lines, that said: 'Thank you for your inquiry, but you must understand that we already have women's hockey in the Olympics in the Summer Games. It's called field hockey.'"

Bush quickly learned that two official World Championships would be needed to establish legitimacy, and he joined forces with Canada's Murray Costello to officially launch those in 1990 in Ottawa.

"We took movies of the tournament and sent them to the IOC, and they said, "You sped these movies up,'" Bush recalled. "I sent them footage of Canada vs. USA, and it wasn't anything like it is today, but it was pretty impressive. They could see that these women could skate."

Bush recalls that the late Gunther Sabetzki, then president of the International Ice Hockey Federation, supported women's hockey at the Olympics but had odd concerns, such as whether the women's long hair would lead to hair-pulling during games.

The second IIHF-sanctioned World Championship was in Finland, and Bush said he got "lucky" that Finnish women on the International Olympic Committee liked the sport and gave him another ally.

"We wanted to put them in the Norway Olympics [in 1994], and we pushed hard," Bush said. "It was too quick, because they already had their programs set. The Japanese also had their programs set too for 1998, but they said they could make it work as long as they had a team in there."

Knowing that the Olympics would generate increased interest in women's hockey, USA Hockey executive director Dave Ogrean wanted the NCAA to immediately sanction a women's national tournament. "But the NCAA decided there weren't enough college teams to justify a women's Frozen Four, so we said, 'Fine we will do it ourselves,'" Ogrean recalled.

The American Women's College Hockey Alliance was formed in 1997–98. A national poll was developed, and the top four teams were brought together

Dick Kazmaier, the 1951 Heisman Trophy winner, poses with his hockey-playing daughters—Kathy of New Hampshire and Patty of Princeton. Patty Kazmaier, a standout player at Princeton, died of a rare blood disease in 1990 at the age of 28. In 1998, USA Hockey introduced the Patty Kazmaier Memorial Award as the women's version of the Hobey Baker Award. The award is given annually to the top women's college player in the country. (USA Hockey)

to play in a national tournament. In 1998 the first AWCHA tournament was held and New Hampshire defeated Brown 4–1. Winny Brodt, the former Minnesota Ms. Hockey, was named the tournament's Most Valuable Player. During the regular season, Brodt, a defender, had produced 11 goals and 34 points in 39 games. That was her only season at New Hampshire. She transferred to Minnesota, where

she finished her career. She played for U.S. National Teams in 2000 and 2001.

Under that format, Harvard won the title in 1999 and Minnesota won in 2000. The NCAA took over the tournament in 2001, and Minnesota-Duluth, coached by former Canadian Olympic coach Shannon Miller, won the first three tournaments and five out of the first 10.

"We had a few people internally that didn't want the NCAA to take it away from us," Ogrean recalled. "And I said, 'You are missing the point...that has been the goal all along. The sport will be elevated.'"

With an idea of growing the game, USA Hockey also introduced the Patty Kazmaier Memorial Award in 1998, as the women's version of the Hobey Baker Award. It would be given annually to the top women's college player in the country in recognition of Kazmaier, who had been a standout player at Princeton in the 1980s. The daughter of former Heisman Trophy winner Dick Kazmaier, Patty had died of a rare blood disease.

The first winner was New Hampshire standout Brandy Fisher in 1989, and of the first 14 award winners, six were from Harvard. Jennifer Botterill is the only two-time winner.

"Sometimes I get grief that a Canadian wins it," Ogrean said. "But the purpose was to honor the best player in women's college hockey, not the best American player in women's college hockey. It's been good for the college game. Today, it's known by one name. Everyone now says, 'Who are the finalists for the Patty.' It's taken on a life of its own, and we are proud of it."

U.S. Olympians who have won the award include A.J. Mleczko (Harvard), Krissy Wendell (Minnesota), Angela Ruggiero (Harvard), Julie Chu (Harvard), Jessie Vetter (Wisconsin), and Meghan Duggan (Wisconsin).

Although women's college hockey still doesn't draw as well as its men's counterpart, it continues to grow steadily. On January 29, 2011, a new women's college attendance mark was set when Wisconsin defeated Minnesota 3–1 in front of 10,688 fans at the Kohl Center. The previous mark was 8,263 set during an outdoor game between Wisconsin and Bemidji State at Wisconsin's Camp Randall Stadium on February 6, 2010.

Julie Chu was a member of the 2002, 2006, and 2010 U.S. Olympic teams. While playing for Harvard, she won the Patty Kazmaier Award in 2007. (Bruce Kluckhohn)

Before the record went over 10,000, the previous high for an indoor women's college game was 5,377 when Wisconsin entertained St. Cloud on January 26, 2008.

Milestones along the way have marked women's hockey as a sport on the rise. In 1992 Minnesota became the first state to recognize girls' hockey as a varsity sport. In 2010–11, there were 124 girls' teams competing to play in the 17th annual high school tournament.

In 1996, before women played at the Olympics and before there was a national women's college championship, there was a one-for-the-ages Eastern College Athletic Conference championship game between New Hampshire and Providence. The Wildcats defeated Providence 3–2, but it took five overtimes. The elapsed time of 145 minutes, 35 seconds made it the longest ice-hockey game in NCAA history. The previous record of 102 minutes, 19 seconds was set December 21, 1968, when North Dakota defeated Minnesota 5–4 in a men's game.

New Hampshire sophomore Brandy Fisher drove home a rebound for the game winner after Providence netminder Meghan Smith had stopped Dottie Carlin's initial shot from the point.

"I've coached in three World Championships, and I've never seen a game like this," said New Hampshire coach Karen Kay. "I don't think anybody at this game can say they have ever seen a better hockey game, men's or women's."

New Hampshire's win ended Providence's four-year hold on the Eastern College Athletic Conference title and completed a 24–0–2 season for the Wildcats. Goaltender Dina Solimini also tied New Hampshire's school record for wins in a career, previously held by Cathy Narsiff and Erin Whitten.

"The women's game has been elevated by leaps and bounds," said goaltender Kelly Dyer, a four-time member of the U.S. National Team.

Dyer was the goaltender in the first World Championship gold-medal game in 1990. That tournament ignited passion for women's hockey more than any other previous experience. The level of play and player enthusiasm proved women were ready to take their sport to a higher level.

"I remember looking at the crowd of 10,000 and saying, 'This is amazing,'" said Granato, who was 18 at the time. "We were used to playing in front of 200 people."

The Americans actually took a 2–0 lead in the gold-medal game before the Canadians came from behind to win in front of the home fans. The Canadians outshot the Americans 41–10, although Team USA dominated the first period.

"I'll never forget when Canada got its first goal, my whole rib cage was vibrating from the force of their [the Canadian fans'] cheering," said Dyer, named Most Valuable Player of that gold-medal game.

What the Americans learned in Ottawa was that their top players—such as Granato, Bye, O'Leary, Dyer, and others—could compete evenly with the Canadians. But they couldn't match the Canadians' depth. It was the same lament that the American men had when they played the Canadians in the Canada Cup series.

In the first Women's World Championship, full body-checking was allowed. After watching that event, International Ice Hockey Federation officials decided body-checking slowed the game, and the Women's World Championship has been played under no-check rules since 1992. Most players applauded the decision. It wasn't that they minded being hit, but the women hit so much that the game was very slow in the third period because players were weary from hitting and getting hit for two periods.

The no-checking edict allowed the women to sharpen their passing and shooting skills. As a result, the international games became quicker, particularly in the third period.

"But if you are watching, it probably still seems like there is some checking out there," Bye says. "Sometimes it's hard to tell whether it was a collision or a check."

Erin Whitten, Kelly Dyer, and Angela Ruggiero have become important figures in American women's hockey history because they brought more awareness to female players by signing with men's minor league teams. Their ability to play men's professional hockey, even for a short time, brought attention to the idea that female players had impressive hockey talent.

Canadian goaltender Manon Rheaume broke the gender barrier by appearing in an NHL exhibition game for the Tampa Bay Lightning against the St. Louis Blues in 1992. At the time, Whitten played for the University of New Hampshire. "I hope she makes it because maybe I will be next," Whitten told USA Today.

Only 14 months later, Whitten was playing for the Toledo Storm in the East Coast Hockey League. On October 30, 1993, she made hockey history by becoming the first female goaltender to record a win in a pro game. Replacing the injured Alain Harvey in the second period of a game against the Dayton Bombers, Whitten stopped 15 of 19 shots to record a 6–5 win. "I'm in the record books, and that's great," Whitten said. "But that's not what I'm concerned about. I'm just doing what I love to do."

When she entered the game, the score was tied 1–1. Whitten impressed teammates with her grit and determination. "Erin is developing more rapidly than we had anticipated," Storm coach Chris McSorley said at the time. "We feel strongly that she can be a solid backup for this team."

McSorley had signed Whitten after her impressive four-day tryout with the Adirondack Red Wings of the American Hockey League. It was an appropriate launching pad for Whitten, who was lured into the sport by the Red Wings' prominence in her hometown of Glen Falls, New York. After one day of practice with the Red Wings, she was drawing favorable comparisons to Rheaume.

"This is not a marketing scheme," Adirondack coach Newell Brown said. "She deserves to play. This is not something where we're sacrificing the integrity of the game."

His initial scouting assessment of Whitten supported that statement. "She's quick and agile moving around the net. You'd think at this level, a female goaltender might flinch. But at the end of practice, players were drilling the net, and she was standing in and making the save. Whether she is good enough to play at this level, I doubt. But she's worthy of a game. I have no reservations about giving her ice time."

Whitten received that playing time in an exhibition game against the Cornwall Aces. She received a standing ovation from the crowd when it was announced she was entering the game in the second period. She surrendered a goal to Paul Brousseau when she was screened on the first shot she faced, but her instincts, talent, and training quickly overcame the nervousness she was feeling that night. She stopped 10 of 12 shots, including a dazzling stop when Niklas Andersson and Pat Nadeau came down the ice on a two-on-one break. When Andersson batted a rebound out of the air toward the net, Whitten spun post-to-post to rob him with a glove save. The crowd erupted in delight.

"I was nervous before she played, because I'm the father—I've been nervous since she was eight years old," quipped her father, Peter, after the game.

Whitten said her focus wasn't shaken by the first goal. "I had pumped myself up for that one period," she said. "I don't know what would have happened had I played more than that."

Mental preparation was always one of Whitten's strong suits. As a young player in Glens Falls, New York, she needed mental toughness to compete against the boys, although Whitten says she never really experienced any gender bashing until she began playing for Glens Falls High School. Before that, her teammates, many of whom had played in front of her for many years, had no problem with a girl being their starting goaltender. But the taunting in high school didn't prevent Whitten from leading her team to the Division II state semifinals, where they lost 4–2 to Salmon River, the eventual state champion.

Peter Whitten said he never worried about seeing his daughter play against boys. "She learned to take care of herself," the elder Whitten said. "She wouldn't let anyone intimidate her."

Accustomed to playing against boys, Whitten was surprised to discover during her junior year in high school that women's varsity college hockey actually existed. Teams in the Eastern College Athletic Conference, which had been crowning a champion every year since 1984, wanted Whitten, but she wasn't sure she wanted ECAC hockey. "I was skeptical," Whitten said. "I thought about playing Division III men's hockey."

But Whitten never regretted her decision to play women's college hockey, where she was able to develop into an elite-level netminder. In four years at New Hampshire, Erin posted a 51–14–4 record, with a 2.62 goals-against average. She won two ECAC titles, the women's version of the national championship.

Another member of that New Hampshire team was Karyn Bye, who is also considered among the world's best players. In the early years of women's hockey, Bye and Kelly O'Leary were said to have two of the hardest shots in women's international hockey.

Kelly Dyer also played boys' high school hockey at Acton-Boxboro in Massachusetts, first as one of the backups to Tom Barrasso, who would jump directly from high school to the NHL with the Buffalo Sabres in 1983. As a senior, Dyer would earn a chance to play eight games.

Dyer started out in the Boxboro figure-skating program, the same program where Nancy Kerrigan began her skating career. But Dyer quickly discovered she liked diving for loose pucks more than she liked cranking up for double axles.

By the time she reached Northeastern University in 1985, Dyer was receiving considerable recognition as perhaps the world's best female netminder. (Erin Whitten hadn't yet reached high school, and Manon Rheaume was still four years away from earning any notoriety.) Dyer posted a 47–6–2 record at Northeastern, with 10 career shutouts and a career goals-against average of 2.01.

"She was so awesome," said Granato, who played against her in college. "It was like playing against Mike Richter. She was intimidating. Just her presence was intimidating."

At 5'11", Dyer was physically imposing to most of her competitors. Her pro opportunities didn't come immediately after college. She played for the Assabet Valley women's senior team in Massachusetts and helped them win two USA Hockey national titles, while keeping in shape for international competition. Dyer was 4–1 in the first Women's World Championship with a 3.60 goals-against average. In her international career, she is 8–1 with a 1.91 goals-against average.

Her performance in international competition drew some notice from minor league men's teams. Dyer followed Rheaume and Whitten as the third woman to play in the minors when she appeared in a Sunshine League game for the West Palm Beach Blaze on January 4, 1994. She played nine games that season and posted a 3–0 record and 5.25 goals-against average. In the 1995–96 season, she played nine games, posting a 3.41 goals-against average.

In 2005–06, Bill Ruggiero was playing for the Tulsa Oilers in the Central Hockey League when he dialed up his older sister Angela and made a pronouncement that was clearly designed to convince her to visit him. "You are better than our defensemen—you should come and skate with us," Bill Ruggiero said.

Angela took Bill up on his offer, skated with his team, and was surprised to later receive a call that the Oilers wanted her to play a game. She jumped at the opportunity. "I saw [Canada's] Hayley Wickenheiser was playing in Europe, and I'm bigger than Hayley. I could knock her over any second I wanted," joked Angela Ruggiero, who is 5'9" and weighs 185 pounds.

On January 8, 2005, she played for the Oilers in a 7–2 victory against the Rio Grande Valley Killer Bees. She played more than six minutes, recording an assist and a plus-2 rating to become the first woman other than a goalie to make more than a token appearance in a North American men's pro league. (Whitten had skated 18 seconds at forward for the Flint Generals in 1996.)

"No one said anything to me," Ruggiero said. "Everyone was respectful to me. But they were physical in the corners. To be honest, I blended into the men's game. Remember, this is minor pro, not the NHL. There were guys who were shorter than me, or skinnier than me. I was in the middle."

Ruggiero, one of the more physical players in the women's game, delivered several body checks in her pro debut. She came away feeling satisfied but regretful that she didn't accept the offer she

Angela Ruggiero poses with the silver medal she earned as a member of the 2010 U.S. Olympic Team. (Warren Little/Getty Images/USA Hockey)

received to play in the CHL on a regular basis. She wishes now she would have tried that after the 2006 Olympics in Torino, Italy.

"I felt like I fit in," Ruggiero said. "I do actually think I could have played there. Like any new athlete playing a first game in a new league, you have to adjust to the speed...but at the end of the day, I said I could definitely do this." ■

Cammi Granato and teammates celebrate after the USA won the 1998 Olympic gold medal. (USA Hockey)

1998 WOMEN'S OLYMPICS
Stinging Like a Bee

As coach Ben Smith prepared his U.S. team to deliver a knockout blow to Canada in the first women's Olympic tournament in 1998, he decided to let Muhammad Ali show the women how it was done.

Before the Americans launched their pre-Olympic tour, the team's sports psychologist Peter Haberl had suggested players watch *When We Were Kings*, Leon Gast's Academy Award–winning documentary film about Ali's 1974 triumph over George Foreman in Zaire. The 89-minute journalistic tour de force spells out in rich detail how underdog Ali rode emotion and creative tactics to seize Foreman's heavyweight crown.

"When you see a documentary like that, it plants the seed that anything can happen if you believe in yourself," U.S. player Karyn Bye recalled.

Smith's objective from his first day on the job was to keep the motivational campfires burning at all times for his players. He wanted them to appreciate the passion, dedication, and work ethic Ali poured into his quest to win the World Boxing Title that had been stripped from him when he had refused to be conscripted into military service. Detailed in Gast's work was Ali's decision to embrace the innovative "rope-a-dope" and a risky "right-hand lead" strategy in the early round. Boxers don't like to lead with a right hand because it exposes them to the possibility of a heavy counterattack.

Anyone who watched the documentary understood the "all-in" conviction that Ali took to Zaire. It was the same level of conviction that Smith wanted the U.S. players to take to Big Hat Stadium in Nagano, Japan. He wanted his American players to want the gold as badly as Ali wanted his championship belt. Smith wanted his players to float like a butterfly and sting like a bee.

In theory, the decision to have women's hockey at the Olympics offered a clean slate for determining world order in women's hockey. But the reality was the Canadians had been the heavyweight champions of women's hockey longer than Foreman had owned the boxing crown.

Before the Olympic tournament in Nagano, the IIHF had hosted four World Championships in

Karyn Bye, who was inducted into the IIHF Hall of Fame in 2011, celebrates after scoring one of her team-leading five goals in the 1998 Olympics. (USA Hockey)

women's hockey, and the Canadians had won them all.

The good news for the Americans was that by 1997 there seemed to be a narrowing of the continental hockey divide between the USA and Canadian women's programs. At the World Championship in 1997, the Canadians had barely survived a 4–3 overtime victory.

The American program seemed to be adding more dominant players quicker than the Canadian changeover, although Cammi Granato and Bye were still stalwarts of the U.S. program.

"They were both great athletes," Smith said. "Cammi was a crafty, wily, sniff-it-out type player while Karyn was a power forward. She had a bomb of a shot if you gave her time for the big windup. Cammi was a little deke, a little pull. She was slippery, all finesse."

But there was a buzz about several young Americans, including defender Tara Mounsey, a teenager who had been New Hampshire High School Player of the Year after leading the Concord High School boys' team to a state championship.

Heading into the 1998 Games in Nagano, Smith believed Mounsey, a freshman at Brown, was the world's most dominant female player. "I think everyone on our team would agree that she was in a class physically that was different." Smith said. "Her on-ice skills were way above the rest. Skating. Strength. Shot. Puck handling. Toughness. She seemed like a woman among girls."

High school player Angela Ruggiero of Harrison Township, Michigan, had also made Team USA's defense. She turned 18 just a month before the Olympic tournament, but she was 5'9", 180 pounds, and she had the skill level that made her an easy choice for Smith.

Smith seemed like the right fit for the Americans in 1998. He had a strong résumé in men's sports, and his style seemed to play well with female players. He was a practical coach, with many sides to his personality. The women seemed amused with his frequent use of video to illustrate points, although his choices often dated him. He was making a point using the movie *Butch Cassidy and the Sundance Kid*, when he realized that none of his players had seen it. However, sometimes it didn't matter that the players were unfamiliar with his dated cultural references. For instance, when Smith used Jackie Gleason in a *Honeymooners* episode to explain a problem with his national team's offense, it received a very favorable response. Smith compared the women's reluctance to shoot the puck to Ed Norton sitting down to write. He would crack his knuckles, prepare his paper, stretch his shoulders—and then never quite get down to the actual writing. "That used to drive Ralph Kramden nuts," Smith said, perhaps suggesting that it was also making him nuts that the women did all the preparation and then never shot the puck. Players liked his style in 1998.

In the pre-Olympic tour, it was clear that the Americans were finally in a position to push back against Canada's dominance. The two teams played 13 times, with Canada winning seven and the USA winning six.

"I never really felt like an underdog," Bye admits. "I felt like we had just as good of a chance of winning as Canada did."

It was a memorable, sentimental journey for the Americans heading to Nagano. Of the 54 players invited to the eight-day training camp at Lake Placid, only 25 made the pre-Olympic roster. Some of those who were cut in the first wave were veterans from the first women's World Championship. Bye recalled the strangeness of feeling personally elated for making the pre-Olympic roster and being "sick to [her] stomach" because several longtime teammates had been sent home.

"It was brutal," Smith said. "There were a bunch who had been involved long before I got involved. It's tough when you are cut from the women's program. You can't slam the door, say 'Screw you,' and go to your NHL club. When you are cut in women's hockey, it usually marks the end."

The final cuts included goalie Erin Whitten, who had already played men's pro hockey, plus defenseman Kelly O'Leary, who had played in four World Championships. Although players who made the final roster were ecstatic, some had survivor's guilt. They were going to battle another day, while teammates were left behind.

"That last cut is something that I will never forget because of the emotions that we went through...people you had been with eight months were getting cut," said 1988 U.S. Olympian Katie King, who was head coach at Boston College in 2011.

Whitten had probably been the favorite to be the No. 1 goalie, but youngsters Sara DeCosta and Sarah Tueting had simply played too well to be left off.

"I'm sure that surprised us as much as it surprised Erin," Smith said.

As difficult as these situations were, those emotional moments may have helped bring the team together. Statistically, all of the players had come to camp with less than a 50-50 chance to make the roster. They had all run the gauntlet and had come out the other side stronger for the experience.

A key test of the team's mental toughness had come in the fall of 1997 during the Three Nations Tournament in the United States. The first USA-Canada game was played in Burlington, Vermont. The game was televised nationally by the Lifetime

Network, a rare occurrence for that era. The Americans built a 4–1 lead only to have the Canadians storm from behind to win. The angry Americans wanted to retreat quickly to their dressing room, but Smith ordered the door to remain closed. He wanted the hurt to be remembered. "I want you to listen to the Canadians celebrate in our building," Smith said.

Today, Smith admits his intent was "to rub their noses" in it. "I wanted them to absorb what had happened to us," Smith said. "It was a televised game, and it wasn't like women's hockey was too big of a deal back then. I thought that maybe the next time we [wouldn't] let that happen to us."

The tournament moved to Lake Placid for the championship game, and the Americans claimed a 2–0 decision to win their first championship against the Canadians.

"Winning that tournament started to make believers out of some of the older players," Smith recalled.

By the time the Americans arrived in Nagano, even the raw players had become seasoned veterans. The Americans respected the Canadians, but they didn't fear them.

"If I think back, there were people saying this is it, this is our time," Bye said. "To be honest, I was getting sick of losing to the Canadians at every World Championship."

The Rumble in the Jungle title that was attached to the Ali-Foreman bout also could apply to the Canada-USA rivalry in women's hockey in the years leading up to the first Olympic meeting.

"In most of our games against Canada, my No. 1 concern was the health of our players," Smith said. "We had kids knocked out," he said. "The sport then was not for the faint of heart."

Smith had a background in the Harvard vs. Yale rivalry and the Boston College vs. Boston

University rivalry and has often said, "For my money, the Canadian and U.S. rivalry has been every bit as heated."

Although the rivalry remains intense even today, it seems as if there was more animosity in the first decade of women's international hockey because players didn't know each other as well outside the competition. Today, the vast majority of Canadian players come north of the border to play at U.S. colleges. In today's international tournaments, U.S. and Canadian players are often playing against teammates or even roommates from their college teams. In the 1990s there was no such fraternal bond between the players.

Also, in the earlier years of women's hockey, there was still indecision about how the game should be officiated. In 2011 Ruggiero, still an active player, watched a replay of the 1998 gold-medal game for the first time and was struck by how much physical play was allowed.

"[Officials] were letting things go that in today's game would be called in a second," Ruggiero observed. "It was a rougher game back then. In the Canada-U.S. rivalry...you wouldn't want to call it hatred. But it was so intense that you would do anything to beat Canada. I mean anything. When Shelley Looney threw her face in front of a shot in the World Championships, it wasn't a surprising thing."

Given the hostility between Canada and the USA, it was not surprising there was controversy heading into the gold-medal game. The Canadians claimed Sandra Whyte had made an insensitive remark regarding Canadian player Danielle Goyette's late father. He had died of Alzheimer's disease two days before the opening ceremony.

The boiling-over that happened in Nagano was not unexpected, because Canada had lost a 7–4 decision to the USA in the preliminary round. The

Canadians built a 4–1 lead and watched as the Americans scored six times in the third period. There were 48 penalty minutes in the game, including seven infractions for checking. The accusation against Whyte seemed like a symptom, rather than a cause for the hostility.

Whyte vehemently denied that she said anything about Goyette's father, and the Americans were infuriated by the accusation, saying the Canadians were simply trying to upset Whyte before the big game. "Anyone who knows Sandra Whyte knows she is the sweetest person in the world," Bye said. "She wouldn't say 'boo' to anyone. And I think she was hurt by that. When you get accused of something like that, and you didn't do it, it is hurtful."

Today, the Americans can look back and see a pattern of the Canadians accusing the American women's team of some alleged insult at every Olympic Games. In 2002 Canada accused the Americans of stomping on their flag, which was also vehemently denied by the U.S. women. At another Olympics, the Canadians said the Americans disrespected them with their comments.

The Americans view the traditional Canadian Olympic accusations as part of Canada's psychological warfare. "They always have something," said Ruggiero, a veteran of four Olympic Games. "I always say, 'What's it going to be this year to detract from what's really going on?'"

Ruggiero remembers she was "dumbfounded" by the accusation against Whyte. A bioanthropology major at Harvard, Whyte was considered among USA's quietest players. "My teammates all found it humorous that I would get into a controversy," Whyte told the *New York Times*.

There was no question in Ben Smith's mind that Whyte had been targeted because she was central to USA's strategy against their Northern neighbors. He has often referred to Whyte as "the best player you have never heard of." "Sandra Whyte was probably the unsung hero of that group," he said. "She was probably the best forward we had in terms of skating. She was the fastest. She was the one who could push the pace for us."

Hayley Wickenheiser was Canada's dynamic presence up front, and Smith liked to use Whyte on the ice against Wickenheiser. "She was sensational in the tournament," Smith said. "She could outskate the Canadians...as strong as [Wickenheiser] was, she couldn't keep up with Whyte. She was the straw that stirred the drink for us."

In hindsight, the accusation directed toward Whyte may have spurred her to the best performance of her career in the chase for the gold medal. "She wasn't in the media like Cammi or Karyn, but she could be the best player on the ice and make the difference," Ruggiero said. "And she could make a difference without being noticed. She did that in the gold-medal game."

The game was 0–0 for more than 22:38, until Whyte created the first goal of the game, on the power play, when she guided a left-to-right pass to Gretchen Ulion, who redirected it past goalie Manon Rheaume to give USA a 1–0 lead.

"Gretchen was one of those dependable players who was always where she needed to be," Ruggiero said. "She never took a shortcut."

It would remain a one-goal game for almost 28 more minutes, but the Americans felt like they were controlling the game as Ali had managed Foreman in Zaire 24 years before.

"I just remember on the bench having a feeling that we were going to win this," Bye said.

The game remained that way until the 10:57 mark of the third period, when Whyte sent a goalmouth setup pass to Shelley Looney, who banged it

The 1998 U.S. women's Olympic team celebrates after winning the gold medal in Nagano, Japan. (USA Hockey)

into the net to make it a 2–0 lead. "When I watch Mark Recchi at the end of his reign in Boston, I'm reminded of Looney," Smith said. "She wasn't the best skater in the world, but she was crafty and she was so tough."

It was at the 1997 World Championship where Looney had gone low to block a shot and suffered a broken jaw when the puck struck her face mask. "Three minutes later on the bench, she was ready to go back on the ice," Smith recalled. "She wasn't going to back off."

As if fate had a sense of drama, Danielle Goyette scored just about five minutes later to make it a 2–1 game.

With a few minutes left in the game, the Canadians dialed up their energy. Tueting would say later that it seemed as if time was moving slower. She felt as if it was taking two or three minutes for one minute to move off the clock. "I thought, *Who is messing with the clock?*" Tueting

said. "That's the kind of paranoia you get in the final five minutes."

With 1:06 remaining, Tueting had to make a memorable stop against Canada's Lori Dupuis.

With Canada's goalie pulled, Whyte had her opportunity to make a statement about what the Canadians had said about her. As the final seconds began to tick down, Whyte gained control of the puck along the left-wing boards and fired the puck about 40 feet into the empty net with eight seconds remaining. That goal was the hockey equivalent of Ali knocking out Foreman in the eighth round in Zaire.

"When she scored that goal, everything in my body erupted," Bye said.

When it was over, the final scoring summary showed that Whyte had contributed on every USA goal, netting a goal and two assists in the 3–1 win. "She had the biggest game of her life," Smith said.

The on-ice celebration for the women of 1998 was every bit as emotional as the on-ice hoopla for the men in 1980. Ruggiero skated the length of the ice to pick up the puck in the Canadian end. Tueting showed up in the press conference with a foam-rubber two-foot Uncle Sam hat on her noggin. Bye even wrapped a flag around herself, much like Jim Craig had done in 1980.

"We do not have a National Hockey League for women's hockey, so this was our chance, maybe for a lifetime, to show how great hockey can be," U.S. defenseman Sue Merz told reporters after the game. "I've seen the Miracle on Ice of Team USA in 1980 on TV, and I had the memory of that moment in the back of my head when we went out on the ice for this gold-medal game."

Canadian players seemed stunned when the game was over, clearly tortured by what probably seemed like a squandered opportunity. "It was a real empty feeling to lose," Canada's coach, Shannon Miller, said. "But when they showed Cammi Granato's face on the big screen and the medal around her neck, my feelings changed completely. I realized a gold medal was being hung around the neck of a female hockey player, and I couldn't believe the effect it had on me."

There were many reasons for the USA's success in Nagano, but players stress intangibles being most important. "I truly believe that one of the reasons we won that game is that the players on this team accepted their roles," Bye said. "Our team chemistry was amazing."

Alana Blahoski echoed that sentiment, saying in Nagano, "I can't think of 19 people I'd want to share this with more."

Although there hadn't been much focus on goaltending during the tournament, Smith believed the goaltending tandem of Tueting and DeCosta was crucial to the team's success. Tueting had made 21 saves, including some major ones in the 3–1 triumph over Canada. "You can't talk about our team without starting with our goaltending," Smith said. "You never thought about goaltending because you knew it would be solid."

Smith considered Tueting and DeCosta to be "interchangeable parts." He liked rotating the goalies, and he said the real reason why Tueting received the start in the gold-medal game was, "We just felt DeCosta was better coming in in the middle of the game if something happened."

The rotation had worked because Tueting and DeCosta put their egos into storage for the duration they were on the team. They were friends, teammates, unified in a single objective of bringing home the gold medal. They did that knowing that it was inevitable that one was going to be playing and the other would be cheering during the gold-medal game.

Before the gold-medal game, DeCosta approached Tueting and presented her with the guardian angel pin that had been a standard part of her equipment throughout the season. DeCosta had worn it on the front of her jersey. In the gold-medal game, Tueting wore the guardian angel—and her heart—on her sleeve, knowing that she carried the strength of two goalies into that contest.

"Goalie partners can have such volatile relationships," Tueting told the *New York Daily News*. "That's not how we are. We made a pact when we first made the team to backstop the team to the gold medal together."

When the gold was won, the two goalies met in an embrace in front of the net and then took a lap together around the arena.

Smith believes the battles that U.S. players fought for their right to play years before had helped them on the big stage at the Olympics. He felt his players could handle anything the Canadians could throw at them because they had already witnessed all measures of hostility in their athletic careers. Most American players had to prove themselves in boys' leagues, often after some long debate in local leagues about whether they should be there. "They knew how to battle through adversity," Smith said.

Most of the American players believed that lining up against boys had made them stronger players. "Playing against boys helped me with competitiveness and the mental toughness side," King said. "You always wanted to prove yourself against the boys."

This American team was rich in top athletes, players who had excelled in other sports. According to Smith, Whyte had played youth baseball in boys' leagues. "A supposed adult, a grown man, supposedly went out on the pitcher's mound and sat down and said he wasn't leaving until she left the field," Smith said.

Hours after the gold was won, 10 American players were on the *Late Show with David Letterman* reading the "Top 10 Cool Things About Winning a Gold Medal."

A couple months before the Nagano Olympics, USA Hockey executive director Dave Ogrean had spoken to the players about what to expect should the Americans win. He had been the media relations director for the U.S. men's team that won in Lake Placid.

"You have no idea what is ahead of you if we win the gold in terms of the attention you will receive," Ogrean told the players. He had been right. The American women were the darlings of the Nagano Games. Within a couple days, General Mills announced that the American women's players would be on a Wheaties box.

"My dream had started when I was eight years old and glued to the TV watching the Miracle on Ice," Bye said. "When you dream of winning the gold, you dream of scoring the game-winning goal, jumping on the goalies, and having the medal put around your neck."

That's where her dream always ended. "I never dreamed of being on a Wheaties box," she said. "I never dreamed of being on the front page of the newspapers or going to the White House and meeting the president. I never dreamed of our team being inducted into the U.S. Hockey Hall of Fame. I never dreamed of being inducted into the IIHF Hall of Fame."

After the 1996 U.S. Summer Games, soccer player Mia Hamm had appeared on Pert commercials. Ogrean warned players that it was possible that a couple players could be singled out for special marketing opportunities. "If one player gets the Pert commercial, there should be 20 of you celebrating that," Ogrean said. "Because it's good for the sport."

Not every U.S. player could be on the Wheaties box because a handful of them still had college eligibility remaining, and appearing on the box would be a violation of NCAA rules. Ruggiero, Jenny Potter, A.J. Mleczko, and DeCosta were among those unable to appear on the box.

"Everyone said, 'Don't worry, you will be on a box someday,'" Ruggiero said. "'There will be another gold medal.' But I'm 31 now."

The Wheaties fame was important to Ruggiero because her dad had given her a Wheaties box with the Olympic rings, and she had put it on her dorm room wall as motivation.

"To this day, people bring me the Wheaties box with the team on it and ask me which one I am," Ruggiero said. "And I have to say I'm not there."

The Americans, post-Nagano, haven't had the amount of women's international success that they were expecting after the gold-medal splash. In 2002 the Americans, with Smith still coaching, won eight of nine meetings with the Canadians in pre-Olympic play only to lose the gold-medal showdown in the Olympic Games in Salt Lake.

In 2006 Smith made the controversial decision to cut both 34-year-old Granato and 36-year-old Looney six weeks before the Olympics in 2006. Neither player saw it coming, and media coverage of the Granato dismissal boiled for several days.

Northeastern coach Laura Schuler, an 11-year veteran of Canada's national team, said Smith's decision was akin to "cutting Wayne Gretzky from the Canadian team."

Earlier that spring Granato had been captain of the U.S. team that had beaten Canada 1–0 to win its first World Championship. Smith's explanation was that he did what he thought was in the best interest of the team. Granato and her supporters also criticized Smith for how the cut was handled.

Although it's impossible to know what impact Granato's absence had on the U.S. team, the Americans didn't even reach the gold-medal game in Torino. Thanks to the stingy goaltending of Kim Martin, Sweden defeated the USA 3–2 in the semifinals. The Americans settled for the bronze medal.

By then Smith had been USA's coach for 10 years, and Ogrean decided to make a change. The U.S. National Women's Team coaching job went to Wisconsin coach Mark Johnson, who had been one of the standouts of the 1980 men's team. With Johnson behind the bench, the Americans still couldn't beat Canada at the 2010 Games in Vancouver. They again took home the silver.

Going into the 1998 Games, there had been a small amount of buzz about the possibility of a women's pro league, but that didn't materialize.

"There is no question that the medal in Nagano was a very catalytic event for the membership in USA Hockey, but that didn't mean people were willing to go pay $10 per ticket," Ogrean said. "If it wasn't U.S. vs. Canada, it wasn't the same."

But none of that diminishes the value of the Americans winning the first women's hockey gold medal. When the American women went to Nagano, there were less than 29,000 registered women players in USA Hockey. Today, there are more than 61,000. Women's college hockey has a much stronger foothold.

Since 1998 Granato has been inducted into the Hockey Hall of Fame, the International Ice Hockey Federation Hall of Fame, and the U.S. Hockey Hall of Fame. Bye has been selected for induction into the IIHF Hall of Fame.

A.J. Mleczko produced 114 points for Harvard in the 1998–99 season and won the Patty Kazmaier Memorial Award as the nation's top collegiate player.

Ruggiero has played in four Olympic Games and appeared on the television show *The Apprentice*. Another member of that 1998 squad, Jenny Potter, has played in all four Olympic Games and will attempt to make the 2014 team in Sochi, Russia. She has said jokingly, or not, that her objective is to play on a U.S. National Team with her daughter.

"Not to take anything away from anyone else's medals," Bye said. "But we were the pioneers on that first team. It was a special team. It truly was, and that's something we will have forever." Katie King says players do keep in touch with each other even today.

"What these women can always be proud of is that they did it first," Ogrean said. ▪

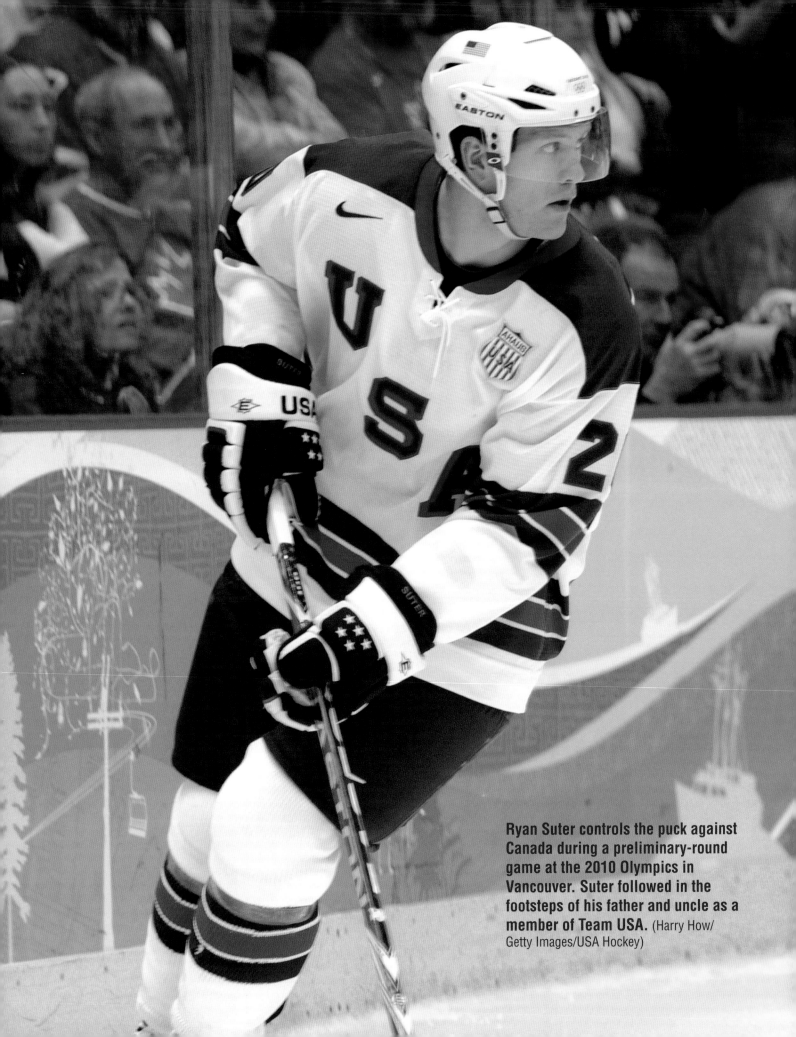

Ryan Suter controls the puck against Canada during a preliminary-round game at the 2010 Olympics in Vancouver. Suter followed in the footsteps of his father and uncle as a member of Team USA. (Harry How/ Getty Images/USA Hockey)

ALL IN THE FAMILY
America's Top Hockey Bloodlines

When a Czechoslovakian player laid a nasty blindside hit on Mark Johnson during the 1980 Olympic Games in Lake Placid, everyone in the building could hear U.S. coach Herb Brooks screaming, "Number three, I'm going to shove that goddamn Koho [stick] down your throat! You are going to eat that Koho, three!"

When Brooks sent Bob Suter over the boards on the next shift, Suter didn't need his orders in writing. He knew his job. The 5'9", 175-pound Wisconsin graduate delivered several booming checks. Bob Suter made a statement: he wasn't going to allow Johnson or any of his teammates to be abused in this game.

"If you had to go to war, you'd want to go with Bobby Suter," said U.S. captain Mike Eruzione.

Eleven years later, in the 1991 Canada Cup, his younger brother Gary Suter was playing for USA against Canada when he delivered a thunderous body check on Wayne Gretzky in Montreal that put the Great One on the injury list for the next game.

As Mike Modano says, "Gretzky was the head of the snake." And Suter had tried to cut it off. Gary Suter had made a statement: the Americans were tired of being pushed around by the Canadians. "He was a wanted man until we got out of Canada," Modano said.

In 2002, at the World Under 18 Championship, coach Mike Eaves called his players together with two minutes remaining in a game against Russia. The Americans were leading 2–1, and under the tournament format they needed to win by two goals to claim the gold. If they won by one goal, they would receive the silver. If they tied or lost, they would earn the bronze. Eaves asked his players what they wanted to do, even though he already knew the answer. The Americans pulled their goalie. Moments later, Ryan Suter, Bob's son, carried his puck from behind his net, with Russians all over him, to the offensive blue line, where he dumped the puck off to Zach Parise, who scored the game-winning goal. Ryan Suter had made his statement.

When it comes to international hockey, few American hockey families have had as many signature moments as the Suters. After Bob earned the gold in Lake Placid in 1980, Gary earned a silver with Team USA at the 2002 Games in Salt Lake City and Ryan played for Team USA when the Americans captured Olympic silver in Vancouver in 2010.

"It's a remarkable story when you consider that the Suter family has had an Olympic presence for 30 years, between Bob, Gary, and now Ryan," said USA Hockey executive director Dave Ogrean. "The Suter family embodies what USA Hockey is all about in passing the game down from generation to generation."

The only other family story of equal weight in American Olympic hockey history is Bill and Roger Christian playing on the 1960 gold-medal U.S. Olympic team and Bill's son, Dave, playing on the 1980 gold-medal team. Bill and Roger's brother, Gord, played on the 1956 U.S. team.

"Hockey is our business, and it is in our blood," Bob Suter said. "We run rinks, sporting goods stores, and coach hockey. That's all we have ever done and probably ever will do."

When Nashville Predators defenseman Ryan Suter was growing up in Wisconsin, the 1980 gold medal was not a frequent topic of conversation in the Suter household.

"The gold medal was always wherever," Ryan said, laughing. "In the dresser, or on the kitchen counter, and once I left it in a kid's locker at school...and when I left it there, no one even asked me about it at home. "

Playing defense also seems to be in the Suter blood, because Bob, Gary, and Ryan are all defensemen, and another brother, John, also played defense. All four played at the University of Wisconsin. Their father, Marlow, played some defense for the Madison Cardinals and Wagon Wheel Cardinals in a famous senior league in the 1950s.

"When I coached the boys, if you could see the ice good, I liked to have you on defense," Marlow said. "That's why the boys ended up playing there."

Ryan's stature has grown significantly in the NHL as opposing teams have started to realize that he was Nashville's version of Nicklas Lidstrom in terms of his poise and polish. "He's not a flamboyant, high-offense guy," said Nashville general manager David Poile. "But he's a complete player."

There is no comparison between the playing styles of Bob and Ryan, says Marlow Suter. "Bob was kind of a reckless player. He might make a mistake on defense, but the next shift he would go down and score a goal."

Johnson said if there was an opportunity to stick up for your teammates, "it would always be Bobby Suter leading the pack."

Gary played 17 seasons in the NHL and had 10 or more goals 11 times in his career. Bob never played in the NHL, but last summer Bob, Ryan, Gary, and their wives played together on a volleyball team, and they signed a Wisconsin jersey for the sponsor.

"Gary wrote his stats down, and I wrote mine down, and we had to look up my dad's," Ryan said. "When I saw his stats, I thought if he were just around today."

Bob Suter had 16 goals and 28 assists in 40 games during his second season playing for Wisconsin, much better stats than either Gary or Ryan had produced.

"He was a good skater," said Johnson, now women's coach at the University of Wisconsin. "He was tenacious taking the puck to the net. He was the classic Bobby Orr type—take the puck to the net, and if he couldn't get by the defensemen, he would crash into the goalie."

In 1980 Bob's teammates nicknamed him "Bam Bam" because he looked like the Flintstone character and seemed to enjoy playing the physical role.

Although Gary became a dominant NHL player, he said he "idolized" Bob growing up. He was inspired by his older brother. Ironically, it was Gary who inspired Ryan because Gary was still playing when Ryan was old enough to watch.

"If I passed along anything to Ryan, it is a work ethic," Gary said. "I could see at an early age that he had the drive."

Toronto Globe and Mail columnist Eric Duhatschek recalls that when Gary showed up for the first training camp, he was first in all aspects of physical testing. "It struck me that his gene pool was tremendous," Duhatschek said.

He recalls Flames player Brad McCrimmon telling him, "This Suter kid is going to win the Norris Trophy."

It didn't happen, but he helped USA win the gold medal at the 1996 World Cup and the silver in Salt Lake City in 2002. He was named NHL Rookie of the Year in 1985–86 after producing 18 goals and 50 assists.

"He was one of the best American defensemen in U.S. history," Berglund said.

According to Duhatschek, the Flames' decision to draft Gary in the ninth round came about only because scout Ian McKenzie ran into him in the hallway at Wisconsin's arena and realized that the NHL's Central Scouting Report on Suter was inaccurate. It listed Suter at 5'9", and McKenzie could see that Gary was 5'11" or better. "Remember, this was a time when being big was what mattered," Duhatschek said.

Gary was known for his high level of conditioning throughout his career. He would run the stairs at Camp Randall Stadium in Madison to the point of exhaustion. "I guess we pass it down from generation to generation," Gary said, as Ryan is also known for working hard at his game.

Nashville coach Barry Trotz said Ryan's development started on a steep rise the moment he stepped into the NHL. "In his first year, he came in with a lot of confidence," Trotz said. "Even in his first year, he thought he could play better than Kimmo Timonen right out of a junior program. But he wasn't quite ready. We challenged him, and he responded.... He has great escapability."

Ryan said now that he has watched the HBO documentary *Miracle on Ice*, about the 1980 Miracle On Ice team, he has a better understanding of his dad's place in hockey history. It's always been meaningful to his father, even though he didn't always know where his medal was. Right after Bob returned from Lake Placid in 1980, two teenagers broke into his van and swiped his gold medal, hockey sticks, and souvenirs from the tournament. "A couple of girls who were with them told on them, so I got it back the next day," Bob said.

But Suter still refuses to put the medal under lock and key. "We don't have it in a safe or anything. What good is it if people can't see it?" Suter said.

Here is a look at some of the other important American hockey families:

The Christians: The Christian family has an Olympic medal collection that is second to none in American hockey history.

Brothers Bill and Roger Christian were members of the 1960 team that won the gold medal

The Christians won Olympic hockey medals over three Olympics and two generations. Brothers Bill (left) and Roger Christian were members of the 1960 gold-medal team. Bill's son Dave won gold as a member of the 1980 Miracle on Ice team. Bill and Roger's brother, Gord, was on USA's silver-medal team in 1956 at Cortina, Italy. (USA Hockey)

at Squaw Valley, while Bill's son Dave won gold at the 1980 Games in Lake Placid. Bill and Roger's brother, Gord, was on USA's silver-medal team in 1956 at Cortina, Italy. Although the least-known of the Christian family, Gord had five goals in six games at those 1956 Games.

Dave was the only member of the family to play in the NHL. He netted 340 goals in 1,009 NHL games. His best season came in 1985–86 when he netted 41 goals for the Washington Capitals.

"He was like the basketball player who learned his game on the playgrounds," said former U.S. National Team coach Tim Taylor. "Dave learned hockey on the pond, and he could play anywhere. On the power play, he could play on the point, or in front of the net, or along the boards."

Although Christian was primarily a forward, Herb Brooks had used him at defense during the 1980 Olympic games. Occasionally, NHL coaches would do the same.

"He was a very smooth player," said David Poile, who was GM in Washington when Christian was there. "He had great hands. He could skate, and he had great hockey sense."

The Mullens: With a combined 762 NHL goals, New York City natives Joe and Brian Mullen are the highest-scoring American brother tandem in NHL history.

"The Mullens weren't tough guys, but they didn't let physical play bother them," said former NHL player Tom Laidlaw. "They were real smart players."

Although Joe is viewed among the top players in NHL history, former New York Rangers stick boy Brian carved out his own place with 260 goals and 622 points in 832 NHL games.

One highlight of the Mullen brothers' career was playing against each other in the 1989 NHL All-Star Game. "I remember I found out first, and my dad put on his New York Rangers jacket and went down to the pub and told all of his buddies that I was playing in the All-Star Game," Brian said. "Then Joey found out he was going, so my dad put on his Calgary Flames jacket and went down and told his buddies that."

The Hatchers: Although brothers Kevin and Derian Hatcher had contrasting styles, both have to be considered among the top 10 American-born defensemen in NHL history, but for different reasons.

Derian was a tough, heavy-hitting defensive-minded player whose offensive skill was better than most fans realized. Kevin was a gifted offensive defenseman who was probably tougher than fans realized. Former Dallas Stars general manager Doug Armstrong calls Derian the "American version of Scott Stevens."

"What always impressed me most about Derian Hatcher was that he walked softly and carried the big stick," Armstrong said. "He never said anything controversial or ever drew a line in the sand; he just always let his actions speak for him."

Kevin had 10 or more goals for 12 consecutive seasons, and he is the only U.S.-born defenseman to score 30 or more goals in a season. He netted 34 for Washington in 1992–93.

"He gave us an offensive weapon that few teams had," Poile said.

Although he was known as a puck-moving defenseman, he was also 6'3" and 235 pounds, and he could play mean when required. He fought 31 times, which is about half the number of fights that Derian had. Poile tells the story of a Capitals' practice in Edmonton when Hatcher and Caps tough guy Dwight Schofield decided they would fight. Players surrounded them, creating a human boxing ring. The players signaled the start of the fight, "and Hatcher [threw] one punch, and Schofield [went] right down," Poile said. "It was over."

The Bennetts: The sons of Canadian-born former NHL goaltender Harvey Bennett, Curt, Harvey Jr., and Billy Bennett grew up in Rhode Island and all played in the NHL in the 1970s. Another brother, John, played briefly in the World Hockey Association for the Philadelphia Blazers. A fifth brother, Jimmy, played at Brown and was drafted by the Atlanta Flames but never played in the NHL.

Curt was the most accomplished NHL player among the brothers, scoring 152 goals in 580 NHL games. He scored more than 30 goals in a season twice for the Atlanta Flames, with a high of 34 in 1975–76.

He was also known for his eclectic personality. "He was the NHL's hippie," said David Poile, who worked for the Flames when Bennett was there. "He was always on the cutting edge. He was the first player I ever heard of who was into yoga or transcendental meditation."

Supposedly, Bennett also dabbled in karate. The 6'3" Bennett is also remembered for decking New York Rangers player Dave Maloney with a punch without removing his glove.

That punch, coincidently, ended up opening the door for Staten Island, New York, native Nick Fotiu to become the Rangers' tough guy. After watching the Rangers not responding to Bennett's knockdown, then-Rangers coach and GM John Ferguson started scheming to land WHA tough guy Fotiu to protect the Rangers. Legend has it that Ferguson agreed to play two exhibition games in Hartford to acquire Fotiu's rights from the New England Whalers. Fotiu became a Rangers hometown hero.

Harvey Bennett Jr. was 6'4" and played 268 NHL games with Pittsburgh, Washington, Minnesota, Philadelphia, and St. Louis. His best season came in 1975–76, when he netted 12 goals for the Capitals and 3 goals for the Penguins for a total of 15. Brother Billy, who was 6'5", played 31 NHL games with Boston and Hartford. At the end of their careers, Curt and Harvey played pro hockey in Japan. Jimmy Bennett was drafted out of Brown by the Atlanta Flames. He never made it, but his son Mac was drafted by the Montreal Canadiens in 2009.

The Roberts: Former Michigan State standout Doug Roberts was one of the rare Americans to play regularly in the NHL in the 1960s. His younger brother Gordie signed with the World Hockey Association at age 17 and played four seasons in the WHA and 15 seasons in the NHL. Doug's son, David, was an All-American at the University of Michigan and had a brief NHL career.

During the 1967–68 season, Doug, who played football and hockey at Michigan State, was promoted to the Detroit Red Wings, where he played on a line with Gordie Howe and Alex Delvecchio. Old-timers remember the New Year's Eve game when the 6'2", 215-pound Roberts laid a body check on famed tough guy Eddie Shack that rocked both Shack and Olympia Stadium. In a 1968 *Sports Illustrated* article written by Gary Ronberg, Detroit coach Sid Abel said of Roberts: "He's got size, and we need it. He has always had the shot, and he's working well with Gordie, too." Roberts didn't last long in that stint with Detroit, but he ended up a full-time player with the Oakland and then California Golden Seals and ended up having a solid WHA and NHL career. He played 419 NHL games and 140 in the WHA.

Gordie was 15 years younger than Doug and played 1,097 games in the NHL and 311 in the WHA. Atlanta Thrashers president Don Waddell was playing youth hockey in Detroit when Gordie Roberts was there, and he says, "Gordie was the best player in Detroit for a long while."

Gordie left Detroit to play in the Western Hockey Association and then signed with the New England Whalers in 1975–76. His best WHA season came in 1977–78, when he had 15 goals and 46 assists for 61 points. "He was a cocky, talented player," said his former Whalers teammate Larry Pleau. "He could do everything."

But his most important seasons may have come in 1991 and 1992, when he helped the Pittsburgh Penguins win back-to-back Stanley Cup championships. In two regular seasons and two playoff runs, Roberts posted a plus-minus of plus-49 in Pittsburgh.

The Penguins made some major trades that season that made a huge difference, such as bringing in Ulf Samuelsson, Ron Francis, and Bryan Trottier. Because of that, Roberts' accomplishments in Pittsburgh sometimes are overlooked.

"It was a ho-hum thing when the Penguins picked up Roberts," said Tom McMillan, a beat reporter for the *Pittsburgh Tribune-Review* at that time. "He didn't bring superstar qualities, but he was an essential part of that group. Badger Bob wanted a veteran defenseman, and Scotty Bowman found him."

David Roberts played 125 games in the NHL with St. Louis, Edmonton, and Vancouver. His best pro season may have been 1998–99, when he netted 32 goals for Kalamazoo in the International League. He also played in Switzerland and Germany.

The Brotens: Brothers Neal, Aaron, and Paul Broten from Roseau, Minnesota, combined to play

2,169 NHL games and produce 521 goals and 1,018 assists.

"If you are living in the shadow of Neal, it's pretty tough because of who he was and what he accomplished," said former 1980 U.S. Olympian Mark Johnson. "But Aaron was a very good player."

Both Neal and Aaron are members of the U.S. Hockey Hall of Fame. Neal was almost a point-per-game scorer in his NHL career, but Aaron managed to have a pair of 26-goal seasons for the New Jersey Devils and finished his career with 186 goals.

"As I like to say, the year that Neal won the Hobey Baker, Aaron had a quiet 106-point season," former 1980 U.S. Olympian Mark Johnson said. "How many college players have a quiet 106-point season and [don't] get noticed?"

Johnson and Aaron were linemates for the New Jersey Devils. Paul Broten managed to play in 322 NHL games. "Paul obviously learned from his brothers and figured out how to get to the National Hockey League," Johnson said. "And it's amazing that Butsy Erickson came out of the same neighborhood [in Roseau, Minnesota], and they all made it to the NHL."

The Millers: The Miller family is to college hockey what the Sutter brothers are to the NHL. The Sutter family of Viking, Alberta, sent six brothers to the NHL, and the Miller extended family sent 10 players to play at Michigan State, five of whom played in the NHL. Their run was highlighted by Buffalo Sabres goaltender Ryan Miller, a Vezina Trophy winner and a member of the silver medal–winning 2010 U.S. Olympic Team. Ryan Miller's grandfather, Butch, was the first to go to MSU, coming from Saskatchewan to play there from 1955 to 1959. His brother Lyle followed, starting in 1961. Ryan's father, Dean, played at MSU from 1977 to 1979. Lyle's sons Kelly (1981–85), Kevin (1984–88), and Kip (1986–90) all played

Aaron Broten totaled 515 points in 12 NHL seasons. He and brother Neal Broten are both members of the U.S. Hockey Hall of Fame. (O-Pee-Chee/Hockey Hall of Fame)

at Michigan State and combined for 39 seasons in the NHL.

Two other cousins, Curtis and Taylor Gemmel, also played at Michigan State before East Lansing, Michigan, native Ryan went there in 1999. Ryan's brother Drew followed in 2002 and was playing for the Detroit Red Wings during the 2010–11 season.

Ryan idolized his cousins Kelly, Kevin, and Kip, who were all forwards. The three brothers combined for more than 2,000 games played in the NHL, led by Kelly, a hard-working two-way forward who spent most of his career with the Washington Capitals.

"Kelly was the guy that coaches loved all of the time because he was dependable in all situations," said former Washington GM Poile. "He was on the ice in all of the important times of the game."

Kevin played in 620 NHL games. "He had great hands in traffic, and he was deceptively physical," said Jim Johannson, who played with Miller on the 1988 U.S. Olympic Team.

Kip netted 48 goals in 45 games in his final season at Michigan State, and he once boasted a 46-goal season for Denver in the International Hockey League. He played for eight different NHL teams. His best NHL campaign came in 1998–99, when he had 19 goals for Pittsburgh.

Of course, their cousin Ryan became the family's biggest star in 2010 with his memorable performance in Vancouver.

The Sheehys: Brothers Neil and Tim Sheehy were different kinds of players during their hockey careers. Tim was one of the top scorers on the 1972 U.S. Olympic Team and went on to be a premium scorer in the World Hockey Association.

He had 178 goals and 351 points in 433 WHA games. His best season was 1972–73, when he had 33 goals and 71 points playing for the New England Whalers. He had a productive playoff that season, scoring nine goals and adding 14 assists in just 15 games as the Whalers won the Avco Cup.

Former Harvard player Neil was a rough-and-tumble shutdown defenseman, remembered for doing better than most at bothering Wayne Gretzky. He had 1,311 penalty minutes in 379 NHL games. Twice he played for the USA in the World Championship. Always difficult to play against, Neil was highly respected during his playing days.

The Fuscos: Scott and Mark Fusco are the only brothers to win the Hobey Baker Award. They also both played on the 1984 U.S. Olympic Team.

5'8" Scott was a center, and 5'9" Mark was a defenseman.

"Mark was Brian Rafalski before there was Brian Rafalski," said USA Hockey's Jim Johannson, who played against Mark in college.

Scott is Harvard's all-time leading scorer, and he also played on the 1988 U.S. Olympic Team. "Scott had a deceptive scoring touch," Johannson said. "He was sneaky tough around the net...he was a master of creating odd numbers. His conditioning level was his strength. Late in shifts he could still play."

The Drurys: Chris Drury has averaged better than 20 goals per season during his NHL season, and yet it is intangibles that put him on the list of best all-time American players.

He was a member of both the silver medal–winning 2002 and 2010 U.S. Olympic Teams. Coaches consider him highly valuable because he is equally comfortable playing a checking role or playing in the top two lines. "He has those Mike Eruzione–type qualities," 2010 Olympic coach Ron Wilson said. He does a lot of dirty grunt work that oftentimes gets overlooked, but not by coaches."

But he wasn't the first Drury in the NHL. His older brother Ted was playing in the NHL with the Calgary Flames in 1993–94, before Chris was even in college. Ted also played for the U.S. Olympic Team in both 1992 and 1994.

The Clearys: Any argument about who the top American-born players were before 1960 has to include Harvard graduate Bill Cleary, whose 89 points in a season is still a school record at Harvard. In helping the USA win the silver medal at the 1956 Olympics and a gold in 1960, Cleary had 11 goals and 10 assists in 14 games. Anyone who saw Cleary play in that era believed he could have played in the NHL.

His brother Bob also had six goals and four assists in helping the USA capture the gold medal in 1960.

The Granatos: When it comes time to argue about the best female player in international hockey history, Cammi Granato is always in the debate. She holds the International Ice Hockey Federation record for career goals (44), points (78), and career hat tricks (5). In her 11 games played over two Olympics, she netted 10 goals and eight assists for 18 points. Her three brothers—Don, Rob, and Tony—all played college hockey at Wisconsin.

A four-time 30-plus goal scorer, Tony had a strong NHL career. He also played for the USA in the 1988 Olympics and 1991 Canada Cup. Cammi always idolized her brother, who also doted on her. "She is the most natural athlete in the family," Tony says.

The Granatos, Cammi included, played some summer hockey together, although the closeness of the family often caused problems, according to Cammi. If someone touched their younger sister, the Granato boys became riled up. "It [was] a little ridiculous," Cammi says, laughing. "A minute into the game, and they [were] all kicked out. I [would] tell them, 'You gotta just let me play. I can handle it.'"

The Michelettis: The Micheletti family earned its place in American hockey history by sending four brothers to the University of Minnesota's team and two to the National Hockey League. Joe, Pat, Don, and Tom Micheletti of Hibbing, Minnesota, all played for the Gophers, and Joe and Pat made the NHL.

Joe was the most accomplished of the players, competing for three seasons in the World Hockey Association and three more in the NHL. He signed with the WHA's Calgary Cowboys in 1976 when Americans were just starting to have a foothold in pro hockey. The ratio of American players to Canadians in that era was about 1-to-20. "[Then Minnesota coach] Herb Brooks called me into his office after my freshman season," Joe Micheletti recalled. "He said, 'I want you to know that you were drafted by the Montreal Canadiens in the seventh round. But don't worry or be concerned about it, because you will never make it anyway.'"

At the time, the Canadiens were among the few NHL teams aggressively scouting Americans. But the WHA seemed to be opening its doors wider for Americans. Joe decided to sign with the Cowboys because he believed he had a better opportunity to play.

"I got a $15,000 signing bonus in Canadian funds, and I got a contract for $40,000 my first year and $45,000 my second year," Micheletti said. "What I was comparing that against was a two-way contract offer from Montreal for $12,000 to play in the minors and $78,000 if I made the Canadiens. The problem was the Canadiens, at the time, had Larry Robinson, Guy Lapointe, and Serge Savard… on defense. The WHA was going to give me a chance to see if I can play."

Herb Brooks recommended that Micheletti take the WHA offer. "He said, 'I don't think you are going to make it, but go ahead and take it,'" Micheletti recalled, laughing at the memory.

Micheletti played with the Calgary Cowboys and Edmonton Oilers in the WHA before signing with the St. Louis Blues in 1979–80. Today, he is a television analyst for the New York Rangers and works nationally for NBC/Versus.

Joe's younger brother Pat was a major goal scorer at Minnesota, netting 48 goals in 44 games in his junior season and another 32 goals in his senior season. He played 12 games in the NHL for the Minnesota North Stars. ∎

With 561 career goals through 2011, Mike Modano has scored more NHL goals than any other American. (Glenn James/NHLI via Getty Images/USA Hockey)

AMERICA'S TOP SCORERS
Leaders in Goals and Points

Joe Mullen's hockey skills were developed in Hell's Kitchen, and Mike Modano's skills seemed like they were made in heaven. Michigan native Modano was a 6'3" center with a divine skating style, an all-powerful shot, and magical hands. New York City–bred Mullen was a 5'9" winger with a short, choppy stride; a minor leaguer's body; and a lifetime supply of hockey sense. Modano was the NHL's No. 1 overall draft, and Mullen was never drafted.

But these two players, with sharply contrasting tools, will forever be linked at the top of the list of the greatest American-born goal scorers in NHL history. Mullen beat Colorado Avalanche goalie Patrick Roy with a shot on March 14, 1997, to become the first American to net 500 NHL goals. Modano scored his 500th on March 13, 2007. On March 17, 2007, Modano scored his 503rd goal to pass Mullen and become the top American-born goal scorer in NHL history. Mullen only needed 1,052 games to reach 500, while Modano needed 1,225 games.

"Joe Mullen is probably the best example I've ever seen of a player who had a nose for the net,"

said *Toronto Globe and Mail* hockey writer Eric Duhatschek.

Duhatschek chronicled Mullen's career in the mid- to late-1980s, when Mullen was playing for the Calgary Flames during the best seasons of his career. Mullen had his most memorable offensive season playing for the Calgary Flames in 1988–89, when he registered 51 goals with 59 assists for 110 points in the regular season, plus 16 goals in 21 playoff games to help Calgary win the Stanley Cup. He also won two Stanley Cup titles while playing with the Pittsburgh Penguins in 1991–92.

"All along the way he had to fight obstacles and an industry that looked at him and thought, *minor leaguer at best*," Duhatschek said. "And what he proved was that he had the innate ability to find open ice and score goals that only the truly greats have."

Mullen was signed by the St. Louis Blues out of Boston College in 1979 and had to spend two full seasons, plus a half season, with Salt Lake City in the Central Hockey League before receiving his first chance to play in the NHL.

"His skating was deceptive," said Jim Nill, who played with Mullen at Salt Lake. "He would look like he was going to fall down when he made a move, and that's when he would go by you."

Mullen began his career as a roller hockey player on the streets of Hell's Kitchen in New York City, where uneven payment forced players to be balanced on their skates or face the consequences of spending the entire season scabbed over from too many spills.

Whenever the late Flames coach Bob Johnson found himself practicing on chopped-up or poor ice conditions he would call it "Joey Mullen ice." Mullen never earned many style points, but he always racked up scoring points. "Guys would always think they had him, and he would get by them," Duhatschek said. "He was just slippery."

NHL scouts had ignored Mullen when he was a teenager, but they were fascinated by Modano's opulent skill package. "Some players look like they are digging into the ice when they skate, and Modano looked like he was hovering just above the ice," said St. Louis Blues general manager Doug Armstrong. "He was so graceful and elegant, and his acceleration was phenomenal."

To go along with his majestic talent, Modano owned a wickedly hard slap shot that has been clocked north of 100 mph.

"He's the jack of all trades and master of all of them," his former linemate Brett Hull once said. "He can shoot, pass, skate, play defense, kill penalties, and run the power play. And he's one of the top three physically fit individuals I ever played with."

Modano was still playing in the NHL beyond his 40th birthday, and he was still speeding down the ice like he was Dale Earnhardt Jr. on the backstretch at Daytona.

"You can always see his jersey flapping behind him," said retired NHL player Keith Tkachuk,

another in USA's 500-goal club. "He is setting the tone for American hockey."

Modano's willingness to leave home and play in the Western Hockey League as a 16-year-old added to his reputation. "It's freezing cold in Prince Albert. When you go there, you are going there for hockey," said Detroit Red Wings general manager Ken Holland, then an NHL scout. "He was going to a small town in Saskatchewan and to a league known for long bus rides and lots of physical play. That's the commitment he had to play hockey."

Modano endured "razzing," some good-natured and some not, as an American playing in a league that then was exclusively Canadian. "When I got there I felt like I had something to prove," he said. "That was the motivation to do well. I was in Canada where they love their sport. They expect nothing less than your best. I felt like I had to make an impact."

Trying to determine the history of the U.S-born NHL goal-scoring record requires debate about who qualifies as an American. The NHL would count Cecil Dillon as the first American-born goal scorer of note. Dillon was born in Toledo, Ohio, and had 167 goals when he retired after the 1939–40 NHL season. According to the NHL and Elias Sports Bureau, Dillon held the goal record for more than 45 years until Minneapolis native Reed Larson moved past him. But Dillon moved to Canada when he was six and developed through the Canadian system. Meanwhile, Hull, while clearly an American in terms of national team eligibility and commitment, doesn't count in recognizing the highest-scoring Americans because he was born in Canada and was developed in the Canadian system.

Probably the true American record holder throughout the 1940s, 1950s, and into the 1960s was Minneapolis-bred Carl "Cully" Dahlstrom,

Unofficial History of Modern American NHL Scoring Records

Goals*:

1944–45: Chicago Blackhawks center Carl "Cully" Dahlstrom (Minneapolis) retires from the Chicago Blackhawks with 88 NHL career goals.

1967–68: Boston Bruins right wing Tommy Williams (Duluth, Minnesota) scores his 89th goal during the 1967–68 season.

1975–76: While playing for the Washington Capitals, Williams retires from the NHL with 161 career NHL goals.

1984–85: Detroit Red Wings defenseman Reed Larson (Minneapolis) scores his 162nd career NHL goal.

1986–87: On February 16, 1987, Calgary Flames right wing Joe Mullen (New York City) caught Reed Larson at 203 goals. Larson actually scored his 203rd on this day, and Mullen netted his 202nd and 203rd career goals.

1986–87: On February 24, Mullen scores his 204th goal to pass Larson permanently.

1996–97: Mullen, then playing for the Pittsburgh Penguins, retires with 502 NHL goals.

2006–07: On March 17, 2007, Modano, then playing for the Dallas Stars, scores his 502nd and 503rd NHL goals to pass Mullen and become the highest-scoring American-born player. In 2010–11, he still owned the record and was still actively playing with the Detroit Red Wings.

Points*:

1939–40: Elwyn "Doc" Romnes (White Bear Lake, Minnesota) retires from the New York Americans with 67 goals and 136 points for 203 points earned over 10 NHL seasons with the Chicago Blackhawks, Toronto Maple Leafs, and Americans.

1944–45: Carl Dahlstrom picks up his 204th point late in the season and then retires from the Blackhawks with 206 points.

1967–68: Late in the season, Tommy Williams registers his 207th point to pass Dahlstrom.

1975–76: Williams retires with 430 points.

1983–84: Reed Larson picks up his 431st point to pass Williams on February 18, 1984.

1988–89: Larson retires with 685 career points.

1989–90: Joe Mullen, then playing for Calgary, registers his 686th point on January 13, 1990, to pass Larson.

1993–94: On March 13, 1994, St. Louis Blues defenseman Phil Housley (St. Paul, Minnesota) picks up his 1,064th point to pass Mullen.

2002–03: Housley retires with 1,232 points over 21 NHL seasons with Buffalo, Winnipeg, Calgary, St. Louis, New Jersey, Chicago, Washington, and Toronto.

2007–08: On November 7, 2007, Mike Modano scores two quick goals in the opening minutes of a game against San Jose to give him 1,233 points to pass Housley.

---

* In determining the U.S. record, the NHL counts Cecil Dillon because he was born in Toledo, Ohio. But he was not factored into this list because he moved to Canada when he was six and was developed in the Canadian program. This list also does not factor in Brett Hull, even though he is clearly American for the purposes of national teams. However, Hull was born in Canada and trained in Canada until he came to the U.S. to play college hockey.

In 21 NHL seasons, Phil Housley totaled 334 goals and 898 assists for 1,232 points. He held the American points record for more than 13 years before being passed by Mike Modano. (Steve Babineau/ NHLI via Getty Images/USA Hockey)

who had 88 goals for the Chicago Blackhawks from 1937–38 to 1944–45. He held the mark until 1967–68, when Tommy Williams scored 18 to give him 92 for his career. He finished his career in 1975–76 with 161 NHL goals, meaning he was the American record holder until Larson moved past him in the 1983–84 season.

Williams was also the first true American to score 20 or more goals when he netted 23 for the Boston Bruins in 1962–63.

"He was an electric player," said Lou Nanne, who played with and against Williams. "He had terrific speed. He was a good puck handler. He was charismatic on the ice. His hair was always flying.

He was always bubbly. He was the guy that a crowd would become attached to. He was exciting."

In the middle of the 1975–76 season, Larson left the University of Minnesota and signed with the Detroit Red Wings. He became an instant NHL sensation because of his heavy, frightening slap shot. Even today, Larson says he hears from former players who inform him of an injury he caused with his big boomer.

"Even into the 1980s, the guys you remember with the big shots were Al MacInnis, Doug Wilson, and Reed Larson," said former NHL player Tom Laidlaw. "Those are the ones you didn't like to block."

Larson had 17 or more goals each season for his first nine full seasons in the NHL. "After being asked by many people why I had such a hard short, I finally thought about it," Larson said. "It was stick design, repetition, practice, technique, timing, and strength in certain muscles."

On every shot, Larson tried to hit the ice six to eight inches before the puck. "It leaves divots in the ice, and thus the stick flexes like a bow," Larson explained.

Larson once fired a puck hard enough to knock the skate blade right off Dennis Hextall's boot. In the early 1980s a police officer came to Joe Louis Arena and timed Larson's shot at 130 mph with a handheld radar gun. Obviously today's radar-gun technology is more advanced, and Zdeno Chara set the official league record of 105.9 mph to win the hardest-shot competition at the 2011 NHL All-Star Game.

When it comes to American-born point production, Phil Housley (South St. Paul, Minnesota) is as distinguished as any of the aforementioned goal scorers. When Housley was drafted sixth overall out of South St. Paul High School (where he was coached by Doug Woog), no one was thinking that Housley would jump immediately to the NHL. But by early in the season, *Sports Illustrated* was suggesting he was the "first American-born Bobby Orr playalike." "He may be Bobby Orr, maybe not," said the *SI* headline in the issue dated October 25, 1982.

Housley reportedly signed a four-year deal worth $400,000 to give up his thoughts of playing college hockey to play instead for the 1984 U.S. Olympic Team. (Can you imagine what Housley could have done playing with Pat LaFontaine, Ed Olczyk, and Chris Chelios in 1984?) His deal was considered lucrative in those days, and it turned out to be money well spent.

According to the late Jack Falla's article in *SI*, Buffalo general manager Scotty Bowman originally said Housley was "the nearest thing to Bobby Orr I've seen" and then modified his statement by adding, "I mean he plays a style similar to what Orr played. He can rush the puck. He's an outstanding passer and he's creative."

After watching him early in the 1982–83 season, Bowman told Falla, "[Housley] has that knack of finding the open man, like [Denis] Potvin and [Brad] Park."

But Housley was only 5'10" and 180 pounds, and NHL streets were lined with fans and opponents believing that the smallish redheaded teenager would be devoured by the league's roughhouse tactics or, at the very least, that his offensive flair would be strangled or scared out of him.

When Housley played well in training camp, his critics said, "Wait until the preseason games start." When he played well in exhibition games, they said, "Wait until the real season begins."

"When I was doing well at the beginning of the year, they said, 'Wait until January,'" Housley said.

Housley ended up playing 21 seasons in the NHL, and no one ever did figure out how to prevent him from being a factor in NHL games. When he was done, he had 338 goals and 894 assists for 1,232 points in 1,495 NHL games. He held the American points record for more than 13 years. It took Modano 18 seasons to pass Housley to become America's NHL points leader. Modano picked up his 1,233rd point in his 1,253rd game.

"[Housley's] offensive instincts are with the best we ever had," said Jim Johannson, USA Hockey's assistant executive director. ∎

Herb Brooks, the coach of the 1980 Miracle on Ice team, returned to the Team USA bench in 2002 to coach a team of NHL players in Salt Lake City. (Doug Pensinger/Getty Images/ USA Hockey)

THE 2002 OLYMPICS
Brooks Leads the USA in Salt Lake

When the telephone rang at 4:00 in the morning in Herb Brooks' South Bend, Indiana, hotel room in 1999, he probably could not have guessed the caller was someone asking him to perform an encore.

"Herb, you got to coach the Olympic team in 2002," the caller said.

Even in a groggy state, Brooks recognized the voice.

"Sheehy, you're messed up," Brooks said.

"I know, Herb, but I haven't been drinking," former NHL player Neil Sheehy said.

"You're crazy, Sheehy," Brooks said, "I'm not coaching at the Olympics again."

Sheehy, one of Brooks' close friends, was in Florida for USA Hockey's executive board meetings and had spent a sleepless night thinking about how to sell USA Hockey officials on the idea of Brooks reprising the role he made famous in the 1980 Olympics at Lake Placid.

"Even though Herb said he didn't want to do it, I knew he would love it," Sheehy remembers.

The next morning Sheehy attended the meeting. "And everyone was open to the idea," Sheehy said. "But they said, 'It will be NHL players, and we have to have an NHL coach.'" At that point, Brooks had not coached in the NHL since 1992–93 with New Jersey.

Then fate threw its support toward the Sheehy plan. The Pittsburgh Penguins fired Kevin Constantine, and Penguins general manager Craig Patrick, Brooks' assistant in Lake Placid, named Brooks as interim Penguins coach. Suddenly, the idea of Brooks coaching the 2002 U.S. Olympic Team had legs to stand on. There was never any doubt in Sheehy's mind that this was the right idea. Brooks was held in such high esteem in America that both the Democratic and Republican parties courted him to run for public office at various times. No approval-rating poll was necessary to know that Brooks' defiant, fiery style in Lake Placid had won over Americans. He was a cultural icon. There were many in the country who wouldn't be able to name a single NHL player, but they could identify Brooks as an Olympic hockey icon. Americans loved Brooks because he had toppled the Soviets by using boys against men. He helped restore American pride at a time when his country needed a psychological boost.

There was every reason for Brooks to be involved more with USA Hockey after Lake Placid, and yet it didn't happen for two decades. It might not have happened at all if Sheehy, who grew up in Minnesota and played at Harvard and for U.S. National Teams, hadn't persevered. Attorney Sheehy realized quickly that the perceived gap between Brooks and USA Hockey wasn't as wide as it appeared to be. USA Hockey officials were far more willing to consider Brooks for the 2002 Olympic job than Brooks would have guessed.

"There were some issues that Herbie had in the past with USA Hockey," Ron DeGregorio said. "Actually, they weren't major issues...[but] there was a thawing out of the relationship, or maybe the lack of relationship, between Herbie and USA Hockey."

Even today it's difficult to pin down exactly what happened between Brooks and USA Hockey, but lack of communication exacerbated the situation.

"It was real from Herbie's perspective," DeGregorio said. "And the relationship needed to be built up a little bit, actually quite a bit."

Sheehy said he asked Brooks point-blank about what had prompted his disillusionment with USA Hockey, and Brooks told him a story about being "fired" by USA Hockey during a celebration party immediately after winning the gold medal in Lake Placid.

"All of the guys were partying after they won the gold medal, and Herb wanted them to get to bed because they were going to the White House," Sheehy recalled. "And someone connected with USA Hockey, but someone who was not on the board, told Herb, 'You've been in these kids' heads long enough. They won. Leave them alone.' Herb's concern was that he didn't want them showing up at the White House hungover. And the guy like said, 'Herbie, you are done, you are fired. And Herbie took that to be a statement across the board.'"

Not knowing exactly what happened at that party, USA Hockey's position was that no one at that time would have been authorized to speak for the executive board in that situation.

Despite Sheehy's lobbying, Brooks didn't immediately embrace the idea of being the U.S. coach again. This was a complicated issue because Brooks had always said that 1980 was his time, and he was moving on. Plus, Brooks didn't love the idea of NHL players playing in the Olympics. He preferred the Olympics staying for amateurs. Sheehy and Brooks argued the way brothers argue, when both parties are still confident they will remain close regardless of how the disagreement plays out.

At one point, Sheehy recalls Brooks said, "Darn it, I'm not doing it" and slamming down the phone.

Sheehy sat down and crafted a letter to Brooks, paraphrasing some passages from Brooks' speech to the 1980 Olympians. "You were born to coach, and this was an opportunity you were meant to have," Sheehy wrote. "You have the uncanny ability to make 20 men believe. The only tragedy I see is that I'm not sure you believe yourself."

After Brooks received the letter, he dialed up Sheehy and called him a "sonofabitch." Sheehy was starting to get to him. He was getting inside Brooks' head, the way Brooks always got into the players' heads.

"I said, 'Herb, sometimes if you want to change the world...you have to change yourself,'" Sheehy said.

That was the argument that worked on Brooks because he mentioned that conversation with Sheehy when he was announced as coach in 2001.

When USA Hockey hired Brooks in 2001, it did not receive the same dictatorial personality that it had hired in 1979. Brooks' strength as a coach is that he adapted his methods to fit his audience. In 1980 he was leading college kids against hardened pros. In 2002 he had 17 NHL veterans over the age of 30 on his roster. The college kids had needed tough love to harden them for the climb up the mountain, but the 2002 American team needed an experienced guide to help them find the right path for the journey.

"I thought everything would be real regimented at the orientation camp, and it was the exact opposite," USA Hockey's Jim Johannson said. "It was light skates and Herb just being around the players."

Not long after he took the job, Brooks began his work, calling Mike Richter unexpectedly to discuss his injury. At first Richter thought it was one of his New York teammates, maybe Brian Leetch, pulling his leg.

"He got me so motivated. I couldn't wait to get my leg better and to get going," Richter recalled. "He said, 'You will see Modano and Leetch, won't you.'"

When Richter said he would see them, Brooks said, "Tell them the legs feed the wolf."

"Sure," Richter said.

"Do you know what that means?" Brooks asked. "Sure...no, not really," Richter admitted.

"What it means is, in order for the wolf to get his prey, his legs have to get him there," Brooks said. "He has to be in excellent condition. And we are going to achieve our goal of winning the gold medal. We will have a lot of older players. We are going to have the legs to get us there. We need to be stronger than the next guy."

Pulling together a team of veterans is never an easy task, but Brooks knew how to do it. "He got to us because we all had so much respect for him," Richter said.

But this group of Americans also needed less motivation than most teams because they played for each other. "This was probably going to be this group's last time together, so the guys were pretty desperate to do whatever they could to make it a good showing.

Brooks had frequent discussions with captain Chris Chelios about strategy, tactics, and motivating the team. He solicited opinions from several players about how to approach the tournament. This was not the same guy who had marched his players through hell on the way to Lake Placid 22 years before.

"He knew who he was coaching," Roenick said. "He knew who he could push and who he couldn't. He respected where people were in their careers. He was very positive. He didn't scream. He inspired us through his knowledge and experience."

NHL general manager Craig Patrick and Larry Pleau plus USA Hockey international director Art Berglund were the U.S. management team. But, as was the case in 1980, Brooks called the shots. His two choices for assistant coaches were Lou Vairo and the late John Cuniff.

Cuniff was a very serious-minded professional who paid attention to the small details of the game.

"He had exceptional knowledge of the game, and he had huge respect for players because he could really [adjust] based on what the game situations were and how his players were performing," said USA Hockey's Jim Johannson.

Johannson says that when Cuniff told players to move up two feet when they were killing penalties, you would see players move up precisely two feet the next shift. "He could really simplify the game for players," Johannson said. "It wasn't a robotic thing, it was more about getting your hand and feet in position."

The choice of Vairo was fascinating because Vairo had been involved with the 1980 team, although Brooks never seemed to want to acknowledge his help. Maybe his selection in 2002 was Brooks' way of saying thanks for Vairo's contributions 22 years earlier.

In 1980 few Americans knew as much about international hockey as Lou Vairo did. "Before anybody knew who Lou was, he paid his way to go over to a clinic with [Anatoli] Tarasov in Russia in the early 1970s," USA Hockey's executive director Dave Ogrean said. "He hung out with Fred Shero. He became a devotee [of the] Russian style of hockey and Tarasov's training principles."

Ogrean was the media relations man for the 1980 team and was in the dressing room before its opening game with Sweden to see Vairo at the chalkboard and answering questions about how the Swedes would play. (A month before, Vairo had coached the U.S. National Junior Team at the World Junior Championship.)

"Craig and Herb were sitting on the bench asking questions," Ogrean said. "And I can tell you that the day before the Russian game Herb was all wound up. He wanted me to find Lou because he wanted to talk to him. I think they talked before every game because Lou was very knowledgeable about international hockey."

Vairo was also a good choice because he was particularly good with veteran teams. He had a colorful personality and was a polished storyteller. Players played hard for Vairo because they liked him and his stories. He had a million of them such as the one about him and Shero going for coffee before a Soviet hockey clinic in Russia in the 1970s.

"We took walks in the morning, and Fred said, 'There's a big, long line over there—that has to be for coffee,'" Vairo recalled. "You couldn't get anything without standing in line in Russia back then. We stood in line for an hour, and we finally turn[ed] the corner, and there was a horse and wagon and some big fat woman with a [babushka] on her head was selling cabbages. Fred thought that was quite funny."

Brooks put his stamp on the U.S. roster with his decision not to include defenseman Derian Hatcher. Whether he used NHL players or amateurs, Brooks preferred a skating team. As much as Hatcher was admired for his toughness and defensive prowess, Brooks didn't believe he skated well enough to be effective on the wider international ice surface. The call on Hatcher was definitely Brooks' call.

Brooks wanted the proven puck handlers, such as Brian Rafalski, Phil Housley, and Gary Suter. Certainly Vairo influenced the decision to take Housley. Although Housley was one of the greatest American players in NHL history, he was nearing the end of the road. In 2000 Vairo was asked to coach the U.S. National Team and asked Housley to play for him. Housley politely declined because his mother had died, and he wanted to spend time with his father, Leroy, who was struggling to deal with the loss.

Mike Richter had a 2.25 goals-against average and .932 save percentage in the 2002 Olympic Tournament.
(Brian Bahr/Getty Images/USA Hockey)

Vairo, who had known Housley since he was a teenager, began thinking about Housley and his father and decided to call him back.

"I thought, *Why not bring his dad with us?*" Vairo said. "He could room with him, be involved in our activities. I told him I thought it would be a good way to get his dad through the grief."

Housley agreed and joined the team. Vairo asked him again to play at the World Championship the following season. Housley said yes. This time, Brooks was in Germany to watch him play. "Herb wasn't sold on him, but he liked how he played in Germany," Vairo said.

The surprise pick by Brooks was Tom Poti, who ended up playing well. But primarily it was American hockey's greatest generation that carried the team, posting a 2–0–1 record in the preliminary round, including a 6–0 win against Finland, an 8–1 victory against Belarus, and a 2–2 tie with a Russian team that probably had the best pure skill in the tournament.

The 2–2 tie with Russia had drawn the best American television ratings for hockey since Brooks' boys had taken down the Soviets in 1980.

Thanks to their No. 1 seeding in the preliminary round, the Americans had a favorable quarterfinal matchup against Germany. But the Germans inexplicably gave Brooks a chance to do what he does best: churn up the passion in his team.

When the German coach, Hans Zach, said he didn't like facing the Americans, Brooks responded by saying, "Maybe that's why they lost the Second World War, guys. So there, I'll draw the line in the sand, and you can take that right back."

The Americans bared their teeth against the Germans, although John LeClair lost one of his in a 5–0 win. LeClair, Brett Hull, Roenick, Tony

Despite being hit by an errant stick against Germany that knocked out a tooth and required 14 stitches, John LeClair scored six goals for Team USA in Salt Lake City.
(USA Hockey)

Amonte, and Chris Chelios scored for the Americans, who had outscored opponents 21–3 at that point in the tournament.

The line of LeClair, Modano, and Hull had played superbly in the first four games. German defenseman Erich Goldmann's errant stick not only knocked out LeClair's tooth but also left a gaping gash that needed 14 stitches to repair. In deciding to play Hull on a line with Modano, Brooks was counting on the chemistry the duo displayed when they played together in Dallas from 1998–99 to 2000–01.

"I can't recall having the feel with a player that I had with Brett in those three years," Modano said. "You just knew that if you could get the puck into Brett, he would find some way [to] get it on the net."

Johannson insists that Modano's passing in 2002 was among the most amazing playmaking he

has ever witnessed. He seemed to set up goals with every conceivable type of pass.

There was a cross-ice feed to Hull for a one-timer; there was a forehand lob over the neutral zone to beat a defensive trap, for the wing to take it in stride.

"The third feed was at full speed, and guys were holding the blue line," Johannson said. "He gains the line going full tilt and feeds a two-foot saucer pass to the right wing breaking in. By not breaking stride, he allowed the right wing to stay in stride."

Just before the Americans' game against Germany, Belarus had defeated Sweden 4–3 in a game that ranks as one of the greatest upsets in Olympic hockey history.

The Swedish fall helped Brooks make a point to his team that David always has a chance to take down Goliath if his passion is high and his aim true. "It helped us in the locker room to get ready," Richter said. "We talked about it before the game, how a great team like Sweden was shocked."

In another quarterfinal, the Russians had defeated the Czechs 1–0 to set up a rematch with USA in the semifinal. Coincidently, the game would be played on February 22, 2002, the 22nd anniversary of USA's win against the Soviets at Lake Placid.

The hockey drama developing in West Valley City, Utah, was a sports columnist's delight: the architect of the greatest upset in sports history had returned to the Olympics to add another layer to his coaching legend.

Brooks refused to play along for the sake of good storytelling. He kept saying it was Chelios' team, not his team. "His stamp is on this team," Brooks said. "What he does and says is respected by quality people, and we have quality people in the room."

The 2002 U.S. team had its 1980-style moment when Brooks gathered them around him at practice and handed out USA Hockey pens to each one of them. "I want you to write your own story," Brooks told everyone.

Young still has that pen, and he cherishes it. "Herb was a great motivator," Young said. "The way he spoke, the tone of his voice. Handing out those pens was his way of saying it wasn't about him. It wasn't about 1980."

Understandably, he had refused to draw any comparison between his mission in 1980 and what he was trying to accomplish in Utah. "There are no similarities whatsoever," Brooks said. "I don't know what else to say."

The Russian forward list read like the who's who list of top NHL scorers: Igor Larionov, Pavel Bure, Sergei Fedorov, Ilya Kovalchuk, Alexei Kovalev, and Alexei Zhamnov. The Russians were a fast team that hoped to turn the ice rink into the Autobahn, with no set speed limit. Nikolai Khabibulin was in the net, protected by a defense that included feisty Darius Kasparaitis, Sergei Gonchar, and Vladimir Malakhov.

The semifinal turned out to be a two-part story. The Americans owned the first 40 minutes, building up a 3–0 lead on goals by Bill Guerin, Scott Young, and Phil Housley. The final 20 minutes belonged to the Russians. When the third period started, it was as if the flood had arrived and the Americans couldn't set up the sandbags quickly enough. Kovalev scored 11 seconds into the third period, and then Malakhov added a goal at 3:21 to make it a one-goal game.

At that point, goalie Mike Richter's survival skills became America's greatest weapon. He made 17 saves, none more important than the post-to-post, back-to-back saves he made against Sergei Samsonov and Alexei Yashin. "It was like holding on for dear life," Modano said. "It was end-to-end against a great Russian team. It was one of most fun games I ever played in."

With respect to how ferociously the Americans had to scrap to hold off Russia in the third period, Roenick called it "the best game I ever played in."

No miracle had been needed to down the Russians in 2002, but Brooks' aura still was important. The players had faith in Brooks' ability to keep their starship in the right orbit. This group of U.S. players had confidence in their own abilities, but they needed a commander who wasn't timid about opening the torpedo tubes. After the 3–2 win against the Russians, Brooks was 10–0–2 as an Olympic coach.

"He was the right person to coach that team," DeGregorio said. "He was different than he was in 1980. He was inspirational without being caustic."

Mike Modano teamed with Brett Hull, his Dallas Stars teammate for three seasons, to lead a potent Team USA line. Modano totaled six assists in the Olympics. (USA Hockey)

The triumph against the Russians meant the Americans would face Canada in the gold-medal game. It was a dream matchup for the NHL in terms of exposing the game.

The Americans hadn't lost an Olympic hockey game on their home ice since the 1932 Olympics. They had been undefeated in winning the gold medals in Squaw Valley, California, in 1960 and Lake Placid, New York, in 1980. Going into the gold-medal game in 2002, the Americans had a 24-game Olympic unbeaten streak (21-0-3) on home ice. Meanwhile, Canada was trying to win its first Olympic gold medal since Edmonton's Waterloo Mercurys won in Oslo, Norway, in 1952. Some streak was going to end in the gold-medal game.

The U.S. did look like a team of destiny when Amonte, the 1996 World Cup hero, scored to give it a 1–0 lead. But then Paul Kariya and Jarome Iginla answered about four minutes apart to give Canada the lead.

In the second period, the Americans were fighting to stay in the game. They gamely killed off a two-man disadvantage power play, and then Brian Rafalski tied the game with a goal.

Even after Sakic scored to give Canada the lead again later in the second period, the Americans made no concession. It wasn't until four minutes remaining when Iginla redirected Steve Yzerman's shot past Richter that Canadian players started to relax. Sakic added his second goal shortly thereafter to make it a 5–2 final verdict.

"It was a lost opportunity," Roenick said about the game. "A couple of mistakes were the difference."

As is always the case, there were multiple factors that led to Canada's win:

Canada boasted a talented team, managed by Wayne Gretzky. His presence certainly added a layer of emotion to the team. Who would disappoint the Great One?

In hindsight, the Canadian forwards probably won the game, wearing down the defense with their constant pressure. Could it have been a different story if Brooks had picked beastly Derian Hatcher for the team? "You can wonder about that, but you can't pick your team based on a chance you might meet Canada in the finals," Johannson said. "You pick your team on your style of play."

The win over Russia had exacted a toll. It was an emotionally draining win for the Americans. Meanwhile, Canada had a much easier semifinal romp against Belarus, a team that already felt like winners because of the upset against Sweden.

The Americans lost Keith Tkachuk to injury in the Russian game, and his physical presence was sorely missed against the always-physical Canadians. Tkachuk was a central figure on the team.

Although the silver medal felt like defeat to the Americans, it had long-term value for the American program and the NHL. No one in the league office would ever admit it, but having a USA-Canada Final provided the league with the most marketing value. In terms of television ratings, the Canada vs. USA Final outperformed the Russia vs. USA game, making it the most-watched hockey game in the United States since 1980.

The strong performance by the Americans also helped mop up the bad karma the U.S. program suffered because of the USA team's poor performance in 1998, coupled with the trashing of the two rooms in the Olympic village.

The silver medal also provided another layer of validation for the belief that the Leetch-Roenick-Modano-Chelios-Hull–led U.S. group was American hockey's greatest generation. After this tournament, Leetch and Richter owned a bronze at the World Junior Championship (1986), a silver at the Canada Cup (1991), a gold at the World Cup (1996), and a silver at the Olympics (2002). Most of the key Americans were involved in three of those events.

Plus, USA Hockey had reunited with Brooks. Considering that Brooks had been the mastermind behind the USA's greatest hockey triumph, this was long overdue.

"Our relationship was never as bad as everyone thought it was," Bush said. "I always felt that Herb got more out of a team in a short tournament than any coach I had ever seen."

To this day, DeGregorio and Bush are thankful to Sheehy for the work he did to bring Brooks back into the USA Hockey family. It would not have happened without his intervention. After the 2002 Olympics, Brooks had interest in coaching the U.S. National Junior Team, but that discussion fizzled.

"He wanted to be more and more involved," DeGregorio said. "But the question was of how he would be involved. We couldn't resolve how that would take place, but he passed away before it happened."

On August 11, 2003, Brooks lost control of his minivan on a highway north of the Twin Cities. He was killed instantly, and America lost an icon.

Mike Eruzione was on a plane traveling home on a short flight from New York, and when he landed, he had 18 messages on his phone. He returned one call and was told Brooks was dead. He had to hang up. "Then I cried," he said.

Brooks' death stunned his players because he always seemed bigger than life. Even into his sixties, Brooks seemed vibrant, imposing, and bulletproof. "It seems like all the great innovators die young," 1980 defenseman Ken Morrow told the Associated Press. "Coach may have been the greatest innovator the sport has ever had." ∎

Bobby Ryan celebrates after scoring the USA's first goal during the preliminary game between the USA and Switzerland on Day 5 of the 2010 Winter Olympics in Vancouver, Canada. The USA won the game 3–1. (Bruce Bennett/ Getty Images/USA Hockey)

THE 2010 OLYMPICS
Taking on Canada in Vancouver

Brian Burke sounded more like a music appreciation instructor than a Team USA general manager when he addressed potential 2010 Olympians at the orientation camp in the summer of 2009.

"When you go to a symphony orchestra, the first violin is elegant, and there is a spotlight on her, and she is in the front row," Burke told players. "But in the back row, there is a guy like me blowing on a tuba. And they don't start the show until we both sit down."

He wanted players to understand that he was going to build the Olympic team like he would any other team, meaning he was going to fill every job on the roster with a player who was accustomed to doing that job. He wasn't looking for America's 20 most-skilled players. He wanted size on the U.S. team. He wanted checkers. He wanted shot blockers. He wanted grunts. He didn't just want star players saying they could fill those roles. He didn't want clarinet players trying to figure out how to beat on the drums all day.

Burke didn't bother with analogies when he delivered his message to the U.S. Selection Committee. When NHL general managers David Poile, Don Waddell, Dean Lombardi, Paul Holmgren, and Ray Shero, plus USA Hockey's Jim Johannson gathered in October, Burke told them, "We cannot make a mistake. We don't have the luxury to be off by one or two players."

The American hockey talent pool was deeper than it ever had been, but Canada still had twice as many NHL players. This is a country rich enough in hockey skill to leave defenseman Mike Green off its 2010 Olympic Team the season after he became only the eighth NHL defenseman to score 30 or more goals in a season. The Canadians also didn't take Steven Stamkos, who was on his way to the Rocket Richard Trophy as the league's top goal scorer.

To beat Team Canada, Burke believed the Americans would have to fit all of the pieces together perfectly. As an NHL general manager,

Burke always loved big, physical teams. As Burke likes to say, he prefers his NHL teams "to have the appropriate amount of belligerence." Sometimes, Burke used the word "truculence," but the point was always the same.

Burke wanted the 2010 U.S. Olympic Team to be fierce, combative, and mighty. He wanted players who viewed themselves as modern-day gladiators. The fact that the tournament was being played for the first time on an NHL-sized rink (200 feet x 85 feet) instead of an international rink (200 feet x 100 feet) simply reinforced his belief that an Olympic roster needed as much spit as polish. Burke wanted players with size on his roster, and he wanted players who didn't mind getting their hands dirty. At the orientation camp, Burke said in his mind there were probably 14 players already penciled in for one of the 23 roster spots, and the nine remaining spots were "wide open."

To accent his desire to have a prickly presence on his squad, he talked glowingly during the camp about Vancouver's Ryan Kesler, St. Louis' David Backes, and Los Angeles' Dustin Brown, all of whom fit the description of bigger, skilled players with a combative nature.

As the roster selection process played out, the most important debate came down to Scott Gomez vs. Joe Pavelski for the No. 2 center position. A factor in that debate was how the group viewed Kesler. If the selection committee saw Kesler as the No. 2 center, then Pavelski had the advantage because he was a much better fit at No. 3 center. He was a better defensive player and all-around player than Gomez. If Kesler was the No. 3 center, then perhaps Gomez was the best choice for the No. 2 center. The decision went to Pavelski, whom Burke referred to as a "Swiss army knife" because he had many functions.

It probably helped Pavelski that U.S. coach Ron Wilson had previously coached him in San Jose. "Watch how he plays—you can play him at any position," Wilson said. "He'll score a power-play goal. He'll win the face off."

When the team was announced, Burke recalls there was criticism of the roster in almost every NHL city where an American played. But nationally the only player who seemed to be a focal point of debate was New York Rangers center Chris Drury. The decision to add him to the team was mildly surprising. Fair or not, the perception of Drury was that he was no longer an elite-level player.

At the press conference, when Burke was asked directly why Drury was on the squad, he said bluntly: "Because he is Chris Drury."

What Burke was saying is that Drury had been a winner his entire life, starting from the time he helped his hometown of Trumbull, Connecticut, win the Little League World Series. He could check. He could kill penalties. He could play on the fourth line or play among the top six forwards. And he would do whatever was asked without complaint. He was a leader.

After the team was chosen, somewhere it was written that Zach Parise might be the only U.S. Olympian who could make the Canadian roster.

When selections were complete, Burke liked his roster. But when it was done, he realized immediately that building a complete team instead of an All-Star team meant that the USA would not be in an advantageous position if it reached the gold-medal game, where overtime would be played four-on-four. The rugged, tough, gritty guys on the U.S. squad weren't all the type of players that you want on the ice in four-on-four when it's all about skating.

"Maybe that's a mistake," Burke told coach Ron Wilson.

"If you are telling me we are going to get to overtime of the gold-medal game, I would take my chances four-on-four," Wilson said.

Neither man knew how prophetic the conversation would be.

As much as the selection committee liked its roster, Burke was constantly saying that the Americans were the underdogs. "If you go to Vegas before the tournament, there isn't going to be a penny bet on us," he would say.

He argued with anyone who questioned whether the Americans were truly underdogs. "We aren't manufacturing this," Burke said. "We are underdogs."

One person who wasn't buying the idea of the USA being an underdog was Team Canada boss Steve Yzerman. He also didn't accept the notion that there was more pressure on Canada playing in Vancouver.

"Honestly, do you think they'll have a parade in Moscow if the Russians go home with a silver medal? They won't," Yzerman said. "The expectation in Sweden is gold and, whether they admit it or not, the [Americans] are in it to win a gold medal."

The Americans had to replace Paul Martin and Mike Komisarek before the tournament. Burke inserted Ryan Whitney, a two-way defenseman, and Tim Gleason, who was more of a stay-at-home guy. "When you lose a hammer, you don't replace it with a wrench," Burke said about the Gleason pickup. "You replace it with another hammer."

Before the tournament, it was clear that this would be the most-talked-about hockey tournament in Olympic history. Nothing less than the gold medal was going to satisfy Canadian fans.

The Russians—with Alex Ovechkin, Evgeni Malkin, and Pavel Datsyuk, among others—were supposed to provide Canada's biggest challenge. No one was talking too much about the Americans,

even after they dispatched Switzerland 3–1 and Norway 6–1. That changed when the USA played Canada in the third preliminary game. The Canadians were also undefeated, although they needed a shootout goal from Sidney Crosby to beat Switzerland.

USA Hockey's executive director Dave Ogrean compared the U.S.-Canadian hockey rivalry to two brothers "who fight but would defend each other if attacked by a third party."

"I don't think this is a very friendly rivalry," said Chicago Blackhawks right wing Patrick Kane, a Buffalo native.

USA center Ryan Kesler said during the tournament that he "hated" the Canadians, although he did back off that statement, adding that he respected the way they played the game.

Before the Olympic hockey tournament began, Jack Johnson rented a private plane to take him to Vancouver to march in the opening ceremony. He asked Los Angeles Kings teammates Dustin Brown and Jonathan Quick if they wanted to go because they were on the U.S. roster. He didn't extend the same invitation to Kings teammate Drew Doughty, who was playing for Team Canada.

Johnson's explanation afterward was that, "It was a very small plane."

Before the game against Canada, Johnson was asked about playing against his Northern neighbors. "Do I dislike them?" he asked. "Yes."

Canadian fans expected their team to thump the Americans, but it never happened. U.S. defenseman Brian Rafalski had a pair of goals to spark a 5–3 win over Canada that gave the Americans the No. 1 seed going into the medal round. This was USA's first Olympic win over Canada since 1960.

"This proves to ourselves, a young team, when we are up against a daunting task we can play our game," U.S. forward David Backes said. "But this is one game, and we had to scratch and claw for everything we had."

USA goalie Ryan Miller made 42 saves, and U.S. coach Ron Wilson said it was probably the best game he had ever seen Miller play.

"Maybe there will be a little less yelling on the streets," Backes said. "Friday night, walking back to the hotel was a little scary at times. I wore a USA Hockey shirt, and I had to get my wife under my wing and scoot through."

In the quarterfinals, the Americans had to again face the Swiss. The Americans had two concerns: Swiss goalie Jonas Hiller (Anaheim Ducks) and the fact that the Swiss had added confidence by pushing Canada to a shootout.

Concern over Hiller was well founded because he stopped the first 35 shots he faced against the Americans before surrendering a power-play goal to Zach Parise early in the third period. Parise added another goal, and USA had a 2–0 win and a semifinal date with Finland.

Against Finland, the Americans scored six goals in the first 12:54 of the game en route to a 6–1 victory that put them in the gold-medal game. Two goals by Kane, plus one each from Ryan Malone, Erik Johnson, Paul Stastny, and Parise was the best single-period offensive production by any Olympic team since 1964. "I've said all along that we have yet to play our best game," said Kane. "We played a great 15 minutes, but I think we [have] more in the tank."

One of the big coaching moves of the tournament was coach Ron Wilson's decision to move Kane off the line with Paul Stastny and Zach Parise and put him with Kesler. That Kesler-Kane combination was crucial to the Americans' success.

But the key to the Americans' overall success was goalie Ryan Miller. Before the season, it was presumed that Miller and Thomas would battle to be No. 1. But that battle never occurred because Miller was clearly the best NHL goalie in 2009–10. Miller's composure seemed to be the foundation of the U.S. team.

"I'm starting to wonder if his heartbeat ever elevates," Backes said as USA entered the medal round. "He's cool, calm, collected. Even after that 42-save performance against Canada, we might have got a half of a smile out of him."

Miller didn't surrender a goal in either the quarterfinals or semifinals.

Miller is a gaunt-looking 6'2" and weighs 175 pounds. "The first time I ever saw him play, I was struck by how skinny he was," Burke said. "He's still a bone rack. I had his brother Drew [on the Anaheim Ducks] by me in his underwear, and I said to him, 'Did they have a weight room at Michigan State?'"

Since the preliminary-round meeting between Canada and the U.S., Canada had made a change in net, replacing Marty Brodeur with Roberto Luongo.

The day before the gold-medal game, Kesler, who plays with Luongo in Vancouver, said he knew Luongo's weaknesses and predicted he would score against him.

The buildup for the game was both intense and festive. Canada men's hockey coach Mike Babcock joked that he was aware of the movie *Miracle*, about the USA's 1980 gold-medal performance. "My kids watch it and think it's great, and I don't think it's that great," he said.

"Hockey is not a sport in Canada—it's a cult. It's a religion," Burke said. "The Canadians view this as their game, and they view this game as planting the flag on the peak."

In the third period of Canada's 3–2 win against Slovakia in the semifinals, fans were chanting, "We want USA! We want USA!"

Ryan Miller guards the net during the USA's 6–1 preliminary round win over Norway. Miller was named the MVP of the 2010 Olympic Men's Hockey tournament. (Jeff Cable/USA Hockey)

"I think a gold medal immortalizes your team," Burke said. "As [Philadelphia Flyers] coach Fred Shero told his team in 1974, 'If we win today together, we will walk together forever.'" Coincidentally, Babcock made a similar point, mentioning the same Shero quote. "Don't get me wrong," Babcock said. "We'd like to do it for our country, but we would like to do it for ourselves first."

The Americans didn't have the start they wanted in the gold-medal game. By the second period, they were down 2–0 on goals from Jonathan Toews and Corey Perry.

Kesler then made good on his promise by redirecting Kane's shot past Luongo for a goal that cut Canada's lead to a single goal. Meanwhile, Miller was keeping the Americans in the contest with save after save. He made breakaway stops against Sidney Crosby and Eric Staal.

The Americans kept pressuring Luongo, and finally Parise scored with 24.4 seconds remaining to send the game to overtime. Wilson had pulled his goalie with over a minute left in the game, and Parise scored after Kane's shot rebounded off Luongo's pad. It was interesting to note that when the game was on the line, Wilson had Pavelski on the ice in the final minute. The selection committee had made the right call on Pavelski.

The building was dripping with tension in the overtime. Miller made key stops against Scott Niedermayer, Jarome Iginla, and Patrick Marleau.

U.S. forward Phil Kessel rang a shot off the crossbar. The Americans were at that point, two inches from a gold medal. That's as close as they would get.

At 7:40 of overtime, Canadian megastar Sidney Crosby fired a shot through Miller to claim the gold medal for Canada.

The play looked innocent seconds before. Crosby lost the puck along the boards and over-skated it, but the puck hit referee Bill McCreary's skate. Crosby pushed the puck toward Jarome Iginla, who seemed to be covered by Ryan Suter.

U.S. defenseman Brian Rafalski reacted to Crosby then heading toward the goal, but it was too late. Crosby had a step, called for Iggy to send him the puck, and Iginla delivered the perfect pass. Miller went for the poke check, and Crosby read his move and fired it past him.

"That was the only time in the tournament in that situation where Miller tried a poke check," Burke said.

Despite the loss in the final, the 2010 Olympic tournament was an important event for the American program. The television ratings demonstrated that hockey was gaining national attention. The 27.6 million television viewers watching the gold-medal game was up 10.5 million over the average audience for the 2002 gold-medal game between Canada and USA in Salt Lake City.

When Parise scored the game-tying goal, it was estimated that there were 34.8 million viewers watching in the United States.

The 2010 gold-medal game was the most watched hockey game in the United States since the 1980 game between the U.S. and Finland. There was a buzz about this game beyond the usual hockey markets, suggesting perhaps that this new generation of American players intrigues general fans.

It was undeniably one of the most entertaining games in Olympic history. "Throughout the game, we thought we would win," Parise said.

Throughout the tournament, there were stories about the veterans on the U.S. team showing the younger players how it was done. But truth may have been that it was the younger players inspiring the veteran players.

"I think the veterans fed off the energy and enthusiasm of the younger players," Johannson said.

The silver medal established, with some certainty, that the class of American players born in the mid-1980s could be a memorable group. "I thought this team played as well as any team I've ever coached," Wilson said.

Suter, Parise, and Kesler, for example, now have won World Championships at the Under-18 and Under-20 levels and an Olympic silver medal. Ryan Miller, born in 1980, is slightly older than the core group, but USA's No. 3 goalie Jonathan Quick's development with the Los Angeles Kings gives the U.S. a premium goalie in that age group. David Backes demonstrated that he could be a key member of that group.

The only missing ingredient of this group might be star power. In comparison to America's greatest hockey generation, it doesn't have the dominant offensive centers like Pat LaFontaine, Jeremy Roenick, or Mike Modano.

After four Olympics using NHL players, the Americans and Canadians are the only countries to reach the gold-medal game twice.

Burke's plan for building a winner was also validated. He assembled a committee of NHL general managers, plus Johannson, to help him on selecting a team. "As it turned out, he was bang on about how we couldn't make any mistakes," Johannson said.

The committee was right about Chris Drury, who turned out to be an essential role player, and Gleason, who was a crucial shot blocker.

Before the tournament, it angered Burke to hear a journalist suggesting that Parise might be the only player on the U.S. roster who could make the Canadian team. When the tournament was completed, there were several Americans who had

Brian Rafalski, who was named the best defenseman in the 2010 Olympic hockey tournament, celebrates after scoring against Canada. Rafalski tied with Zach Parise as the top point-producer for Team USA.
(Bruce Bennett/Getty Images/USA Hockey)

more productive tournaments than some Canadian players.

Miller was the tournament's best goalie, posting a .942 save percentage. Parise was exceptional. Suter was one of the tournament's top defensemen. Kesler was a monstrous force in the middle of the ice. In the end, there truly wasn't much difference between the Canadian and American rosters. Said Burke: "I would like to meet the idiot that wrote that only one of our players could play for Canada."

Burke always comes with the proper amount of belligerence. ∎

Team Captain Derek Stepan and teammates celebrate following the USA's gold-medal win over Canada at the 2010 IIHF World Junior Championship. (Matthew Manor/ HHOF-IIHF Images)

THE WORLD JUNIOR CHAMPIONSHIPS

America's Bright Hockey Future

At the 2011 World Junior Championship, the American roster included 16 players who were drafted in the first or second round of the NHL draft. When the U.S. competed at the inaugural WJC in 1977, USA Hockey official Art Berglund had to borrow two players from Dartmouth's junior varsity team to fill out the roster.

When Berglund begged college coaches for players in the early years of the WJC, it was like he was asking them to send their players to the outer galaxies of space.

"No one knew what the tournament was," Berglund said. "We couldn't get anyone to coach the team the first year. We even asked Denver's Murray Armstrong, and he hadn't even become an American citizen yet. He didn't want to do it, but he gave us his assistant Marshall Johnston."

In the first tournament in the Czech Republic, the Soviets had Sergei Makarov and Slava Fetisov. The late Pelle Lindbergh was in net for Sweden. In hindsight, the most prominent player on the U.S. squad was Richie Dunn, who ended up playing 483 NHL games, mostly with the Buffalo Sabres. Another player on the U.S. squad was Don Waddell, who is known more today as the longtime general manager and president of the Atlanta Thrashers. He actually played for the USA in the first two WJC events in 1977 and 1978. The Americans finished seventh in that first tournament, although it did beat Lindbergh's Swedish team. But that's not what Waddell recalls. He remembers the tanks that were always visible in this closed communist country that was still behind the iron curtain in those days. "When we were coming in from the airport, there was a slew of tanks," Waddell said. "Those tanks were a daily sight. At the time, it was a communist country, and we were guarded about where we could and couldn't go. You felt insecure."

Waddell said the American team only won a game or two, but he jokingly recalls that the American players were the big winners in the country's black market. The stat he remembers: he owned a ski jacket that he paid $30 for in the U.S., and he sold it in Czechoslovakian for $90. "Over there, they couldn't get their hands on that stuff," Waddell said. "Everyone sold whatever blue jeans they had before they came home."

The other memory he has from the tournament: how well the Czechoslovakian people treated the Americans. "The Americans were looked up to in those years," Waddell recalled. "We were looked up to because we were free, and people went out of their way to make us feel at home."

Today, the WJC is a multimillion-dollar event, but in early years, the Americans had to scrape together funds for the trip. Lou Vairo, who coached the USA in the third WJC, recalls soliciting contributions from hockey-minded businessmen and purchasing some windbreakers at Kmart. He stenciled *USA* on the jackets himself. "We just wanted to give the kids something," he said.

Today, games from the WJC are broadcast on the NHL Network, and the Internet provides thorough coverage. In the early years, players didn't aspire to play in the WJC because they had never heard of it. "You took the players you could get," Berglund said. "Coaches didn't even understand how it worked. They would say I have this freshman...and I would have to say, 'Yes, but he is too old.' Today, we talk about having a 1993 or 1994 birthday, and everyone understands. But it took us 10 or 15 years to get there."

It took many years for coaches to understand. The Americans only medaled twice in the first 20

years the tournament was held. Their first medal came in 1986, when Brian Leetch, Mike Richter, Scott Young, Darren Turcotte, Jimmy Carson, Lane McDonald, Paul Ranheim, and others led the Americans to a bronze medal. That was about the time that college coaches began to cooperate more fully in the lending of players. If Richter had not come down with blood poisoning, the Americans may have won the silver medal. Young and Turcotte were the offensive catalysts, combining for 13 goals in seven games.

The following year, the Americans didn't medal, but University of Minnesota goalie Robb Stauber was sensational in net as the USA beat the Soviets for the first time in WJC history. In 1989 Jeremy Roenick became the first American to win the WJC scoring title, producing eight goals and eight assists to capture the crown in a field that included Russian greats Alexander Mogilny and Pavel Bure. Roenick's linemates were future Hall of Famer Mike Modano and Joe Sacco, who ended up playing in the NHL and was coaching the Colorado Avalanche in 2010–11.

In 1991 Doug Weight (five goals and 14 assists) outpointed Canadian megaprospect Eric Lindros to win the 1991 WJC scoring title in Saskatoon, Saskatchewan. Kevin Constantine, the U.S. coach, said Weight outplayed Lindros start-to-finish. "Doug Weight was the best forward, and he was the best defensive forward of all those getting points," Constantine offered.

A native of Roseville, Michigan, Weight said the USA proved a point by tying Canada 4–4. "It was ridiculous how we were talked about before the tournament," Weight said. "[Canadian media] was talking about us being a tune-up for teams, a chance for Canada to get its lines together."

Weight had two goals and six assists in a 19–1 win against Norway. "Everything I shot or passed ended up in the goal," Weight said. "I didn't play that well. My wingers Keith Tkachuk and Chris Gotziaman buried everything for me."

The bronze medal–winning 1993 U.S. team—with Tkachuk, Chris and Peter Ferraro, and Scott LaChance—was one of the USA's best.

Again the spotlight was on the goaltender, in this case University of Maine's Mike Dunham. "When Dunham was in goal," said U.S. coach Walt Kyle, "the team expected to win."

Remembering the tournament, Dunham said, "The puck seemed the size of basketball to me. I was on one of those rolls where I felt I could stop anything."

In terms of visibility, the U.S. junior team has come a long way. Vairo remembers how, when he was hired by USA Hockey in 1978, his first assignment was to attend the college coaches' convention and convince the fraternity that the U.S. junior program was worthwhile.

"I told them, 'Give us your players, and we will give you back a better player,'" Vairo said. "The experience these players get can't be found anywhere else."

It's a better experience today because the Americans are always among the favorites "to bring home some jewelry" as Berglund calls the chase for medals.

The arrival of the U.S. National Team Development Program (NTDP) has undeniably had an impact on the Americans' ability to compete in international tournaments.

From 1977 to 1996, the Americans won two medals at the WJC. In the 15 years since USA debuted its development program, the Americans have won five medals, including two gold. In 1997 the Jeff Jackson–coached Americans won the silver medal, losing 2–0 to Canada in the final. Robert Esche was the U.S. goalie, and the team included future NHL players Mark Parrish, Mike York, Tom Poti, Eric Rasmussen, and Paul Mara, among others. The first hard evidence of the NTDP's potential came in 2002 when Zach Parise and Ryan Suter collaborated on a goal with less than two minutes left in the game to give the Americans their first gold medal in the World Under-18 Championship.

The true turning point in America's participation in the WJC came in 2004 when the group that won the World Under-18 Championship also delivered a WJC championship in Finland with a 4–3 win against a Canadian team that boasted Ryan Getzlaf, Sidney Crosby, Jeff Carter, and Dion Phaneuf. The American squad included Suter, Parise, and Ryan Kesler, plus other future NHL players James Wisniewski, Patrick Eaves, Drew Stafford, and Jake Dowell. U.S. NTDP Coach Mike Eaves was also the coach of that team.

This was a very confident group, to the point that USA was considered a co-favorite going into the tournament. The Americans went 4–0, outscoring teams 21–4 in the preliminary round, which included a 4–1 win against a Russian team that had Alex Ovechkin, Alexander Semin, and Evgeni Malkin. "I think the way we beat them, we must have blocked 30 shots that game," said Parise. "Right there you could see the commitment we had to winning."

Perhaps the team's toughest challenge came in the semifinals when the Americans defeated the Finns 2–1 in front of their home crowd. Finland had defeated USA in a pretournament exhibition game.

USA Hockey Assistant Executive Director Jim Johannson called that game "the most physical junior game" he had ever witnessed. "It was a war," Eaves told NHL.com writer Adam Kimelman in 2008. "You had to be a man to play in that game."

The USA won its first World Junior Championship gold medal in 2004, defeating Canada 4–3 in the final.
(Pekka Mononen/USA Hockey)

Once Finland was dispatched, the Americans turned to the Canadians. Both teams were 5–0 going into the gold-medal game. Future NHL player Patrick O'Sullivan turned out to be one of the USA's heroes, scoring two third-period goals, including a game-winner that was delivered in bizarre fashion.

The Americans trailed 3–1 after two periods, and O'Sullivan pulled the U.S. within a goal at 4:39 of the third period with a nifty wrist shot over Canadian goalie Marc-Andre Fleury. O'Sullivan's second tally, at 14:48 of the period, was far less spectacular and far more meaningful. O'Sullivan was steaming down the ice chasing a loose puck, and he was credited with the goal after Fleury

tried to clear the puck and hit Braydon Coburn. The puck caromed into Canada's goal for the game winner.

"You have to say it was one of the biggest wins in U.S. history, because it was the first at the World Juniors," said Jim Johannson.

Jimmy Howard had been the goaltender at the World Under-18 Championship, but he was sidelined with an infection. It was Al Montoya in net for the USA, and he was named to the tournament All-Star Team. Parise was named the tournament's MVP. Eaves shook every player's hand, thanking them for delivering USA Hockey's first gold medal in 28 years of the tournament.

Revenge was certainly talked about after the game, because 10 of the Americans had lost to Canada 3–2 in the 2003 semifinals. "It has been a long wait to get revenge, but it is sweet," Parise said.

Eaves' message to his players before the third period was simply that their best work was coming in that period. "Some say it's a tournament, but it's really a marathon," Stafford said. "You play your heart out in this tournament."

This triumph cemented the validity of the NTDP as a program that was going to produce results in international tournaments. The 2004 gold medal launched a U.S. run of four WJC medals over eight years. The Ron Rolston–coached U.S. team picked up a bronze in 2007 by beating the host Swedes 2–1 on goals by Erik Johnson and Patrick Kane. James van Riemsdyk, who was also on that bronze-medal squad, was the No. 2 overall pick by the Philadelphia Flyers in 2007.

In 2010 the Americans slayed the dragon in the dragon's lair when they beat Canada 6–5 in a dramatic overtime win in Saskatoon, Saskatchewan, that will put defenseman John Carlson forever among American hockey heroes. He scored at 4:21 of overtime to give the Americans their second title.

"Eventually people are going to ask, 'How many championships did you win?'" Johannson said. "They aren't going to say, 'Boy there were a lot of great games that could have gone their way.' You have to close out championships. We did that [in Saskatoon]."

Coming into the tournament, the Americans had only defeated Canada five times in 35 games at the WJC. "We cut some people that were maybe more talented," said U.S. coach Dean Blais. "We wanted a team that was mentally tough, guys who would block shots. This team had grit and character."

They needed the mental toughness because they squandered a two-goal lead in the closing 2:26 of the game when Edmonton Oilers prize prospect Jordan Eberle scored twice within a span of a little more than a minute. The first came on a power-play goal with Kyle Palmieri in the penalty box for bumping the goalie after driving the net for a shot. "It was a little bit scary when the game

The U.S. team picked up a bronze in the 2007 World Junior Championship by beating the host Swedes 2–1 on goals by Erik Johnson and Patrick Kane. (Andre Ringuette/ USA Hockey)

was 5–5," Blais conceded. "But they regrouped in between periods."

Carlson said players began telling themselves that they would have gladly taken an overtime game with a chance to win coming into the game. "If anything, we showed that this team had character," Carlson said.

Another key for the Americans was Blais' decision to pull goaltender Mike Lee after he gave up three goals and switch to Jack Campbell. "He was the difference," Blais said.

Lee, a Phoenix Coyotes draft pick, had won the quarterfinal and semifinal games. "He was the first guy to come up and hug me when it was over," Campbell said. "It could have just as easily been him making those saves in the third period."

But it was Campbell making the stops, including one big save before Carlson's game-winning goal. "Any time Carlson has the puck on his stick, the goalie should be afraid," Campbell said, laughing.

It was a four-on-four play in overtime, and Carlson said he shot the puck because he thought it was a safer play than making a pass, which could quickly go the other way if it were intercepted. New York Rangers prospect Derek Stepan and Toronto Maple Leafs draftee Jerry D'Amigo combined on two third-period goals to give the U.S. to a 5-3 lead.

Team USA celebrates with the trophy following its 6–5 overtime win over Canada in the gold-medal game of the 2010 IIHF World Junior Championship. (Richard Wolowicz/Getty Images/USA Hockey)

University of Wisconsin player Stepan, the team captain, set up Jerry D'Amigo for a goal a little more than four minutes into the third period, and just over two minutes later, Stepan scored on a backhander with D'Amigo drawing an assist.

When Carlson started slowly at the World Junior Championship last December, U.S. coaches began to push his restart button. He told coaches he was waiting for the games against Canada.

Johannson recalls that coach Dean Blais said he "got into Carlson's kitchen a little bit" and challenged him to take his game to a higher level. Carlson did exactly that, scoring the game-winning overtime goal to give USA a 6–5 win against Canada in the gold-medal game. Carlson fired a wrist shot from the right-wing circle to beat Canada on Canadian ice. "I think everyone in Canada knows who John Carlson is," Johannson said.

"I was on the two-on-one with [Carlson], so I was just thinking, *Don't pass, don't pass.*" Stepan recalled. "To be honest with you, I knew that they had a new goaltender in the net, and my thought process was, the way he shoots the puck, just end it now."

Stepan knew Carlson scored because the building went completely quiet. "It was surreal," he said.

That goal probably ranks among the top 10 goals in American international hockey history. "We challenged [him] during the event, and in the end, he challenged himself to be better," Johannson said. "It was obvious he was tuned in for the big game—maybe what he learned there is that you have to show up every night."

Campbell and Chris Kreider, two members of the gold-medal squad in 2010, also delivered big in 2011. Kreider had a pair of goals in a 4–2 win against Sweden that gave the U.S. the bronze medal. After the game, Campbell said he was surprised Chris Kreider was the hero of the bronze-medal game only because he thought Kreider should have already been in the NHL.

It marked the first time the Americans had ever won a WJC medal on home ice and gave them back-to-back medals for the first time in the tournament that began in 1977. "This is huge for the program," USA player Ryan Bourque, son of Hall of Fame player Raymond Bourque, said. "It means a lot for me and the [seven] other guys who have been part of that."

Campbell (Dallas Stars), John Ramage (Calgary Flames), Bourque (New York Rangers), Jeremy Morin (Chicago Blackhawks), Jason Zucker (Minnesota Wild), Kyle Palmieri (Anaheim Ducks), Jerry D'Amigo (Toronto Maple Leafs), and Kreider (Rangers) were all members of both the 2010 and 2011 medal teams.

Fifteen years after, the NTDP still has critics, but there are fewer of them. It's important to point out that not all top Americans choose to play in the NTDP and still find their way to the NHL.

But since 1996, the NTDP has sent 259 players to Division I hockey on scholarships, and 189 players have been drafted by NHL teams; of those, 38 were drafted in the first round. In 2010 roughly 37 percent of all American players in the NHL had NTDP backgrounds. The U.S. squad has won the World Under-18 Championship six times since 2002.

After the U.S. won the WJC gold medal in Saskatoon, it owned the Under-17, Under-18, and Under-20 World Championships at the same time. USA Hockey has come a long way from the days when Americans competing at an international tournament had a better chance of selling their blue jeans for a handsome price than earning a handsome medal. ∎

Acknowledgments

The most agonizing decisions about writing a book about American hockey history didn't come from deciding what to include in the book, but rather what to leave out.

My estimate is that about 200 people were interviewed for the original manuscript and this update, and it was impossible to include every interesting tale I heard, or every piece of information that was unearthed. But I do believe that every person I talked to contributed to the book because each story gave me a better understanding of why the American hockey culture is where it is today.

Many debts are owned for this work, most too large to ever repay. But there are those who have contributed significantly to this updated version that deserve to be mentioned.

Mike Modano, Mike Richter, Brian Rolston, Scott Young, and Jeremy Roenick contributed greatly to the chapter on America's greatest generation. Former general manager Larry Pleau helped me sum up the contributions of some of the Americans who played in the NHL in the 1960s and 1970s. The great Scotty Bowman told me the story of Phil Housley and Lou Nanne talked to me about why NHL teams were so slow in embracing Americans.

One of my favorite conversations was with Mike "Lefty" Curran who gave me insight on the 1972 U.S. Olympic team, and shared some tales of Americans in the World Hockey Association. We ended our talk with a shared lament about Phil Housley and Mark Howe not receiving Hall of Fame consideration.

Many of the people I interviewed for the original book in 1996 have passed away, including Frank Brimsek and U.S. historian Don Clark and Herb Brooks. This time around I relied on others to provide me with insight about Brooks, and many came through, particularly his friend Neil Sheehy, a former NHL player who is now a player agent.

Thanks also to former NHL player Tom Laidlaw, a Canadian-turned-American, who seems to have at least one story about every NHLer he ever played against.

Some of the best new material for this book was provided by Lou Vairo, the 1984 U.S. Olympic coach and a person who has been involved in U.S. hockey since the 1970s. Thankfully, Vairo is a world-class storyteller with an uncanny ability to remember rich detail.

There is a second helping of USA Hockey legend Art Berglund in the updated version of the book, a look at some of the forgotten U.S. Olympic teams plus more discussion of the USA's participation in the World Championship. Thanks also to USA Hockey president Ron DeGregorio, past USA president Walter Bush, USA Hockey's executive director Dave Ogrean and his assistant Jim Johannson for their stories and insight.

Former U.S. Olympic women's coach Ben Smith, plus players Angela Ruggiero, Katie King, and Karyn Bye also deserve special mention for providing lengthy interviews about the Olympic gold-medal chase in 1998.

Another important contributor is *Windsor (Ontario) Star* columnist Bob Duff , a Canadian who probably knows more about the early hockey history as anyone in North America. As someone who has written about hockey for the better part of three decades, I have learned to trust Duff's memory and research more than any other hockey historian.

This book doesn't include footnotes because I source within the text any reporting that is not my own. Some statistics were gathered from hockey-reference.com or the *Total Hockey* encyclopedia. Some of the original research was done through the *New York Times* articles.

Thanks goes to USA Hockey Senior Director of Communications Dave Fischer for remaining patient while I peppered him with questions and queries for several months. Fischer started out as someone I dealt with in my job, and that work relationship has evolved into a friendship. This project doesn't get done without Fish's willingness to serve as the blocking back while I carried the ball.

Also thanks to Triumph Books, and particularly editor Noah Amstadter, for making the editing a painless process. Still today, there aren't many publishers producing hockey books. But I've now worked Triumph boss Mitch Rogatz for the better part of two decades, and when you give him a good idea, he makes it come to life. The world needs more people like that.

—Kevin Allen

With the increased success the U.S. has enjoyed in international competition, USA Hockey's influence across the globe continues to escalate. The photo below is from a visit paid to USA Hockey's national headquarters in Colorado Springs by the top two executives from the International Ice Hockey Federation in the spring of 2010. Pictured (l to r) are: Dave Ogrean, executive director of USA Hockey; Ron DeGregorio, USA Hockey president; Horst Lichtner, general secretary of the IIHF; Rene Fasel, president of the IIHF; Angela Ruggerio, four-time Olympian; and Tony Rossi, vice president of USA Hockey and a member of the IIHF Council. (USA Hockey)